International Association for the Integrational Study of Language and Communication

2015
David Bade, Rita Harris, Charlotte Conrad. *Roy Harris and Integrational Semiology 1956-2015: A bibliography.*

2020
Sinfree Makoni. *Language in Africa. Selected papers vol. 1*
David Bade. *Efficiencies and Deficiencies: Cataloging and Communication in Libraries.*

In preparation:
Sinfree Makoni. *African Applied Linguistics: Selected Papers*, vol. 2
Sinfree Makoni. *Linguistic Ideologies, Sociolinguistic Myths and Discourse Strategies in Africa. Selected Papers*, vol. 3
Cristine Severo and Sinfree Makoni. *Language in Lusophonia: Perspectives from Bakhtin, Southern Theory and Integrational Linguistics.*
David Bade. *Integrational Linguistics for Library & Information Science: Linguistics, Philosophy, Rhetoric and Technology*

The International Association for the Integrational Study of Language and Communication

The IAISLC was founded in 1998. It is managed by an international Executive Committee, whose members are:

Adrian Pablé (University of Hong Kong), Secretary
David Bade (University of Chicago, retired)
Charlotte Conrad (Dubai)
Stephen J. Cowley (University of Southern Denmark)
Daniel R. Davis (University of Michigan)
Dorthe Duncker (University of Copenhagen)
Jesper Hermann (University of Copenhagen)
Christopher Hutton (University of Hong Kong)
Peter Jones (Sheffield Hallam University)
Nigel Love (University of Cape Town)
Sinfree Makoni (Penn State University)
Rukmini Bhaya Nair (Indian Institute of Technology)
Jon Orman (Brighton)
Talbot J. Taylor (College of William & Mary)
Michael Toolan (University of Birmingham)

Anyone wishing to join the Association can do so by email apable@hku.hk or by sending their name and address to the Secretary:

Dr Adrian Pablé
School of English
Run Run Shaw Tower
Centennial Campus
The University of Hong Kong
Hong Kong S.A.R

David Bade

Efficiencies and Deficiencies
Cataloging and Communication in Libraries

www.integrationists.com

International Association for the Integrational Study of
Language and Communication

This collection ©2020 by David Bade

The Creation and Persistence of Misinformation in Shared Library Catalogs: Language and Subject Knowledge in a Technological Era ©2002 Originally published by the Graduate School of Library and Information Science, University of Illinois at Urbana-Champaign.
Colorless Green Ideals in the Language of Bibliographic Description: Making Sense and Nonsense in Libraries ©2007 Originally published in *Language & Communication*, v.27 nr.1, p.54-80.
Rapid Cataloging: Three Models for Addressing Timeliness as an Issue of Quality in Library Catalogs. ©2007 Originally published in *Cataloging & Classification Quarterly* v. 45, no. 1, p.87-123.
The Perfect Bibliographic Record: Platonic Ideal, Rhetorical Strategy or Nonsense? ©2008 Originally published in *Cataloging & Classification Quarterly*, v. 46, nr.1 p.109-133.
The Social Life of Metadata: Arguments from Utility for Shared Database Management (A Response to Banush and LeBlanc) ©2008 Originally published in *Journal of Library Metadata*, v. 8, nr.2, p.113-137.
Irresponsible Librarianship: a Critique of the Report of the Library of Congress Working Group on the Future of Bibliographic Control and Thoughts on How to Proceed ©2009 Previously unpublished. Originally presented at the Music OCLC USers Group Meeting, February 17, 2009.
Carlo Revelli on the (Non)Autonomy of Cataloging ©2010 Originally published in *Cataloging & Classification Quarterly*, v.48, nr.8, p. 743-756
Jakobsonian Library Science? A Response to Jonathan Tuttle's Article "The Aphasia of Modern Subject Access." ©2013 Originally published in *Cataloging & Classification Quarterly*, 2013, v.51, p.428-438

For my daughter Khaliun Rachel
May she grow to love the world even more than her father does

CONTENTS

Preface: 1

I. *The Creation and Persistence of Misinformation in Shared Library Catalogs: Language and Subject Knowledge in a Technological Era* 5
II. *Misinformation and Meaning in Library Catalogs* 55
III. *Colorless Green Ideals in the Language of Bibliographic Description: Making Sense and Nonsense in Libraries* 59
IV. *Rapid Cataloging: Three Models for Addressing Timeliness as an Issue of Quality in Library Catalogs* 107
V. *The Perfect Bibliographic Record: Platonic Ideal, Rhetorical Strategy or Nonsense?* 157
VI. *The Social Life of Metadata: Arguments from Utility for Shared Database Management (A Response to Banush and LeBlanc)* 191
VII. *Irresponsible Librarianship: a Critique of the Report of the Library of Congress Working Group on the Future of Bibliographic Control and Thoughts on How to Proceed* 225
VIII. *Carlo Revelli on the (Non)Autonomy of Cataloging* 245
IX. *Jakobsonian Library Science? A Response to Jonathan Tuttle's Article "The Aphasia of Modern Subject Access."* 269

Preface

I came to work in libraries entirely by accident. I had studied linguistics but abandoned a PhD because to a young man in love, linguistic theory in the early days of "move alpha" (1979) seemed not only trivial but ludicrously disconnected from real life and the proper language of youth, which is poetry, song and dance. During a chance encounter with another student of linguistics then working in the library I was informed that I should try to get a job in the library because "they hire all kinds of strange people there." And so for many years I worked in libraries while I read, thought about and dreamt of other matters deemed more important. All the while I was paying attention to the world of libraries and learning many things, yet without ever considering these to be serious matters worthy of intellectual engagement. After all, libraries and librarians seemed far removed from philosophy, poetry and dance. Or so I thought prior to giving these matters my full attention in 1997 after reading a paper by Thomas Mann, a librarian of the Library of Congress.

Between 1979 and 1997 when not working I read philosophy, but not the regular curriculum. I also read extensively among those authors who influenced or were influenced by systems theory and cybernetics: Gregory Bateson, Ludwig von Bertalanffy, Kenneth Boulding, Heinz von Foerster, Kurt Goldstein, Humberto Maturana, Francisco Varela, Norbert Wiener and a host of others. During those two decades of reading my thinking revolved not around the library but around three repeated personal experiences: language, love and violence. Reflections on the Shoah and the hatreds racial and ethnic that surrounded me tormented me precisely because I knew that it was possible to love. After reading Hannah Arendt on Eichmann it dawned on me that Eichmann dealt with Jewish people as objects of policy in the same way that librarians deal with books and information: Eichmann's transportation system was identical to Shannon and Weaver's mathematical theory of communication. And as Roy Harris has shown, that theory of communication came straight out of linguistics. Just as the ideologies of National Socialism and International Socialism inexorably gave rise to concentration camps and the GULAG, information science, by disregarding the persons communicating and treating information simply as a thing to be trucked around from one place to another has led to an information science and thence to library policies that seem to me to be frighteningly similar to the world of the 1930s and '40s. Communication is theorized as a mechanical process of transportation, never as a love song from a special someone to someone even more special. In other words, information science validates the world of violent action —the manipulation of objects describable entirely in terms of relations of power and force—and denies the world of the lover and the beloved. Library science, I concluded, urgently needed my full attention.

With these connections raging within my rapidly aging brain, I finally set out on my donkey to confront the world misunderstood as a self-organizing system that can be known statistically—and manipulated on the basis of that knowledge—with the world of Martin Buber's *Ich und Du*, Rosenstock-Huessy's *Respondeo etsi mutabor*, and Rosenzweig's *Stern der Erlösung*. Along the way I discovered three thinkers who provided me with the theoretical approaches that have informed all but the first of the papers that follow: Roy Harris, who brought me full circle back to linguistics; Erik Hollnagel who taught me to think about machines as things that *people* use for their varied and often conflicting purposes; and Michel Meyer, who put questioning right at the beginning as well as at the end. Eichmann was guilty of accepting orders without asking questions, guilty of misunderstanding transportation systems, and guilty of creating a language that denied his involvement in what was happening. When put in those terms, it is clear that Eichmann's name could be replaced by many of our contemporaries, both within and without the scientific community.

The first paper reprinted here—*The Creation and Persistence of Misinformation in Shared Library Catalogs*—brings together most of the concerns that occupied me in 1997 and still occupy me today. Originally inspired by Thomas Mann's 1997 paper *Cataloging Must Change! and Indexer Consistency Studies* and written in 1998 in a fit of exasperation at the cataloging I had to deal with in OCLC, it was not published until 2002 because the first publishers to whom it was submitted objected that it was satire, not science, that it lacked any quantitative basis and therefore any scientific value, and that (in its earliest versions) it did not discuss the literature. It was only in following up on that "literature" that I realized how seriously deficient library science was (and remains) in asking questions that deserve our attention. The literature on cataloging quality and errors available in 1997 was almost without exception worthless on methodological grounds alone. My own paper was written in an effort to understand the practical situation in which I found myself as a cataloger, but I could not place the problems I identified in any theoretical perspective. In her review of this paper Alenka Šauperl remarked that the author could probably write quite a bit more on the topic, and it was at that point that instead of turning my attention back to philosophy and Mongolian studies, I set out to ask the kinds of questions that I found so woefully lacking in library and information science.

The theoretical basis upon which I would develop my ideas for the next decade had come to me unexpectedly precisely at this point. When reading Prof. Šauperl's remarks in December 2002, I decided to pursue these matters primarily because I had stumbled upon the work of Roy Harris in January of that year and in his writings I had found the profound combination of ethical and theoretical critiques of current (and past) theories of communication that I needed in order to proceed with something other than another lament. In pursuing a literature search beyond the literature of library science, I decided to read the ergonomic literature on error and thus encountered the work of Erik Hollnagel. Then a few years later when I began to focus on the rhetoric of library science I came across the work of Michel Meyer.

The second through sixth papers owe an obvious debt to both Harris and Hollnagel, but their influence runs throughout everything I have written in these fields since 2002. I remain baffled that no one else in the world of library and information science appears to have grappled with—much less grasped—the profound implications of their theoretical arguments for these related fields. Perhaps it is because their ideas force the reader to engage directly questions of labour and ethics, and the conditions of labour in libraries today is far more apalling than it was when I entered the field in 1979. To me, that suggests an intimate connection between the development of computers for "communication and control," the degradation of labour in libraries, and the poverty of ethical inquiry in library science. It is just such a connection that Roy Harris saw clearly in the model of communication upon which modern linguistics was founded, a model which was incorporated into the foundations of computer science, library science and information science.

With the exception of the second and seventh paper, the papers in this volume have been previously published as indepent publications or in journals devoted to library and information science or linguistics. In reprinting these papers together it is my hope that readers may see more clearly the theoretical issues that underlie them all, and thus they may contribute to reorienting the discussions in library science towards the people who are involved in libraries rather than towards the abstractions and fictions that have dominated the discipline since the Second World War.

David Bade
Rachel's Farm
6 April 2020

I

The Creation and Persistence of Misinformation in Shared Library Catalogs: Language and Subject Knowledge in a Technological Era

ABSTRACT

Misinformation science is an evolving discipline arising from the productive and eliminative activities of *Homo bibliotecario inadaequatio* using efficient and powerful information technologies in the library ecology of a market economy. The forms of misinformation inhabiting large data reservoirs are briefly described, and the natural history and epidemiology of two important parasitic species (*Incompetentus linguisticus* and *Subjectus incorrectus*) outlined. A variation of Malthus' law is proposed to account for the dynamic population growth of all species of the genus *Oopsus*—i.e., the growth of misinformation will be directly proportionate to the incompetence of the misinformation providers. The author rejects the use of metadata pesticides and the genetic engineering of librarians and proposes, instead, stricter environmental management and rigorous natural selection to deal with these persistent miscreations.

INTRODUCTION

Perhaps the earliest recorded instance of misinformation is in a narrative about a garden party conversation concerning epistemology and the consequences of a little knowledge. The human agents had been informed by one authority that to partake of the fruits of knowledge would certainly mean death. Yet, in the tree of knowledge itself, there was another authority who contradicted the first and insisted that, far from bring death, the pursuit of knowledge would make the knower an authority equal to any. This misinformation was distributed globally, the ensuing experiment caused the system to crash, everyone blamed someone else for importing corrupt files, the Chief Executive Officer fired everyone including a third of the angelic hosts, and to this day humans are dropping like flies after a lifetime of ignorance.

Misinformation, as the common origin of evil and ignorance, prompts two opposite responses: the authoritarian and the democratic. Most institutions in the western world (church, governments, universities, corporations and, of course, libraries) have experimented with both over the years. The authoritarian responses have been to exclude everyone except the infallible ones (e.g., those with a master's degree in library science), drown everyone but the righteous, and outsource any work that causes headaches. The democratic model has expanded over the years to include most anyone willing to pay membership fees and usage charges, sign loyalty oaths, and put up with incompetence. It is unlikely that the kinds of misinformation that librarians produce and distribute will entail such dire consequences as the above case. It is still often useful to investigate the librarian as misinformation provider and to consider how best to respond to this evil phenomenon, misinformation.

PURPOSE AND PLAN

The main concern here is with two fundamental types of misinformation found in bibliographic and authority records in library catalogs: that arising from linguistic errors, and that caused by errors in subject analysis, including missing or wrong subject headings. Bibliographical and authority records with such misinformation enter shared databases in several ways; all are originally the work of human agents. This article does not address misinformation in databases due to the misfunctioning of software or mechanical procedures beyond the reach of the cataloger, nor does it address issues related to the many other kinds of shared databases, though many of them increasingly find their way into library catalogs in their Web versions. The discussion should still be relevant to a wide range of issues in the expanding universe of shared information.

  A discussion of other kinds of errors will help to show why they present problems unlike those errors associated with language and subject knowledge. These errors, briefly treated, are typographical, International Standard Book Description (ISBD), MARC, and those in applying and interpreting rules, notably the Anglo-American Cataloging Rules (AACR). At the end, I include a personal response to a critical situation, namely, the vanishing intellectual in the academic library.

VARIETIES OF MISINFORMATION

The four broad categories of errors discussed here each have a considerable literature devoted to them, but since these do not represent the main focus of the paper, they are not discussed.

Typographical Errors
Typographical errors are troublesome, for a single error can render a document virtually irretrievable, but these are easy to correct. The inadequacy can best be addressed by better typing and proofreading skills. If typographical errors are not eliminated while the item is still in the cataloger's hands, it will be noticed

only by chance in the future. The chances for correcting misspellings—as opposed to typing the MARC tags incorrectly—are small enough when the language is common; such an error in a language that few librarians and library staff cannot read will be neither noticed nor corrected.

General Description: Basis, Order of Elements, Punctuation
The general description of books as well as materials in other formats is based on the International Standard Book Description (ISBD) and is outlined in Part One of AACR. These conventional rules for the basis of the description, the order of elements, and punctuation serve to standardize the presentation of the bibliographical information, originally on a catalog card but now usually in electronic form. With cards, the user could expect to find the author at the top of the card, the co-author(s) at the bottom after Roman numerals, and so on for all the bibliographical details. The information given on the card was encoded in this prescribed order and punctuation, enabling the librarian to determine author, title, edition, series, and all other elements of the description based solely on the appearance on the card: knowledge of the language or script written on the card was not necessary for comprehending the purpose and significance of each block of text or numbers. In a MARC-coded electronic catalog, all of this information is explicitly coded in the various fields and subfields (fixed fields 020, 100; subfields 'a,' 'b,' 'c,' and so on). Many library systems now identify each element of the record in the display; order and punctuation retain their value as conventions facilitating easy use through familiarity, as well as for those users who do not know or have no access to a MARC display. Like cataloging rules, these rules for order and punctuation have varied during the course of the last century, have often been applied incorrectly, and many users of databases other than catalogers ignore them anyway. These conventions no longer bear as large a load of information as they formerly did; the choice of the basis for description remains, but punctuation is essential in only a limited number of instances—

e.g., in those cases where an exact match is necessary to link a bibliographic heading to its proper authority record. Punctuation, in most cases, affects neither searching nor comprehension of the description. If ISBD punctuation really mattered, the coexistence of retrospectively converted records, old cataloging copy, and plain old errors would have combined to make large shared databases unusable. But that is not the case, and users and librarians can almost always correctly interpret the records they find, no matter what form of punctuation they display. And as long as there are some general standards and the order of elements remains roughly the same, ISBD errors will never be a barrier to bibliographic comprehension.

MARC
Mistakes in the MARC coding of bibliographic and authority records, whether as typographical mistakes or improper coding, is a greater problem since they can seriously disrupt a user's ability to find and interpret bibliographic information. Corporate names tagged as personal names do not work. Subfields 'b' and 'c' determine the domain of title searches. Example: *Trianon. A magyar béreküldöttség tevékenysége 1920-ban. Válogatás a magyar béketárgyalások...* [Trianon, the work of the Hungarian peace delegation of 1920: anthology of etc.]. This book may be searched in the Online Computer Library Center (OCLC) database with a derived title search such as: tri,a,ma,b. If the title has the subfield 'b' placed after "1920-ban," this search will succeed. If the subfield 'b' is placed after the word "Trianon," the same search will not succeed, for the derived title search is limited to the main subfield 'a.' It would be necessary to do the search as: tri,,, and qualify the search by date of publication, since the OCLC system will not display the number of records retrieved under this search without a qualifier. A scan title search will retrieve either variation in the same fashion. If after "Trianon" one were to wrongly enter a subfield 'c,' all words of the title after "Trianon" would be unavailable in any title search. In this example, placement of the subfield 'b' is a judgment call, and the dif-

ficulties for the user can be overcome by adding an additional title tracing for the option not chosen. A subfield 'c' would not be a matter of judgment but a simple error. These errors are preventable by rather simple means. Many a ten-year-old should be able to sit down and learn MARC coding in a short time and so could any librarian. MARC format should be learned (like ISBD and AACR) as a matter of every librarian's initial library education.

Misinterpreting and Misapplying Cataloging Rules
Interpreting and applying cataloging rules (e.g., AACR2, LCSH manual) presents greater problems. Correct use calls for thought and judgment, especially for catalogers who are inexperienced and who deal with all formats, subjects, or types of material in a profusion that makes it hard for them to recall examples and acquire the instincts of the specialist. Unlike the preceding kinds of errors, the improper application of cataloging rules can lead to the creation of forms of entries that the users will neither find nor search for, as well as improper tracing or non-tracing of important items in the record and the failure to associate one work with another (e.g., adaptations and translations). Whereas the earlier kinds of misinformation can often be identified and corrected with only the bibliographic record in view, errors in the application of cataloging rules often require looking at the item in order to determine what should be in the record and in what form. Typographical errors and ISBD and MARC errors can usually be corrected quickly by the cataloger, a supervisor, a database administrator for the shared utility, or any other cataloger who looks at the record and notices the problem. Errors in cataloging rule applications are not always easy to spot and, even when evident, fixing them usually requires looking at the item. No mechanical fixes here.

Prevention and Correction of these Errors
All of these errors have in common the possibility of being corrected by anyone who is looking at the title page (in the case of

typographical errors), or who knows the standards and conventions of bibliographical description (ISBD, MARC, AACR). Any librarian can spot the errors and report them to the appropriate person. These errors are prevented primarily through a knowledge of cataloging rules and MARC coding, which should be thoroughly learned as part of a general library education. The cataloging experience itself should continually inform the practitioner as to their interpretation, modifications, and clarifications. All these kinds of errors belong to those specific activities for which librarians are trained and responsible. Catalogers should be on guard against these kinds of errors, and misinformation arising from such mistakes should be minimal. They can and should be identified and corrected by any librarian who encounters them in the database. Of course, most librarians do not have time to worry about the millions of typographical, ISBD, MARC, and AACR errors. These records are usually handled by copy-catalogers anyway, staff who may or may not be able to identify the errors, and who may or may not be allowed to make such corrections-should they want to in the first place. Catalogers usually fix only those that matter to them and leave the rest for database managers or for those who have no more pressing concerns.

A Note on Retrospective Conversion
Retrospective projects differ from day-to-day cataloging in that their staff has often been deliberately instructed not to think but merely to transcribe what they see. This, of course, permits the institution to hire otherwise less qualified persons and pay them less than folks who are expected to think. The reasons given are sound: the library has already cataloged the item; all that is needed is to take the information found on a card and key it into a database in MARC format. There is no need to alter elements to fit current rules, no authority work, no checking for obsolete headings. The result is to dump many thousands of records, errors and all, into a database for all to share. Often the authority form of name/title will differ from all entries in the database ex-

cept the one on which the authority record was based. Such discrepancies may not be seen as errors, but they do result in misinformation insofar as the authorized form is the anomaly in the bibliographic file. Users must keep this in mind if they are not to be misinformed. Objecting to retrospective conversion is unwarranted, since all libraries and shared utilities benefit greatly. When retrospective conversion is cost-effective, it often carries a high price in misinformation.

LINGUISTIC ERRORS AND WHY THEY MATTER

Most catalogers today contend with unusual items (books, periodicals, videos, computer files, maps, scores) that they have been asked to catalog but which they cannot read. Often they are even unable to determine the language in which the item is written. Library schools do not teach languages. Since most libraries collect at least some materials in languages other than English, the typical monolingual American will face a dilemma: catalog them the best one can (e.g., Georgian books, vols. 1-44); learn 5 (10, 40,...)[1] languages; hire more catalogers, staff, or students

---

[1] The number of languages suggested may shock some readers but, by 'learn,' I mean acquiring a reading knowledge sufficient to work competently even if slowly. A sound knowledge of the writing system, basic grammar, and critical function words suffices to work competently for the purposes of cataloging. Description does not require reading, understanding, and critically engaging the text. It is usually the practice that catalogers are hired to work with language groups (Romance, Germanic, Slavic, etc.). Anyone who works with groups of related languages knows that the initial investment made studying one language pays off in the ease with which one can acquire a reading knowledge of the other related languages. If one has a prior knowledge of Russian, it is much easier to attain a working knowledge of all the Baltic and Slavic languages than it is to acquire a similar ability with Armenian, Hungarian, and Romanian. I take it to be a professional responsibility that if one is hired to catalog in certain languages and language groups, these languages will be studied and learned in a manner adequate to the library's specific needs. Obviously, if libraries establish positions for catalogers, who will be responsible for "European languages," or worse, "Eurasian languages." They are asking too much, at least if they get materials in many of these languages.

and make them responsible; outsource what cannot be read; lock these items in a back room and forget about them. Many well-meaning librarians do attempt to catalog materials for which they are inadequately equipped linguistically. It is praiseworthy that some librarians have a dedication to access that leads them to provide some kind of record even though they are well aware of the probabilities of errors in both description and subject analysis. My objective here is not to decry the efforts of catalogers (like me) who boldly catalog what they cannot read. Rather it is to point out the disastrous effects on the library community of ill-equipped librarians, working in libraries with little linguistic depth in their catalog departments, providing bibliographical and authority records for other libraries to use.

Varieties of Linguistic Errors
What kinds of errors appear in databases when catalogers lack linguistic skills? I have seen incorrect transliteration; improper identification of the language; names established in other than nominative singular; table of contents treated as title pages; series authority records established for dedication statements or other non-series-like statements (e.g., "Workers of the world unite!"); "Book 3" treated as part of title proper and cataloged separately from "Book 1," "Book 2," instead of cataloging all volumes as a multivolume set or each individually with "Book 3" in subfield "n"; real words treated as articles and vice versa; author entered in 245, title in 100; and improper class number and subject assignment due to inability to read the text. Some of these errors do little harm as they add useless information to the database (e.g., "Workers of the world unite!" entered into the database as a note, a traced series, or other title). Useless misinformation in the form of notes can be tolerated, or in the form of tracings deleted by knowledgeable catalogers and ignored by users. Are all linguistic errors this insignificant?

Extent of the Problem
Even trivial mistakes like those just mentioned can take on a more troubling character if the misidentified phrase is duly entered into the authority file as a uniform title, traced series, corporate name, or other heading. Such authority records are in fact made, and the ill-informed cataloger of Hausa may waste an enormous amount of time tracing "Abin da ke ciki" [Table of contents] in a 440 if she or he should have discovered it was actually an established series.[2]

Such trivial, useless, annoying, and—to the uninitiated—misleading information is usually entered into bibliographic and authority files solely because of linguistic ignorance (but see section "Intellectual Errors" below). A more complex problem involves diacritics, special characters, and transliteration. Such errors do not affect access when the special characters and diacritics are ignored in indexing and searching, but they do create havoc when imported into local systems that link the bibliographic records to the authority records. Thus, a *miagkii znak* or an acute accent in Russian, a cedilla or left hook in Romanian, ligatures or no ligatures accompanying the Ukrainian 'zh,' has caused few problems in the past because, in systems like OCLC, authority records were not linked to bibliographical records. That is changing and will only get worse. A much more serious problem will arise when the Romanized records are mechanically converted to display in the vernacular script. A small number of Arabic records that I provided on worksheets for a library some years ago were input by that library with all the diacritics following the associated letter rather than preceding it.[3] Those readers who know Arabic, or any language with a significant number of diacritics, try to imagine what such records will look like when they are dis-

---

[2] At the time of this writing in spring 1998. Checked in January 2001, the authority record has been deleted, but the 490/830 tracing remains in the bibliographical record.

[3] I am happy to say that the presiding librarian in this case caught the errors and quickly fixed them.

played in vernacular scripts: I do not see how any computer could make sense of such garbage. The library patron is likely to see little more than a string of hex set symbols interspersed with seemingly random letters. Conversion will present tremendous problems on any account because of the changes in transliteration schemes in use over the years.

Word division (e.g., Thai), voweling (e.g., in languages using scripts derived from Arabic), ambiguous letters (e.g., Amharic) often lead even knowledgeable catalogers to disagree. Even where standard reference sources are agreed upon as establishing the authorized form, productive processes within the language still cause trouble, as do new words, dialect words, and borrowings. Ambiguities and other problems inherent in the languages and scripts themselves can lead not so much to errors as to difficulties for users at any level: several different headings may need to be searched if transliterated forms are not to be overlooked. Even though some will argue that there is only one correct transliteration, catalogers who know the language well, even native speakers, will often disagree due to optional, archaic, or dialectal variants, one of which must be supplied but which is not specified in the writing itself. When they are brought into the authority file, transliteration differences are often partially resolved but also partially exacerbated. Subsequent catalogers may not notice authorized forms established in older romanization schemes or with different vowelling or word divisions.

Another kind of misinformation in shared databases that arises out of linguistic incompetence is the malformation of names, titles, and series that results when the morphology or syntax of the language is misunderstood. A recent example I encountered was for a book in Polish where the surname was recorded in the plural as it appeared in the statement of responsibility. The cataloger simply traced the plural form and compounded the error by establishing an authority record.

In records in the "lesser known languages" written with a Latin-based alphabet, there are often instances of a number, part, section, or even separate work treated as subtitles rather than sub-fields 'n' or 'p' or, in the case of a separate work, being adequately traced. Authors and titles may appear as the 245 and 100 respectively, and tables of contents, dedication pages, or even advertisements may be used as the chief source of information on which the description is based. Related to these gross errors are the much more common errors in the major European languages where articles are treated as significant (filing and searchable) words and vice versa (Nielsen and Pyle give an excellent discussion and a heretical suggestion for dealing with this problem[4]). Catalogers are often too quick to rely on layout, typography, or other common publishing formats. It is the common format of title at top then author that is the primary reason some books with author at top followed by title get these two mixed up—the format itself, not any statement of the publisher to assign the elements of the record—when they are catalogued without knowing the linguistic facts.

When languages are so poorly understood that such mistakes are made, one can expect errors in subject analysis and classification as well. Unfamiliarity with the language of the text is a frequent, but by no means the sole, factor in errors of subject analysis and classification. Misanalyzed titles coded as full level cataloging are common, and other errors in the record indicate a linguistic inadequacy.

This discussion has focused on the different kinds of linguistic misinformation. What about extent—i.e., the numbers or percentages of records? Do these errors represent a half dozen bad records stumbled upon during the course of one librarian's nearly 20-year career? I know of no studies examining errors directly attributed to linguistic incompetence, nor any articles

---

[4] Nielsen, Ralph, & Pyle, Jan M. (1995). Lost articles: Filing problems with initial articles in databases. *Library Resources & Technical Services*, 39(July), 291-292.

that directly address language competence as a factor in database quality other than Nielsen and Pyle. A few studies have looked at the availability and quality of copy in major utilities for Slavic,[5] East Asian,[6] and Latin American imprints,[7] but the main problem they note is simply that copy was not found for most items in their samples.

Linguistic misinformation exists and is growing as cataloging positions are eliminated. The main problem is simple: If the data we share are provided by persons who can neither read the language of the item nor understand its subject, then the growth of misinformation will be directly proportionate to the incompe-tence of the misinformation providers. A corollary is that catalogers with no linguistic and subject skills will not see the problems, since discovering that something is wrong usually takes the same skills needed to describe an item correctly.[8]

Causes of the Problem

Linguistic misinformation may be directly traced to individual catalogers, but it results from more than simply ignorant librarians. Both libraries and the shared utilities are also responsible, thanks to policies that contribute to the problem of poor cataloging and linguistic misinformation. They affect the cataloger's

---

[5] See Gurevich, Konstantin. (1991). Russian monographic records in the OCLC database: A crisis in shared cataloging. *Library Resources & Technical Services*, 5(October), 459-461.

[6] See Tsao, Jai-hsya (1994). The quality and timeliness of Chinese and Japanese monographs in the RLIN database. *Library Resources & Technical Services*, 38(January), 60-63.

[7] See Grover, Mark L. (1991). Cooperative cataloging of Latin-American books: The unfulfilled promise. *Library Resources & Technical Services*, 35(October), 406-415 and Sercan, Cecilia S. (1994). Where has all the copy gone? Latin American imprints in the RLIN database. *Library Resources & Technical Services*, 38(January), 56-59.

[8] For those readers who were appalled at the Pig Latin of the abstract, its significance should now be clear. Those who overlooked this detail should recall that Pig Latin, or its modem equivalent, is the heart and soul of pseudoscience, and the only sure way to distinguish between the two species is a sound knowledge of, in this case, Latin.

ability to do accurate work and have a drastic negative effect on both the library and the common database. Even now, some large libraries input bibliographical records into the OCLC database without diacritics. Catalogers in major research libraries are often reassigned responsibilities in ways that minimize their language and subject skills and experience, and they are forbidden from working with materials that previously had been their primary responsibility.

Library hiring policies also adversely affect database quality when they result in unqualified catalogers. Positions for cataloging in foreign languages (be they uncommon, like Indonesian, or common, like Russian, German, and Latin, especially when several languages are involved) often go unfilled for lack of qualified candidates (where are the catalogers who have linguistic expertise? Are there none graduating from library schools? The circle of responsibility expands ever outward). Are positions not being filled? Are language and subject requirements being dropped or replaced with other qualifications when the positions are advertised? Are catalogers with one or two languages hired and then called on to catalog other things? Is LC maintaining a linguistically competent cataloging staff? Are there too many people like me who claim we can do everything when in fact we cannot? The lack of linguistic capabilities among catalogers is the primary source for linguistic misinformation in our databases.

Prevention and Cure

Catalogers and library policy have been criticized without mentioning the actual linguistic situation which libraries and librarians face. How many languages are there? How many characters does a keyboard handle? How many Romanization tables have been approved by the library community? How many catalogers are necessary to catalog an East European, South Asian, or Africana collection? How many catalogers apply for jobs requiring Russian and then find they have to catalog everything published east of Germany and Italy, up to Chinese Turkestan and Alaska?

The person responsible for Romanian, Kazakh, Hungarian, Balinese, Hausa, Estonian, and Vietnamese often does not know these languages but relies on what can be learned from dictionaries, transliteration tables, and other reference sources.

This situation can be prevented, of course, by hiring catalogers who either know or take it upon themselves to learn all the languages for which they are responsible. Hopes and expectations are occasionally raised with agreements for cataloging cooperation, but most such ventures have brought disappointing results.[9] Rather than cooperating through cataloging according to institutional abilities, libraries appear to stop cataloging, hire no one, and wait for another institution to provide copy—which every other institution does, and eventually the copy is input as a minimal level record for acquisition purposes at some library, and all others download that record because something is better than nothing and that is the last anyone ever sees of that book.

This is the situation today: too few catalogers in the country to do a greatly increasing load of publications in an increasing number of languages. The cataloger for Classics retires and the Germanic cataloger also becomes the Classics cataloger and next year may add Romance languages to his or her responsibilities. This situation is common and serious. As long as this situation exists, there are a few things that can be done and a few things that should not be done. What can be done:

* learn some languages. Given the way things are, part of any cataloger's professional development and continuing education

---

[9] See Gurevich, "Russian Monographic Records" on cooperation in Slavic cataloging; Sercan, "Where Has All the Copy Gone?" for Latin America; and Leazer, Gregory H., & Rohdy, Margaret. (1995). The bibliographical control of foreign monographs: A review and baseline study. *Library Resources & Technical Services*, 39(January), 29-42, for the general state of the bibliographical control of foreign monographs.

should be a continual broadening of language (and subject) capabilities;

* wait for good copy (and learn how to distinguish it, and study a language while waiting);

* utilize students and other library and institutional personnel;
* subcontract or outsource to persons or organizations that have a reputation for providing the linguistic skills;

* cooperate with other institutions, like the agreement between the University of Minnesota (Scandinavian materials) and the University of Washington (Arabic).[10] Such agreements seem to work better than large-scale agreements among groups of libraries, perhaps because the books end up on the desk of one person, who is held responsible and who usually knows what is right and cares about accuracy.

What not to do:

* input records coded to suggest the cataloger knows what she or he is doing when he or she does not;

* routinely make authority records without knowing how the language works or what the crucial statements really mean; and

* add subjects and class numbers to the shared record without justification.

---

[10] See El-Sherbini, Magda. (1992). Cataloging alternatives: An investigation of contract-cataloging, cooperative cataloging, and the use of temporary help. *Cataloging & Classification Quarterly*, 15(4), 67-88, for a note on this agreement and Ohio State University's decision to pursue a similar path.

INTELLECTUAL ERRORS: CLASSIFICATION/SUBJECTS

As in the case of linguistic misinformation, class number and the choice of subject headings (though not form) depend on knowledge of things that are assumed in library school (and, of course, usually the faculty and the students both know that too often the assumption is incorrect and that there is little they can do about it). The rare cataloger whose position is limited to cataloging materials only in his/her specialty (e.g., Latin American law or Greek and Latin classics) is enviable. Most catalogers need to work in many languages, many formats, and in every subject anyone ever thought of. The specialist can keep up with a particular field; the general cataloger will more than likely not even try to keep up with anything other than personal passions that may never enter into his or her work.

In shared databases with bibliographical information contributed by thousands of catalogers, the cumulative effects of linguistic and subject misinformation presents a greater problem than all the typos, MARC, ISBD, and AACR errors combined. The reason for this is that the former kinds of misinformation can be eliminated only by one who both notices the error and can correct it. Compounding the problem is the absence in most shared databases of any mechanism for sharing the corrected records with other databases that have reproduced the misinformation.[11]

---

[11] Several utilities and information services offer such automatic upgrades. Many problems remain, however, not the least being a need to wait until upgrades are available. If the upgrade is a Dewey call number, it is useless for institutions using another classification system. Even if the number is usable, how long should one hold onto a book before giving it a call number (subjects, etc.) and shelving? Paying for unusable enhancements (sometimes even incorrect ones!) makes no sense. Waiting for desired and necessary enhancements is a disservice to users: the enhancements may never appear. As long as libraries must pay for these enhancement services, they will remain uneconomical as well as being too little too late.

Linguistic ignorance and errors are a primary source, but not the only source, of intellectual misinformation. Two principal sources of misinformation may be distinguished—those that result from linguistic disability and those that result from a weak general education or a lack of specialist knowledge—but the results are identical: incorrect subjects and classification.

Extent of the Problem
There are many discussions of cataloging as a subjective practice, of how no two people can be expected to assign the same subject heading to the same books. The point of such articles is usually to say that we spend too much time on something that does not merit it, and that we should give up sooner and not try to find a heading that truly fits. Could one who held such a position ever have tried to compile a bibliography or write a seminar paper? Wrong subjects waste a reader's time; lack of the right subject can prevent readers from finding what they want. Subject headings that are too broad leave the record lost in the large number of items retrieved. How often a search calls up the response "Too many matches. Please qualify your search." General headings are often the only answer, and often the system cannot handle these. For many kinds of material (e.g., periodicals, congresses, and general textbooks), only a general heading will adequately cover the contents. But the general rule is to describe the item as precisely and narrowly as possible.

Methodological Considerations for Evaluating Subject Analysis
Before introducing the examples in the next section, I will first propose a rule outlining the necessary conditions for any studies evaluating subject analysis:

> For all evaluation of subject analysis, including classification, the items must be evaluated with the item in hand, and the evaluator must have an adequate knowledge of: (1) standards (LCSH, Dewey Decimal System, etc.);

(2) language(s) of the text; and (3) subject of the text.[12]

The examples below were selected according to this rule from among the many that pass through my hands each day. No corpus of random items was selected with each item judged and the percentage of mistakes in each category tabulated and analyzed: this is the method underlying all of the studies that I have read and although this is never stated, other comments suggest that in these studies the evaluations were based on the catalog record alone. The only common methodological grounds between the studies mentioned below and the selection of materials discussed in the following section are the authors' knowledge of professional conventions and standards. For readers who are aware that each of these records was cataloged by a cataloger who is probably adding 100 or more records into a national database each month, a statistical count is as unnecessary as it is irrelevant: no counting is necessary to see such an obvious problem. Science and scholarship should not be limited to quantification; it is the quality that is under scrutiny, and such evaluation is done, like cataloging itself, one item at a time.

Seven Examples

Of the following seven examples from the OCLC database, the first five were all cataloged between the years 1996 and 2000, all were input as "I level" records, and all from the same part of the world—Eastern Europe (materials for which I am responsible). These examples should make it clear how wrong subject headings can misinform the reader. The final two examples are not given in full since they were taken from memory—they were my own errors, and I no longer remember the details, only my shame upon discovering them. Discussion will follow in the next section.

---

[12] This rule is a slightly adapted version of the rules for the compilation of bibliographies drilled into me many years ago by my thesis adviser Donald Krummel.

Example 1. Manuscrisele de la Cîmpulung. Reflecţii despre ţărănime şi burghezie / Constantin Noica. [The manuscripts from Cimpulung: Reflections on the peasantry and the bourgeoisie]. The descriptive portion of the record is flawless, the classification number and subject given for local history of Cîmpulung, Romania. Constantin Noica was a Romanian philosopher who spent many years under house arrest in Cîmpulung. This volume contains several previously unpublished essays on Werner Sombart's *Der Bourgeois*, Georg Simmel's *Philosophie des Geldes*, and other works by Dilthey and Tönnies, all written during his confinement in Cîmpulung.

Example 2. In genul lui Cioran, Noica, Eliade /N. Steinhardt. Two records for this book may be found in OCLC: 1) The cataloger provided no subjects, but included the note "Parodies of Cioran, Noica, Eliade, and others". Classification for Steinhardt as literary author, PC839.S; 2) Subjects given: a) Philosophy, Romanian--History--20th century; b) Cioran, E.M.; c) Noica, Constantin; d) Eliade, Mircea; e) Romania—Intellectual life--20th century. Classification is B 4822, 20th century Romanian philosophy.

Example 3. Psychological ideas and society: Charles University, 1348-1998 /Josef Brožek, Jiří Hoskovec. Cataloged as a book by Brožek and Hoskovec. The subjects given: 1) Charles University--History--Sources; 2) Philosophers--Czechoslovakia--History. The book was classed in LF under Charles University. The correct story: the book, as edited by Brozek and Hoskovec, is in fact an anthology of writings in several languages, translated into English on the topic of psychology, by politicians, doctors, sociologists, psychologists, and others, all of them one time or another associated with Charles University. Two pages in the introduction deal with the history of the university, nothing else on the topics given in the record, no reason at all to class in LF A title keyword search could bring up the book for someone—if the system could handle terms like "psychological," "ideas," "society," and the patron had a lot of time to waste. Even if they found the record, would they bother looking at it seeing it really had nothing to do with psychology but rather was about Charles University history?

Example 4. Title transliterated: *Vidimost nezrimogo: IV Peterburgskaia biennale = The visuality of the unseen: IV St. Peterburg biennale.* The romanization and tracings in the record are impeccable. Subject given: Philosophy--Congresses. Class B20. The actual theme of the conference was aesthetics and cyberspace, virtual reality, and the arts. Since the real topic was neither in the title nor in the conference name nor in the subject headings, who will ever find this book? Only those who look for it by exact title—that is, those who already know that the book exists and is of interest to them.

Example 5. Title transliterated: *Gosudarstvennyi teatr imeni Vs. Meierkhol'da (GOSTIN)-(1926-1938g.g.): "TeatrRSFSR-I" (1920-1922 g.g.). "Teatraktera" (1922g.), "Teatr Gitis" (1922-1923 g.g.), "Teatr im. Vs Meierkhol'da" (TIM)-(1923-1926 g.g.).* The book was cataloged as an open multivolume microfilm reprint of something published in Moscow by Tsentr. gosud. arkhiv SSSR, 19-. The subjects given were: 1) Theater-Soviet Union--20th century--Archives; 2) Meierkhold, V.E. (Vsevolod Emilevich), 1874-1940--Archives--Statistics [this was coded as a topical subject-not name-with no subfields 'q' or 'd', with Archives and Statistics both subfield 'x's]; 3) Theater-Soviet Union--20th century--Statistics. The actual title of the set is: The Meyerhold Theatre, 1920-1938 from the holdings of Russian State Archive of Literature and Art, Moscow, Russia / microfilmed in 1999 by Research Publications. This 165 microfilm reel set is the first publication of the archives of the Gosudarstvennyi teatr imeni Meierkholda, whose name with subfield 'v' Archives should have been the first subject. Subjects two and three are wrong: this is not a collection of statistics about the archives, anyone, or anything else.

And, finally, to make it clear the author is not sitting on a throne, two whopping mistakes made by the author himself and caught later:

Example 6. Collection of praise poems in Yoruba. Ignorant of both Yoruba culture and language, I relied on a dictionary for the meaning of "oriki" and, instead of realizing that the book was a collection of praise poems and treating it accordingly, I assigned classification and subject for Names, Yoruba. A linguistic error that led to a grievous error of subject analysis and, hence, classification.

Example 7. History of Maluku. I thought Maluku was Indonesian for Malacca and did not bother looking it up. (Or did I think Malacca was Portuguese for Maluku? I do not remember.) A lack of geographical knowledge that was at the same time a linguistic error. The bigger problem is: how many more had I cataloged before I discovered my mistake? How does one correct mistakes one does not know one has made?

Discussion of the Examples
These examples show how wrong subject headings mislead and direct the reader away from investigating the book further. These and many other cases are not examples of subjective differences or reasonable divergences of cataloger's interpretation. They are wrong. "Stop the massacre" is completely different from and opposed to "Slow down the massacre." In all of these examples, the error was probably due to the cataloger not bothering to open the book past the title page. Might this suggest haste to fulfill a quota or carelessness? The table of contents and the first page of each book made it clear what the subjects really should be. Might the cataloger really not have known who Simmel, Dilthey, Tönnies, and Sombart were, that they were more than good old boys working in local history? These examples did not reflect on specialized knowledge so much as on negligence or lack of basic education. If one assumes that the

catalogers had done graduate work, at the very least toward an MLS, negligence seems likelier.

In Example 1, a knowledge of intellectual life in post World War II Romania would have introduced the cataloger to Noica even if the details of his residence were not known. To produce the subject given, the cataloger had to assume a good deal from the title and look no further for justification. And if the cataloger did not even know the language, the book should have been set aside to wait for some other cataloger to do.

We shall let the reader evaluate Example 2: The first question to be answered is: Which record accurately reflects the contents of the work? For the readers who have difficulty choosing between these two analyses, we must further ask: What information is necessary in order to make the choice? Will a knowledge of Romanian suffice? "In the style, or manner, of Cioran etc." the title states. There is a difference between parody and philosophy, and that difference should be reflected in the library catalog. Is the first record one of the many cases where a book, not being understood, is declared to be literature (parody in this case) and thus sent on its way? Or did the cataloger for the second record see the names Cioran, Noica, and Eliade and assume the work to contain studies of the essayist, the philosopher, and the historian of religion respectively? Does "in the style of" here mean the same thing as "imitation" or "parody"? There is still another possibility; perhaps each cataloger registered only one aspect of the book's contents. Might it not be a discussion of the ideas presented by these writers, written in the same style as that in which they each wrote, or even a true parody that was seriously concerned with their style as much as with their ideas, as one might write a Platonic dialogue about Plato's Dialogues? I hope any reader who has not already read this particular book would want to open it up and read a bit before choosing between these two records.

Yet Example 2 yields more matters of interest: one of these records was provided by the Library of Congress. Most libraries have a general policy of preferring full LC records to any others when these are available. Would 'that be the correct choice here—i.e., is the LC record correct? And if it errs in subject analysis, may we close our eyes and accept the authority of LC anyway? There are really only two options for the cataloger: (1) for the cataloger who does not know Romanian, choosing the LC record acknowledges the authority that the Library of Congress has and the fact that most catalogers rely on the knowledgeable catalogers there to provide the expertise that few other libraries support; (2) the second option is available only to the cataloger who knows Romanian or has access to someone who both knows Romanian and understands what the issue is in deciding between these records: that person can take the book and read it until the light dawns—there is no other way to analyze this book properly.

The cataloger who provided Example 3 has not even a language barrier as an excuse. Librarians must ask the question: are we in so much of a hurry to move our books and other items onto the shelves that we will settle for such hack work? Is this the work of a professional cataloger? If so, just what does "professional" mean?

The fourth example presents the problem of general versus specific headings. As in the previous example, the book was in English (and Russian), so language should not be the problem. In order to find a specific heading and class number that would both match the contents and not be so general as to be worthless, it was necessary in this case to browse the table of contents. This simple step does take a few minutes, but the nature of the contents in this case was easily identifiable and, while it needed more than one subject heading, the book clearly belonged in BH under aesthetics, rather than in B, general philosophy.

Example 5 is particularly distressing because the only correct lines in the entire record were for the Physical Description Fixed Field (007). This record was done wrong primarily because the cataloger determined that the chief source of information was not the leading frame but the first item microfilmed: the 1938 catalog of the archives published by the Tsentr. gosud. arkhiv SSSR. Hence, the publisher in Moscow rather than in Woodbridge, Connecticut. Furthermore, the nature of this first item in the collection was mistakenly identified as a volume of statistics rather than a catalog. The MARC coding was wrong in all of the subject fields, the latter two subjects being completely wrong in the first place: the archives pertain to the theater that happened to be named after Meierkhol'd, but the archives were not his nor do they pertain in any way to him.[13]

On checking the catalog of the library that provided the record, it became clear that someone had corrected a few of the mistakes, so some errors were noted and corrections made at the home institution, even if these corrections were not made in the record on OCLC. What is more, as is often the case when bibliographical records are reviewed by someone not doing the original cataloging, the errors were only those that could be spotted from the catalog record itself—i.e., the name subject for Meierkhol'd was changed from a 650 into a 600 with the appropriate subfields added and the "x"s of the subfields changed to "v"s. The one essential subject is still missing from the record, and the two wrong subjects—the name and the statistics—remain. The title, imprint, and reproduction note are still based on the analysis of the entire set as a reprint, which analysis was also based on the wrong source.

Such errors as are noted above enter the database through the original record but often remain there even when the record shows several, even dozens, of holding institutions. It is often the case that such gross errors in both description and subject analysis go undetected, while the records are enhanced

---

[13] Note to this edition: The immediately preceding sentence is an example of an error on my part. What I learned one week before this paper was to be printed (too late!) was that the theater was in fact founded and directed by Meyerhold, and not simply named after him. I would have preferred to silently correct my error for this edition, but honesty forces me to leave it as it originally appeared and acknowledge the part that ignorance plays not only in my cataloging but also in my publications.

by changes in the capitalization or punctuation in a note, or the addition of unnecessary notes—such as "'Nauchnoe izdanie'—Colophon" or "In cyrillic." In such instances, the phrase "cataloger's judgment" comes off looking mostly like an excuse for inadequate intellectual analysis of contents, and the kinds of additions and corrections that are made represent an obsession with trivia.

When Two Heads are Better Than One: Complex Problems, Specialized Knowledge, and Interdepartmental Cooperation
So far, problems arising from basic inattention and general educational deficiencies have been discussed. These problems may loom large, but some problems are even more disconcerting. General catalogers may need to deal with Aztec literature with established titles for particular texts that are incorrect. Often the errors are repeated with no inkling of the problem. Catalogers working with German and Scandinavian titles may be confronted with a commentary in Swedish on a section of the Burmese version of the Tripitaka. While the second (Burmese) situation is hypothetical, the Aztec (Nahuatl) example is not: I stumbled upon it myself and, being no Nahuatl scholar, I could not determine the correct form nor would I attempt to. The matter was referred to the Library of Congress, whose catalogers could and did correct the matter. Most experienced catalogers, however, in dealing with subjects and forms of headings for works in law, Buddhist writings, Islamic subjects, medicine, Russian music, finance, and many others, have needed help from personal or written resources. Some areas—medicine, law, and music—often have specialists in these fields in the library, but who gets the book, the subject or the language cataloger and, both of them being busy, how can they be persuaded to take the time to talk to each other?

Virtually all of the literature on cataloging and on database quality is concerned with technologies or methods and standards. Acknowledgment that cataloging is an intellectual activity that requires an ability to understand what an item is about, and prior to that, an ability to read the specific language of the text, is so rare as to be disturbing. However librarians may have thought in the past, in the present climate of technological possibilities and the excitement they generate, librarians increasingly see themselves as information scientists, and their work as information handling, brokering, and management. What must not be forgotten is that information always has a specific content. Catalogers, bibliographers, and reference librarians in fact work not with abstract information devoid of content, but with autopoiesis, prosopography, logotherapy, Rechtsextremismus, amparo, Ujamaa, sultawiyya, *Babad Buleleng*, *Yuan chao pi shih*, arianism, Brownian motion, Empfindungslosigkeit, chocolate chip cookies, and anti-semitism. Information science knows nothing of these matters, in any language. A few articles touch directly upon this theme, however, and these are discussed next.

A Brief Survey of the Literature
Intner's study of bibliographic quality has a flaw that invalidates its basic point. She states that: "Substantive errors in subject headings and classification numbers were confined to obvious discrepancies between the content of the books and assignments of subject headings and class numbers" as well as absent and outdated headings, and those cases where heading and classification were contradictory.[14] This is a good example of the extraordinary inexactitude and carelessness with which catalogers often approach subject analysis, combined with the most exhaustive attention to details of description in the record, details that are utterly insignificant to everyone except some librarians. Most of the examples cited in her study do not merit the attention of a copy-cataloger, as she appears to argue in a later paper.[15] The obvious examples to which she confines her atten-

---

[14] Intner, Sheila S. (1989). Quality in bibliograhic databases: An analysis of member- contributed cataloging in OCLC and RLIN. *Advances in Library Administration and Organization*, 8, 5-6.

[15] Intner, Sheila S. (1990). Copy cataloging and the perfect record mentality. *Technicalities*, 10(July), 12-15.

tion are just that—obvious. My concern here is with all the misinformation that Ms. Intner ignores.

LeBlanc notes that: "In many large academic libraries, one can find veteran copy catalogers with vast subject and/or language backgrounds... but who, because they do not brandish an M.L.S., are excluded from doing original work." He continues with a description of the recent library school graduate who, "seeing and foreseeing the 'big picture' with regard to cataloging," actually does the original cataloging but, LeBlanc suggests, this "big picture" is no substitute for "the more fundamental factors of language and subject background."[16]

Ewbank, reporting on a talk by Intner, comments that: "One of the most important parts of subject analysis is determining the subject content of an item and this can't be taught."[17] She later notes that, in learning subject analysis, one problem that students have (in a list of four problems) is lack of subject expertise. In another article, Intner sets up the impossible goal of a "perfect catalog," one that requires catalogers with language and subject expertise. Having asserted that this is economically impossible, she then asks: "Who cares if the perfect catalog is doomed?" Her response: "Not I."[18]

Two recent studies have looked at the question of subject appropriateness. Both came to distressing conclusions. Svenonius and McGarry noted that of the non-LC monographic records in their study over 50% had inappropriate, obsolete, or

---

[16] LeBlanc, James D. (1993). Cataloging in the 1990's: Managing the crisis (mentality). *Library Resources & Technical Services*, 37(October), 430.

[17] Ewbank, Linda C. (1996). Untitled report on the program "Crisis in subject cataloging and retrieval" at the American Library Association Annual Meeting, Chicago, June 22-29, 1995, *Cataloging & Classification Quarterly*, 22(2), 92.

[18] Intner, Copy cataloging, p. 15. Perfect is impossible because humans are imperfect; as a goal toward which we strive it is essential. Shall we do what one librarian did when he said to me, "Only 20% of the subject headings in the catalog are incorrect—and that is an acceptable margin of error"? I do not want a lawyer or a doctor or an accountant who is wrong "only 20% of the time," so why lower standards for librarians?

missing headings. They noted: "Subject catalogers should be obligated to understand the meaning of subject headings"[19] and, later on, "Subject catalogers need to be educated in the subject terminology of the discipline in which they are cataloging."[20] Mann, on the other hand, has looked at a series of publications claiming that it does not matter whether the cataloger knows anything, for no two catalogers will agree on the subject anyway. He did not agree.[21] His criticisms of a recent study by Chan[22] could be generalized to most of the literature on subject errors: "According to actual LC policies, a heading that is properly assigned must meet two criteria, not one: (1) it must appear in LCSH, and (2) it must al-so be at the most specific level appropriate to the book in hand rather than at a general level. Chan simply overlooks the second criterion."[23] The fact that a heading is in LCSH does not mean it is appropriate to the item in hand; for it to be appropriate it must reflect exactly the subject of the work.

Subject Cataloging as an Intellectual Activity—Not Anymore?
It may be objected that the inattention to language and subject knowledge as a prerequisite to cataloging has been due to their being seen as prerequisites. The evidence suggests that this is not the case. Many studies of subject errors and indexer inconsistency (like those discussed in Mann's study) fail to ask "What subject is the work about?" and then concluding that the process is subjective, so catalogers shouldn't even bother. Hong Xu, stu-

---

[19] Svenonius, Elaine, & McGarry, Dorothy. (1993). Objectivity in evaluating subject heading assignment. *Cataloging & Classification Quarterly* 16(2), 26.
[20] Ibid., p. 27.
[21] Mann, Thomas. (1997). Cataloging must change! and indexer consistency studies: Misreading the evidence at our peril. *Cataloging & Classification Quarterly*, 22(3/4), 3-45.
[22] Chan, Lois Mai, & Vizine-Goetz, Diane. (1997). Errors and obsolete elements in assigned Library of Congress Subject Headings: Implications for subject cataloging and subject authority control. *Library Resources & Technical Services*, 41(October), 295-322.
[23] Mann, Cataloging must change! p. 30.

dying job advertisements, found that, between 1986 and 1990, only 14% of advertised positions for catalogers asked for any kind of subject background.[24] (She did not give figures for language requirements. Towsey's study of 1995-1996 advertisements in the United States found that "44% of the advertised posts specified language knowledge as necessary or desirable."[25]) In comments on Hafter's Academic Librarians and Cataloging Networks: Visibility, Quality Control and Professional Status,[26] Barnett noted: "The catalogers Hafter spoke with come across as having lost the sense of cataloging as a demanding intellectual activity."[27] Many librarians simply do not see cataloging as an intellectual activity requiring an educated mind. The most telling evidence of this is the assignment of original cataloging to nonprofessionals without regard for their abilities and qualifications to do cataloging. (Many nonprofessionals can clearly do original cataloging. Removing the necessary qualifications from the position description, thus lowering the position rank and abandoning the principle of "Equal work, equal pay," that is distressing.) Trainer went so far as to say that: "More and more libraries are discovering that they can no longer afford to have professional catalogers be mostly catalogers .... cataloging is being turned into an activity for nonprofessionals" so that professional catalogers can become cataloging managers who supervise and train rather than catalog.[28]

---

[24] Xu, Hong. (1996). The impact of automation on job requirements and qualifications for catalogers and reference librarians in academic libraries. *Library Resources & Technical Services*, 40(January), 19.
[25] Towsey, Michael. (1997). Nice work if you can get it? A study of patterns and trends in cataloguing employment in the USA and the UK in the mid-1990's. *Cataloging & Classification Quarterly*, 24(1/2), 70.
[26] Hafter, Ruth. (1996). *Academic librarians and cataloging networks: Visibility, quality control and professional status*. Westport, CT: Greenwood.
[27] Barnett, Judith B. (1988). Bibliographic networks and the cataloger crisis. *Journal of Academic Librarianship*, 14(2), 99.
[28] Trainer, Karin A. (1989). Dollars and sense: Training catalogers. In Sheila S. Intner & Janet Swan Hill (Eds.), *Recruiting, educating, and training cataloging librarians: Solving the problems* (p.368-369). New York: Greenwood.

The implications are clear: what once was an activity seen as professional and requiring expertise, not only in cataloging methods and technologies but also in language and subject, is now seen by many as too unimportant to allow professionals to engage in it and so is now considered nonprofessional by definition. Administrators who take this attitude soon realize that part-time high school students can make the same mistakes working for minimum wage. Once the job is assumed to require no prior knowledge, not even library school, finding catalogers becomes mostly a matter of finding the cheapest typing pool.

Interlude: Why Bother?
The question was raised above: Since librarians lack the intellectual capabilities for working with the many languages and subjects with which they are confronted, why bother with subject analysis at all? Why not rely on keyword searches, as some have suggested? The answer should be clear to anyone who has ever tried keyword searches in Chinese or Burmese, in inflected and agglutinating languages, or in languages with special characters and diacritics to distinguish words that searching mechanisms usually see as identical. But consider the scholars who use several languages: should they search all possibilities in English, then again in German, and again in French and Chinese or any number of other languages? One major advantage of a single controlled vocabulary is that it brings together all materials of a particular topic, regardless of language.[29]

It is often assumed that keyword title searches can replace subjects so why bother with them? The following two kinds of materials are examples where subjects, not title, matter most: (1) language of text is irrelevant, and (2) text is multilingual. First case: you want the Moonlight Sonata, no matter what they call it. For the Moonlight Sonata, the problem

---

[29] For a good discussion of the complementarity of controlled subject terms and free keyword searching, see Taylor, Arlene G. (1995). On the subject of subjects. *Journal of Academic Librarianship*, 21(November), 486.

is solved by a uniform title. But if you want Picasso's Guernica, any book in any language about Picasso will probably have it, as well as a catalog of the gallery in which it resides, books on war in art, etc., yet there will be no uniform title nor subject for Guernica unless the whole book is about the one painting. The subjects will have to be those in which one would expect to find Guernica. Subjects can get at all these materials regardless of the language of the text because the reader only wants the picture—who cares what language the book is in? Second case: symposium on topic x in Russia has Russian title but contributions in English. Monolingual readers looking for articles on x will retrieve this volume on a subject search and see contents in English, Russian, and French. No title search with an English keyword will find it.

There are also items whose author and exact title you cannot remember, but you know what they are about. Readers may be looking for a particular object, wherever they can find it. Proper subject headings may not lead directly to the object, but they can gather together books, computer files, films, and other media in many languages that may contain pictures of the object: catalogs of galleries in which the object is found, monographs on the artist/photographer/place, even subject headings like "Animals in art." In the second case, many periodicals, edited collections, Festschriften, conference proceedings, collected works, and collections of documents have materials in several languages while the title is in only one language.

In a 1991 study, Larson concluded that "Title keyword searching, which provides a limited form of natural-language access to the topics of books, was found to be the primary replacement for subject index use."[30] These are still subject searches. They simply replace searches in the subject index, which did not lead to the desired materials for many possible reasons in-

---

[30] Larson, Ray R. (1991). The decline of subject searching: Long-term trends and patterns of index use in an online catalog. *Journal of the American Society for Information Science*, 42(April), 213.

cluding poor analysis by catalogers. Title keyword searches can be alternatives but with similar and not wholly satisfactory results. Larson begins with a summary of the results of an earlier study by Matthews, Lawrence, and Ferguson, which found that subject searches accounted for as much as 59% of the searching in on-line catalogs, and that "enhancements to subject and topical searching were the most desired addition to the capabilities of existing online catalogs".[31] Knutson conducted an experiment adding subjects and contents to social science essay collections and found a significant increase in circulation as a result.[32] Taylor's 1995 article reproduces a number of arguments for maintaining subject headings as additional access points beyond keyword searches, quoting Dubois' statement that "they both display advantages and weaknesses dependent on a fairly wide range of context."[33]

Subject headings, properly formed and assigned, are clearly very useful to readers, perhaps especially to students and novices in any field (as we all are, outside our own specialties). Our main concern should then be to ask: Are we making correct and, hence, useful headings, or are we proudly and nonchalantly burdening our users with mistaken and misleading misinformation?

Causes of Misinformation Regarding Intellectual Content
Inattention and carelessness must be bluntly condemned. It still helps to remember that haste can lead to both inattention and carelessness, and that haste is often imposed from on high. The story is told of a cataloger who managed to complete only five bibliographical records in a month, being either uniquely un-

---

[31] Larson, The decline of subject, p. 197. The study cited is Matthews, J. R.; Lawrence, G.S.; & Ferguson, D. K. (1983). *Using online catalogs: A nationwide survey. A report of a study sponsored by the Council on Library Resources.* New York: Neal-Schuman.
[32] Knutson, Gunnar. (1991). Subject enhancement: Report on an experiment. *College & Research Libraries*, 52(January), 65-79.
[33] Taylor, "On the subject of subjects." Quotation from Dubois on p. 486.

qualified or burdened with too many other responsibilities. Pressure to increase quantity clearly may be an urgent concern of the administration, and it may well be that the elimination of many cataloging positions has been a direct result of the administration determining that the quality of bibliographical information supplied by catalogers simply did not justify an investment in slowpokes. Will people work faster if they know less, or should not specialists work faster because they have the knowledge they need? Is the general retreat from specialists within libraries due to the dubious notion that the added value previously provided by the specialist can now be replaced by simply relying on shared cataloging? Can someone else really pay for specialists so we can all benefit? Does anyone do this now? Will they in the future? If libraries cannot afford specialists, how likely are commercial vendors to seek and retain the well qualified? Catalogers are needed who work quickly and accurately, not catalogers who have to agonize endlessly over matters they do not understand—and in the end often get it wrong anyway.

Inattention and carelessness, whatever the causes, can be dismissed as simply unacceptable evils. Ignorance remains and, among the unforgivable sins, it is no less frequent a problem for it is the original sin with which all librarians are burdened. Ignorance is in fact uniquely incarnate in each of us—we are all ignorant in all but a few languages, more or less ignorant in all subjects, even when we are exceptionally learned in some specific field. Ignorance may be fought with learning, yet everyone will be ignorant of most everything for their whole life. How can an ignorant librarian become a competent cataloger?

Fitting a cataloger's specific skills and background to a particular collection is a matter of position descriptions, changing collection practices, the need for flexibility, and the amount of materials in need of cataloging. In the past, most research libraries divided the universe of knowledge into attempts at manageable parts: catalogers were assigned a group of languages and a broader or narrower portion of the subject division (e.g., law, music, humanities, or natural science). Sometimes the subject was more specialized, but the languages were fewer; for other positions, the languages were greater in number, but the kinds of materials and their subject matter were more restricted. Africana collections, for example, often acquired materials in many languages, but most of the material consisted of elementary works on language, literature, folklore, religion, history, health, and readings for adult education. They did not require a specialist's knowledge in medicine, literary theory, or nuclear physics.

Times have changed. Today there are fewer cataloger positions, and most of those that remain are in special libraries (e.g., law, music, map, and medical libraries). Outside the special libraries, most positions are now either general positions for catalogers who do everything, or positions determined by linguistic knowledge, such as Romance, East Asian languages, and Slavic languages. Catalogers in these positions are responsible for every kind of material received in these languages. Having too few catalogers responsible for too broad a range of subjects is the same problem as having too few catalogers for too many languages: the cataloger is forced into incompetence, and misinformation is the result. But there are no others with enough knowledge to spot the errors, so we accept our raises, promotions, and tenure, and gradually transform ourselves into misinformation providers.

The initial vision was for a shared database, built from the cooperative labors of thousands of competent well-educated intellectuals and librarians with impressive special abilities and subject expertise among them. It is still a great idea. But the number of librarians with the needed languages and subjects has diminished sharply as libraries have chosen to save money by relying on cheap cataloging. What will happen when the cooperating institutions say "Let us all share one database (or two, or three)," then each library promptly proceeds to eliminate most all of those who could have produced this reliable and accurate database?

Whatever the causes, the existence of such records as the seven examples above indicates that something is rotten in the state of cataloging, and it is irrational, irresponsible, dishonest, and unscientific to refuse to acknowledge this problem in the first person plural: the problem is us. Not one person can work quickly and accurately with the whole world of published scholarship. It is rare that any one cataloger can adequately work with a "narrow" area of responsibility like "Humanities in Romance languages." But let us return to the seven examples above: librarians can do better than that.

Prevention and Cure
Without realistic proposals for achieving a more acceptable state of affairs, a critic is neither useful nor welcome. Hence, these comments for both individual catalogers and library policy makers:

* Libraries need to reexamine the number of catalogers and their responsibilities in relation to the amount of cataloging necessary to prevent the growth of backlogs. Existing and future positions should realistically reflect the needs of the collection in terms of subjects, languages, and quantity of materials to be cataloged.

* A position with responsibilities too general and too broad will be of little interest to the people who can bring a high level of skills and abilities to an institution.

* In a research library, librarians without a commitment to scholarship and continuing self-education are a liability.

* Catalogers should seek/be encouraged to supplement their educational deficiencies through attending classes (auditing at one's own institution is usually free).

* Many catalogers work closely with bibliographers and faculty, and all of them should be if for no other reason than using their

specialist knowledge as a resource. That faculty, bibliographers, and other librarians with subject and language expertise might assist the cataloger in improving the quality of the database and providing access to more specialized materials should not be discounted or rejected on "territorial" grounds.

* Use the many Internet special interest and discussion groups. Questions asked through such forums are often answered by the less than knowledgeable, but the knowledgeable responses will also help with insights that may never be located in published reference works.

ON RESPONSIBILITY

The roles of catalogers and library administrators in the natural history of misinformation have been addressed above; a brief summary and a few additional comments on these perpetrators follows, after which a brief look at the role and responsibilities of database administrators.

Education of Catalogers
The order in which the topic of responsibility for misinformation (or, positively speaking, the quality of information in a database) is presented here may seem a bit backwards. Catalogers enter the picture to do the work only after systems have been designed and purchased, cooperative agreements signed, and position descriptions and duties outlined. What the cataloger puts into the database is what matters. The first and final responsibility for the quality of the bibliographical information and the shared authority files belongs to the cataloger. Thorough, conscientious, and intelligent catalogers may be born and not made. But their education before, during, and after library school is primarily a matter of the cataloger's own decisions. The cataloger with an inadequate academic background as well as the cataloger with a highly specialized background are both in very difficult positions if they are hired as general catalogers, particular-

ly if they are responsible for a range of languages they do not know or know only inadequately. The great advantage of specialized cataloging responsibilities is the possibility of systematic and sustained self-education directed at the requirements of the job, even as that changes over time. For positions with general responsibilities, systematic self-education is far more difficult since the retirement age is generally 65 and the universe of knowledge is rather extensive. However, there are practices that inexperienced general catalogers can undertake, and responsible catalogers are rarely happy doing nothing.

Perhaps the simplest and best way for catalogers to improve their understanding of the meanings, scope, and construction of subject headings is by studying LC copy. Some librarians may feel that copy-cataloging is a waste of a professional's time, but familiarity with current LC practice on a regular heading-by-heading basis is still the best way to keep abreast of changes and usage.

Other means of self-education have been noted above: taking classes, learning languages, and working with other faculty and librarians with areas of expertise. For technical knowledge of AACR, MARC, authority work, and the structure of LCSH headings, there are national seminars, training sessions offered by LC, and local discussions from which to benefit.

Library Administration

Catalogers are ultimately responsible for the keystrokes destined for cyberspace, and the library administration is responsible for finding and hiring the catalogers for the responsibilities they shoulder and for the resources they use. The quantity and quality of people working to build a database depends on the attitudes of the administration toward the work they do. If cataloging is seen as an intellectual added value, the prospects for a quality database are good. If it is something to be acquired from the lowest bidder, quality may be cut as often as the budget. The library and the college or university to whose budget the library is inescapably tied must work with limited human and financial resources. College and university officials in charge of purse strings will know that corners in library staffing can no more be cut than classroom teaching can. Incompetent or over-worked teachers cannot teach well no matter how much they are or are not paid. Physicists are not hired to teach history, or Russian literature, or psychoanalysis. The same applies to catalogers as for bibliographers in such libraries as still have them. Perhaps naively, one hopes that both the university and the library administration set scholarly standards and educational goals first and then decide what to do with available funds. Economic, rather than scholarly and educational matters, however, often explicitly constitute the "bottom line."

Library administration is responsible not only for the number and quality of professional catalogers but, just as important, the procedure for working with shared bibliographical records. In many libraries, any item for which a record is found in a shared utility is not given to a professional cataloger to do but is routed to a copy-cataloger or even labeled and sent directly to the shelves with no evaluation. The decision to accept cataloging provided by an outside source is justified by the same sound reasons as were outlined above in the note on retrospective conversion. The same problems occur here, with the additional problem of internationally and vendor supplied records. If copy catalogers are hired with the abilities to evaluate and correct if necessary the insufficiencies and errors of these imported records and are expected to produce a good record according to local standards, cataloging will proceed more quickly as a result, and the library will benefit from the knowledge of many librarians, while not suffering from the inadequacies. The disaster of our time is that this work is being done more and more by people who can neither evaluate nor correct imported errors and often are forbidden from even thinking about it. If copy-cataloging is to be pursued mindlessly—and I object here that nothing should be pursued mindlessly—then it will result in a usable database only if the records received from these external sources are perfect. If catalog records from these external sources have any inadequacies or errors, the library will be paying for, and living with, a growing body of misinformation.

Database Administrators
Shared databases are, in the most basic sense, computers owned and maintained by corporate bodies: groups of shareholders or members. Decisions on inputting records into the database, the kinds of records the database will accept, entry practices, and price structures for use are all the prerogative of the database owners and managers. Librarians in academic libraries should therefore urge upon them the need for quality. Records already in the database are a difficult matter, since the quality issues of most concern require language and subject expertise for their correction as well as the item in hand.

Institutions and vendors outside the Anglo-American world have recently begun to use OCLC. The result has been a massive influx of records that do not adhere to the standards and headings used in the AACR/LCSH world. These bibliographical records require even more editing than a locally input acquisitions record and wreak havoc with authority control when imported into local systems. International contributions to OCLC, like other databases, are important breakthroughs for those who seek materials published abroad but are not available locally, but this broader use creates new problems. These must be solved individually by member institutions; might it not make more sense for the database administrators to separate these records and revise them before making them generally available? Once again, libraries are all sharing both good and bad records; most institutions most of the time are apparently treating the good and the bad equally, downloading and editing locally, if at all. "See no evil, fix no evil" applies to much of the copy-cataloging done in academic libraries. As a result, bad records persist and are being edited locally by each institution according to "whatever" standards: the exact opposite of how shared databases should function.

Other kinds of problems range from the bad records of habitual offenders to tapeloads from libraries that do not accept certain national standards, to retrospectively converted records that are often rife with errors and invalid headings. By accepting without review these various kinds of records, the quality of the shared database is undermined.

In certain cases and for certain purposes, these incomplete and even incorrect records suffice. For example, when a patron has a complete and correct citation, any librarian should be able to find the item if it exists if even one searchable field is correct (and the searcher does not stop at the first negative result). The vendor Harrassowitz uses a different system of transliteration for cyrillic letters that affects both titles and names. But if the acquisitions librarian searches by ISBN, the record is both there and recognizable, though incomplete and, by local standards, improperly transliterated. But if this record is downloaded into a local database without changing the searchable fields to conform to local practice, few users will search by ISBN and, consequently, the others will fail to find the item.

More often it is the case that the patron has an incomplete or incorrect citation, or a citation appearing in transliteration in some other language, and this is where the problem looms large. Yet even with an incomplete or incorrect citation, if the catalog record has some correct fields, and at least one of these matches the citation, the item can be located by the persistent searcher. With that acknowledgment, it still remains the case that even with correct fields, a vendor or other record without subject fields will be inadequate for the patron who asks for "that book about Einstein reviewed in last month's Atlantic Monthly." It is clear that a subject search could be quick and easy; otherwise finding the item will entail searching a periodical index or, for something so recent, a look into the item in which the citation was taken. The minimal level records without subjects that have been allowed into OCLC for many years are a well-known problem, and we need not elaborate on this here.

It is the ideal of the catalog record to provide a description that can be accessed equally easily by a number of different searches. The more errors and the fewer access points included, the less useful the record can be. For bibliographical information in a shared database to be efficiently used, that information should be qualitatively acceptable without further review. Neither of the major shared cataloging utilities (OCLC, RLIN) can be used in this fashion. Yet many libraries in practice have adopted cataloging procedures as if records from these databases can be accepted as they are.

CONCLUSIONS AND RECOMMENDATIONS

> The results... are now painfully visible: every error, every defect, is now repeated—often instantaneously—on a worldwide scale. The more universal this technology becomes, the fewer the alternatives that will be available, and the less possibility to restore autonomy to any of the components of the system.[34]

For three decades, librarians have lived with promises of what a shared online catalog could be; now most institutions proceed as though the promised state of affairs exists. It does not. Unqualified catalogers, decisions by database administrators, and library policies have all combined to bring about a situation—in spite of programs like PCC—where the quantity of records requiring review is growing rapidly while the quality of the personnel to perform this task and the performance of the task itself is rapidly diminishing.

In my youth, there was a common saying about those incredible new machines, computers: Garbage in, garbage out. Librarians have forgotten this. Library systems with astonishing capabilities are being used with great inefficiency because the

---

[34] Lewis Mumford, *The Pentagon of Power*. New York: Harcourt, Brace & World, 1970, p.159.

data necessary for the more powerful and refined searches were never entered into the database. Because we acknowledge that humans are imperfect and often disagree, we have abandoned any insistence upon exactness and appropriateness as well as fullness of description. The fact that the author of this critique makes mistakes—and the reader can find more than a few, as I have entered perhaps more than 20,000 records into OCLC and RLIN—is no reason to dismiss the problem. On the contrary, if I am doing a poor job of cataloging, that is further alarming proof of the magnitude of the problem.

Although incompetence of catalogers is a large concern of mine —and I shall speak bitterly and from the heart about that in my closing complaint—to err is human, and mistakes, misunderstanding, ignorance, and carelessness are all found in every profession. The crucial issue for librarianship is whether we continue to think that this is no problem, that computers will do their magic, thinking for us, self-correcting and correcting our errors as well, ignoring the true logical nature of computers: Garbage in, garbage out; or, on the contrary, we face the problem in its increasing magnitude, its perpetuation and institutionalization in our hiring policies. To put the matter simply: Is librarianship a matter of intelligence or artificial intelligence? If it is the latter, I want out.

I have three suggestions for catalogers and a bone to pick. The suggestions often seen in the library literature bear repeating since they have been disparaged so often in the era of "cheaper, faster, and maybe not quite so good." These are:

> * Right the first time. In a shared database, it is crucial for the data entered to be correct from the start. Wrong information supplied to any shared database takes on a life of its own and is reproduced and distributed worldwide. Misinformation in a database from corrupt sources requires users to review everything. This is economically unfeasible and rarely happens in practice.

The best possible solution is the only possible solution: get it right the first time.

* Strict self-review. It makes as little sense to hire someone to review the work of catalogers as it does to review bibliographical records imported from a shared database. Obviously, beginners need to be reviewed. But, after that, there is no need for adding layers of qualified persons to make sure everyone is doing things right. If there is money for another position, use it to put another cataloger to the task. Catalogers should not expect anyone else to find and correct errors—they should not make them in the first place (a goal, of course, impossible to achieve, but essential).

*Cooperation. Catalogers must know when they need help and must not be too shy or too proud to look for it. There are many possibilities now that did not exist in the past. Whether catalogers use existing resources or systematically initiate a group of networks for bringing those with responsibilities and problems beyond their grasp in touch with those with expertise, cooperation is a clear key to the problems catalogers face in a multilingual world inundated with publications.

EPILOGUE: THROWING STONES

The process of automation has produced imprisoned minds that have no capacity for appraising the results of their process, except by the archaic criteria of power and prestige, property, productivity and profit, segregated from any more vital human goals.[35]

---

[35] Ibid., p. 192.

And now, the final complaint of a middle-aged cataloger. Unpleasant as it may be to consider, is not the lack of qualified catalogers directly related to our "professionalism"? Intner's comment (noted earlier) concerning the impossibility of employing catalogers with adequate language and subject abilities is outrageously false. Libraries abound with underemployed underpaid staff who have academic credentials, backgrounds, skills, and abilities that surpass those of many librarians. The qualified people are right here among us but are only allowed to be here if they will work for low wages or as volunteers. Many of these staff would prefer the status and salary accorded to librarians but work in the library without these niceties because they treasure the academic environment and would not want to leave the intellectual possibilities that a university provides. Librarians prefer to continue performing their tasks at the height of their incompetence while prohibiting the multilingual doctorate without a library degree from rising above a salary half that of the professionally inept. A professional spends three hours a week in library school for two semesters studying cataloging, 90 hours total. Linguistically challenged, with no experience, a meagre academic background, maybe even no real commitment to scholarship and bingo! she or he is a tenure track Professional Cataloger. I began cataloging in 1982 as a temporary consultant (low pay, no benefits, no security), hired because of my linguistic skills and previous nonprofessional library experience. My training consisted of forty hours a week for three months studying under the principal cataloger, practicing with AACR2 and copy found on OCLC: a 500 hour cataloging practicum. Then I set to work. A good cataloger is not necessarily made in library school; the skills a cataloger needs are primarily intellectual skills and attitudes and broad academic background that are acquired only through a commitment to learning.

While the intellectual activity of cataloging is often given to staff to do, it is only because this activity is devalued by librarians and the administration. Instead of encouraging staff to increase their skills and responsibilities to meet a higher level position—an apprenticeship that could lead to professional competence and remuneration—the position itself is downgraded, and the staff member remains exactly where he or she previously was, the only difference being that the work is now more interesting. (This is a huge bonus that the qualified and academically inclined staff will eagerly accept. Unfortunately, with increasing frequency this "bonus" is forced upon staff who are neither linguistically nor academically equipped to do the work properly and who do not enjoy it.) But generally, in accordance with the devaluing of these positions, university staff policies and librarians' desire for status combine with union activity to ensure that thought, initiative, and responsibility for all nonprofessional staff are strictly regulated. Universities in general, and libraries in particular, prefer to create positions that demand routine and thoughtlessness in staff while proudly proclaiming the virtues and values of knowledge and learning. Universities design positions to require a minimum of intelligence so those employed can be paid less, however well-educated the applicants are. In addition, established positions that require thinking beings are eliminated whenever possible. It is a blatant lie to sing the praises of knowledge, then deliberately structure work responsibilities to eliminate the exercise of intelligence and judgment in as many positions as possible. We create at the same time a gulf between the rich and the poor, and a gulf between those who can exercise intelligence and judgment and those who are forbidden to do so. We set the stage for our comedy of errors by dividing our work according to status rather than fitting skills and abilities to the work that needs to be done.

Which will it be? Shared databases manipulated by obedient but ignorant worker ants where quality means correct punctuation or a community of junior and senior scholars combining knowledge and skills to create a database with accuracy and erudition on a level with the *Oxford English Dictionary*. My stance should be clear: I want a library staff devoted to the general life of scholarship and learning, where everyone is responsible to that "bottom line." If we cannot create such working conditions and work in such an environment, according to the same high standards as other academic disciplines, then bring on the high school students: we should be abolished.

REFERENCES

Barnett, Judith B. (1988). Bibliographic networks and the cataloger crisis. *Journal of Academic Librarianship*, 14(2), 99-100.

Chan, Lois Mai, & Vizine-Goetz, Diane. (1997). "Errors and obsolete elements in assigned Library of Congress Subject Headings: Implications for subject cataloging and subject authority control." *Library Resources & Technical Services*, 41(October), 295-322.

El-Sherbini, Magda. (1992). "Cataloging alternatives: An investigation of contract-cataloging, cooperative cataloging, and the use of temporary help." *Cataloging & Classification Quarterly*, 15(4), 67-88.

Ewbank, Linda C. (1996). Untitled report on the program 'Crisis in subject cataloging and retrieval' at the American Library Association Annual Meeting, Chicago, June 22-29, 1995, *Cataloging & Classification Quarterly,* 22(2), 92.

Grover, Mark L. (1991). "Cooperative cataloging of Latin-American books: The unfulfilled promise." *Library Resources & Technical Services*, 35(October), 406-415.

Gurevich, Konstantin. (1991). "Russian monographic records in the OCLC database: A crisis in shared cataloging." *Library Resources & Technical Services*, 5(October), 459-461.

Hafter, Ruth. (1996). *Academic librarians and cataloging networks: Visi-bility, quality control and professional status.* Westport, CT: Greenwood.

Intner, Sheila S. (1989). "Quality in bibliograhic databases: An analysis of member-contributed cataloging in OCLC and RLIN." *Advances in Library Administration and Organization*, 8, 1-24.

Intner, Sheila S. (1990). "Copy cataloging and the perfect record mentality." *Technicalities*, 10(July), 12-15.

Larson, Ray R. (1991). "The decline of subject searching: Long-term trends and patterns of index use in an online catalog." *Journal of the American Society for Information Science*, 42(April), 197-215.

Knutson, Gunnar. (1991). "Subject enhancement: Report on an experiment." *College & Research Libraries*, 52 (January), 65-79.

LeBlanc, James D. (1993). "Cataloging in the 1990's: Managing the crisis (mentality). *Library Resources & Technical Services*, 37(October), 423-433.

Mann, Thomas. (1997). "Cataloging must change! and indexer consistency studies: Misreading the evidence at our peril." *Cataloging & Classification Quarterly*, 22(3/4), 3-45.

Mumford, Lewis. (1970). *The Pentagon of Power*. New York: Harcourt, Brace & World.

Nielsen, Ralph, & Pyle, Jan M. (1995). "Lost articles: Filing problems with initial articles in databases." *Library Resources & Technical Services*, 39(July), 291-292.

Rohdy, Margaret. (1995). "The bibliographical control of foreign monographs: A review and baseline study." *Library Resources & Technical Services*, 39(January), 29-42.

Sercan, Cecilia S. (1994). "Where has all the copy gone? Latin American imprints in the RLIN database." *Library Resources & Technical Services*, 38(January), 56-59.

Svenonius, Elaine, & McGarry, Dorothy. (1993). "Objectivity in evaluating subject heading assignment." *Cataloging & Classification Quarterly* 16(2), 5-40.

Taylor, Arlene G. (1995). On the subject of subjects. *Journal of Academic Librarianship*, 21(November), 484-491.

Towsey, Michael. (1997). "Nice work if you can get it? A study of patterns and trends in cataloguing employment in the USA and the UK in the mid-1990's." *Cataloging & Classification Quarterly*, 24(1/2), 61-79.

Trainer, Karin A. (1989). "Dollars and sense: Training catalogers." In Sheila S. Intner & Janet Swan Hill (Eds.), *Recruiting, educating, and training cataloging librarians: Solving the problems*. New York: Greenwood, p.368-369.

Tsao, Jai-hsya (1994). "The quality and timeliness of Chinese and Japanese monographs in the RLIN database." *Library Resources & Technical Services*, 38(January), 60-63.

Xu, Hong. (1996). The impact of automation on job requirements and qualifications for catalogers and reference librarians in academic libraries. *Library Resources & Technical Services*, 40:1(January), 9-31.

II

Misinformation and Meaning in Library Catalogs

THE UNIVERSITY OF CHICAGO LIBRARY

September 10, 2004

TO: David Bade, Cataloging Department

FROM: Denise Weintraub, Library Personnel

You, Judith Nadler, Patricia Williams, Janet Fox, Renette Davis, and I met a little over a week ago to discuss the use of the University of Chicago name in connection with your publications.

At this meeting you mentioned that you had included a disclaimer in your materials, indicating that these materials are your own and not those of the University of Chicago. You also stated that you were not distributing these materials from the University of Chicago.

The copy of "Misinformation and Meaning in Library Catalogs" that you provided for your promotion process has a cover and title page with the author information as follows: "by D.W. Bade, Joseph Regenstein Library, University of Chicago."

Page 2 has the following distribution information: "A limited number of copies of this paper are available and may be obtained from the author. Please write for availability to: David Bade, Joseph Regenstein Library RM 170, University of Chicago, 1100 East 57th Street, Chicago, IL 60637."

On page 10 you provide the following signature to the Preface: "David Bade, Joseph Regenstein Library, 20 October 2003." I have included copies of these references with this memo.

We must ask you to remove all references to the University of Chicago with the exception of the disclaimer from your publications and remove the University of Chicago's address as a distribution address.

The Library respects your right to have and publish your opinions. The Library does not support these opinions or want to provide support for these opinions.

Cc: Judith Nadler
      Aneesah Ali
      Patricia Williams
      James Mouw

III

Colorless Green Ideals in the Language of Bibliographic Description: Making Sense and Nonsense in Libraries

Abstract
Cataloguing in libraries was formerly done by cataloguers with a wide range of academic backgrounds and linguistic abilities. With the rise of networked databases much of this work is now automated, outsourced to vendors, or done by persons lacking the requisite skills. The removal of this activity from libraries leads to a generic product produced for a generic user, with no possibility for a library-internal evaluation of the product. Librarians demand "a bibliographic record" of a certain form in a manner analogous to the generative grammar's production of sentences. So long as the form is correct, it is not evaluated for appropriateness or usefulness. The resulting information is often equivalent to colorless green ideas.

1. Introduction
In his 1975 Oxford inaugural address *Communication and language* Roy Harris asked

> why we have no linguistics of the living-room, or of the court room, or of the class room, or of any other form of socially institutionalized linguistic exchange...why the theoretical linguistics of a civilization which depends increasingly on language can apparently tell us so little about how the processes of linguistic communication are shaping the very form and content of that civilization. (Harris, 1990, p. 139)

One such form of linguistic exchange may be found in the library, where a diverse set of library users, many of them bilingual or multilingual, seek to locate reading (listening, viewing) material through the use of a catalogue, whether electronic or printed. In the early 21st century that catalogue is created more often than not by persons far removed from the library in time and space, and frequently by persons who cannot understand the language and contents of the items for which they create catalogue records. That library catalogues remain usable and libraries still used by many is evidence of some measure of successful technologically mediated linguistic communication. Although there has been no shortage of publications concerning hopes, expectations, theories, experiments and implementations, how this linguistic exchange succeeds and whether, when and how it fails have not been the subjects of empirical research, neither in linguistics nor in librarianship. It is the goal of this paper to offer a brief description of the setting, the linguistic activity of the librarian, and the importance of technologies, policies and library users in making sense (and nonsense) out of the library catalogue.

2. The nature of bibliographic description

In a world in which millions of new publications appear each year libraries play a large role in making those publications both known and available to readers around the world. This role requires libraries not only to discover, acquire and house (shelve, warehouse, or store electronically) these publications, but to provide readers with some means of discovering for themselves what publications exist and where they are located. Since readers do not ask to know about all the books available, but rather seek to find particular works by particular authors or on particular topics, one primary task for the library is to describe these publications in a manner in which readers can expect to find what they want.

The work of bibliographic description is generally known as *bibliography*; the particular kind of description performed in libraries has the specific purpose of identifying and describing items located in the library and it is usually called *cataloguing*. The product of this work in the library is in every case a linguistic artefact, whether it appears as a printed catalogue, a card catalogue (which may also be printed in book form, such as the British Library's *General Catalogue of Printed Books*), an online catalogue or an electronic database which may contain citations only or citations with full text, with both the citations and the full text being searchable.

In most electronic catalogues and databases it is possible to search every word and truncated portions thereof, a possibility which has led many information theorists and librarians to suggest and even to believe that the work of bibliographical description is no longer necessary in an online environment. A mindless transcription or optical scanning of the item's title page or table of contents into a database or better yet downloading the entire text into that same database is all that is needed: no interpretation is necessary, what matters is the searching software.[1] Yet even in an automated system, there is still a need to specify at a minimum certain elements since these appear in the publication itself as nothing more than words among other words, or rather, ink spots on paper. If library users are to search for authors, editors, titles, publishers and place of publication, these must be identified and described as such, which requires acts of interpretation. A biography, for example, may have on its title page no more than the name of the biographer and biographee, neither of which is identified as such; unless those marks on the page are identified as having a particular significance, these names are for the computer not names but nothing more than topographical shapes to be analyzed as sequences of numbers representing discrete concatenations of letters. The computer encoding which identifies the significance of each item of information in the electronic bibliographical record, whether it is created by human agents or is the result of the operation of software, is sometimes called *metadata*.

In the era of card catalogues the specification of this information in a bibliographical description was implicit in the layout of the catalogue card: the author appeared on the top left hand side of the card, followed in the next line by the title, subtitle, edition and so on. Each element was printed on the card in a prescribed order and according to a prescribed punctuation, these indicating to the user of the catalogue the nature of the information which followed. Thus subjects were preceded by Arabic numerals while additional authors, editors or societies were entered as the last elements on the card, each preceded by roman numerals. In an online environment, this information about information (i.e. metadata) is input into an electronic record according to a particular system of numerical encoding which permits any number of possible styles of display in the catalogue. For example, in the common MARC form of meta-

---

[1] Svenonius (2000, p. 66) noted this process and remarked that this amounts to transforming 'the theory of bibliographic description into a theory of bibliographical searching'.

data, the author is encoded as "100" if a person, "110" if a corporate body, society or association, "111" for a conference and "130" for an anonymous work or a work of multiple authorship such as the Bible. These will then display in the online catalogue in any manner which a given system specifies: thus the information coded in the 100 field may appear as "Doe, Jane" as the first line (the information implicit, as in the old card catalogue) or perhaps as "Author: Doe, Jane" with the authorship explicitly stated, and similarly for every other element of the description. When the information on the item described is correctly interpreted by the cataloguer, it can be correctly encoded and correctly displayed; if the black marks on the title page are incorrectly interpreted or if the title page is not correctly identified (e.g. an advertisement or dedication is mistakenly identified as the title page) then the resulting information may be completely useless and the necessary information will not be available for searching.

The vast majority of items described and entered into online catalogues in today's libraries are books, serials, maps and various other forms of printed and recorded materials which are not available for full text searching anywhere and therefore require not only the minimum of transcription of information found on the items but in addition some description of the contents, including the format, language of the text or sound recording, the subject/topic and perhaps genre. In spite of widespread hopes, dreams and even beliefs to the contrary, there is not yet any machine into which the librarian can insert the book and receive in return an analysis of these elements – even in the case of electronic documents – and therefore this work of description must still be done by human beings.

3. The communicational goals of bibliographic description

In order to produce a description of the contents of any particular item, whether a treatise on linguistics or a recording of Gabrielli's works for trumpet ensembles, there are a number of prerequisites; these prerequisites vary by institution. There are local, national and international standards and conventions regarding transcription and analysis of materials, as well as the differing goals of different kinds of institutions: music libraries demand far more in their descriptions of sound recordings and scores than do high school libraries or many university libraries, and the desired level of description varies similarly for legal materials, maps, medical books and literature. Research libraries rarely provide subject headings for fiction and poetry whereas many public libraries put this high on their list of priorities. More generally, a knowledge of the standards and conventions of bibliographical description, an ability to understand the language of the item described and a knowledge of the metadata systems and subject terminology used are all required for the successful performance of this work. I do not say the correct performance of this work, for the simple reason that the work can be done successfully even though incorrectly as often as it can be done correctly but unsuccessfully since the meaning of correct is usually determined by library rules but the meaning of successful is uniquely determined by the library user with each search performed. It is on this disjunction between correct and successful description that this article focuses.

In the past, prior to the rise of shared library catalogues and the existence of large international bibliographic databases, the goal of bibliographic description was understood to be an aid to the library user in the activity of finding what the library owned and had available for the users of the library. For many librarians this is still the assumption and orientation which guides the work of cataloguing. The librarian examines each item acquired, determines how users are likely to search for the item (e.g. by author, subject, genre) and provides a description designed to maximize the number of potential users and uses and the ways in which one could be led to the item by the description. This description is always limited by the linguistic and subject knowledge of the cataloguer, by time constraints, budgets, and the technical limits of the catalogue (e.g. the size of the card or the online system's searching capabilities) as well as the nature of the community of users, be they English speakers, Cambodian refugees, migrant laborers, the faculty and students of a private college, or inner city school children. As examples of such limitations, we can imagine that there would be no need to distinguish between authors and editors in the catalogue record if the system cannot distinguish them in its searching or display, nor is there a need for a bilingual catalogue in the absence of a bilingual community. Given these various limitations, the descriptions produced have one purpose: to permit the library's users (including librarians themselves in their work with the collection) to accomplish their own goals involving materials available in the library or through the library's services (e.g. electronic journals).

The immense difficulty which this work creates for any large library is not simply a matter of volume; the most serious difficulties involve the number of languages and the breadth of subjects encountered. In some libraries like the Library of Congress in Washington, D.C., an organizational solution to these particular problems was attempted by dividing the work among specialists in languages and subjects, the former providing "ordinary language" descriptions which are then translated by the subject specialist into the terminology of the specific subject heading systems in use, the Library of Congress Subject Headings (LCSH) and Medical Subject Headings (MESH). But by far the greatest emphasis in the library world has been on the development of technical solutions since these are deemed to be more economical both in terms of time and money than the hiring of a staff adequate to institutional needs. The development of the shared electronic library catalogue in the 1960s and its integration with the Internet in the 1990s led to the common belief that the human labour of bibliographical description was no longer necessary: libraries would no longer be required to create bibliographical information, they would simply download records found online in other libraries' catalogues.

One of the more obvious problems with this approach was that someone had to create that bibliographical record; all the libraries in the world could share a database but if none were inputting records then there would be no records to share. The trend of the past decade has been to input "minimal" records – records which would be sufficient for a machine match but not intended to support the needs of library users – with the expectation that one person somewhere in the world would, upon finding this minimal record, enhance it with all the desired names, subject headings, complete and correct transliteration and so on. At the same time the idea was put forward that if publishers and booksellers could be trained to do this work, they could be allowed to enter such records into the large shared databases and libraries would no longer need to do any of this work; publishers, distributors and booksellers would take over all of this work because of the potential for financial rewards in the form of increased orders due to the order information they input being available to everyone using these international databases. Some have even suggested that everything on the Internet could be catalogued by requiring every Web page to include standardized metadata.

The results of these developments have been predictable: with the library users' needs no longer being considered in the creation of the bibliographical database, there are only two non-economic goals in the production of these records: (1) input of those elements required by the technical system (e.g. certain elements in the record are required, such as title, while others such as author, publisher and subject are not) whether or not they are correct or appropriate to the item described; and (2) ability to locate these items for acquisition or for the purpose of purchasing the enhanced and useful record from a shared database. Everything else is left to the market. The belief that what is now needed in a bibliographic record is simply "a bibliographic record" to link to a particular book by a barcode, call number or vendor number leaves the work of interpretation and all matters of communicative usefulness, appropriateness and errors as strictly technical matters, the responsibility of vendors and outsourcing agencies, not the library. Of course few state this openly[2] but in practice it is impossible to evaluate any description provided for appropriateness without the item which it claims to describe already known or in view. To my knowledge this is never done for records batch imported from a shared database.

These records, known to be inaccurate and useless for most users because created without attention to accuracy and explicitly coded as being minimal or below minimal level descriptions, are coded for enhancement in the individual library catalogues and regularly tapeloaded to be matched against the large shared databases in hopes of retrieving an improved record. That improved record, however, may be and often is the work of a library staff member somewhere or employee of a commercial firm who is under orders to "enhance" any record found, regardless of whether the language or subject of the item is understood. For given a useless record, some administrators assume that their staff can make some improvements and therefore increase the value of the record for their users. Furthermore, there have been handsome financial incentives to do this work, whether or not it is done intelligently. When libraries in possession of the unenhanced useless records send their records out to match against the database and find that someone has fixed it up nice and tidy these records are then downloaded into local catalogues without any awareness that the record being purchased is not an improvement but a farce, yet since the work is done auto-

---

[2] A friend of mine with extraordinary linguistic abilities interviewed for a position as a cataloguer in one of the most prestigious universities in the United States and was told at the interview by the library director that the library did not want cataloguers to waste their time ensuring the accuracy or usefulness of the records created for the catalogue since all of the necessary information would be added later by downloading a good record from the shared database. All that was wanted was that a bar code on the book be linked to a minimal record in the shared database. The fact that the person in that position would be the person responsible for creating and maintaining the records in the shared database from which all knowledge was expected to flow seemed to be of no importance for the library director's understanding of the efficacy of the process.

matically no one in the library ever sees much less evaluates the product.

The current situation [2007] in libraries (at least in the United States) is such that the former focus on the usefulness of the bibliographic record to the library's users has been replaced by a focus on producing a technical object without any communicative purpose;[3] the sole communication required is that the record can be matched by software to a corresponding record in a shared database. This is true in spite of programs such as the Program for Cooperative Cataloging (PCC), a program designed to promote the creation and sharing of bibliographical records of a certified quality at a bargain price. For some librarians, this program was a welcome and necessary means for enabling librarians to make corrections as needed rather than having to initiate a long process of documentation and verification before any correction could be made.[4] But as more and more institutions joined the program for other reasons (e.g. cost cutting, prestige, following the trend) the goals of the programme were reoriented away from supporting increased responsibility towards *decreased* responsibility. The conflict between the goals of quality and economy was "resolved" by focusing on establishing authorized headings and not on their appropriateness or the qualifications of those creating them.[5]

---

[3] In an information economy, the production of information appears to follow the same trajectory as money, from means to end. Galimberti (1999) noted that "Marx had described this transformation of means into ends with regard to money. As means money serves to produce goods and to satisfy needs, but when all goods and needs are mediated by money, then it becomes the end, for which even the production of goods and the satisfaction of needs must be sacrificed if necessary." (p. 37).

[4] I have participated in the programme almost since its inception for precisely these reasons.

[5] Most of what I have written in this essay is corroborated by the following remarks from the PCC page for its proposed revision of its Mission Statement (http://www.loc.gov/catdir/pcc/tgrptPCCMission.html): 'The Task Group began its work by identifying trends and issues that will impact the cataloging environment over the next 5–7 years. The following are the as-

sumptions we made about that environment: Batch acquisition of records will be the norm *Records for e-resources will be generated through macros and loader programs *Records for specialized materials will continue to be created in-house but the records will be short and search engines will rely more on post- rather than pre-coordination of data *Authority records will continue to perform a role of fundamental importance in the development and refinement of finding tools and in the automated generation and receipt of various types of metadata *There will be an increasing coverage of remote access resources, which by their very nature (i.e., varied presentation, imbedded and associated metadata) will require less emphasis on descriptive cataloging and more emphasis on subject access *The lowest level of staff will perform the majority of routine cataloging work *Catalog librarians will focus more of their attention on subject analysis and authority control as opposed to description *Publishers will routinely supply shelf-ready materials to libraries for commercially published materials *Human intervention in cataloguing will shift to a focus on unpublished, often uncataloged material – material that fills the shelves of special collections, archives and institutional storage facilities *A majority of resource discovery activity will occur outside the framework of the OPAC and the Library Information System will be used primarily for the business purposes of ordering, receiving, tracking payments, recording license agreements, etc. *User access to information will occur in a much more diversified environment *Structured data will enter the library sphere from many sources. Based on these assumptions, the group identified the following roles for PCC:Continues to be involved in helping to establish standards and in helping to promote shared ''buy in'' and acceptance of those standards *Continues to be involved in creating good cataloguing and will continue to promote cost-effective solutions in a heterogeneous metadata environment *Promotes certified types of metadata in a diverse metadata framework *Supports efforts to derive standard cataloging records created according to standards established by other communities *Champions creation of records for the vast numbers of unpublished and uncatalogued materials residing in member libraries *Promotes the use of commercially created data for use in local systems *Continues to embraces its core activities but it will find ways to support new access mechanisms *Leads in the education of catalogers *Advocates the needs of the end user and allow the end user perspective to guide future efforts.'

Some of this sounds acceptable or even splendid. However, the implementation of these guidelines in most libraries appears to be motivated by and in practice entirely reduced to efforts to save money and eliminate the time and attention required to identify and satisfy 'the needs of the end user'; in order to satisfy the economic goal library policies require the abandonment of the only goal that matters.

When full records are created at the start, this is frequently done by persons unable to understand the content of the item described. In such cases there is also no communicative context nor intent for the cataloguer has no understanding that would provide a basis for communication. There can be no collaboration between cataloguer and future users because the cataloguer cannot imagine how or why anyone would want to find and read this particular item. The decision to provide descriptions in the absence of any capacity for doing this intelligently is what Morel (2003) would classify as an absurd decision, one with consequences persistently and radically contrary to the desired goal. In the case of bibliographical description the goal ought to be the provision of a useful guide to the available literature and not simply filling in the blanks because they are blank.

What kind of language appears in the catalogue as a result of these absurd policies and the decisions they entail? The grinding of the linguistic machinery with no communicative purposes produces exactly those forms of 'English' (English is the language of American library catalogues) produced by Noam Chomsky's generative grammar: 'Colorless green ideas sleep furiously.' 'S'il y a ni sens ni communication, le tout se réduit à une éjaculation de sons, qui pourraient être autres et n'importe quoi!' (Ellul, 1981, p. 198). In fact it may well be that a study of the generation of the inappropriate and absurd subject headings produced according to the rules for bibliographical description but without any communicational intent could yield significant insights into the nature of the I-language posited by generative theory and the decontextualized linguistic forms that it would produce.

4. Well-formed strings vs. useful descriptions

In many cases – though by no means all – the transcription of title page information and its correct interpretation can be accomplished with very little relevant linguistic knowledge; common publishing conventions throughout much of the world combined with a large database in which one may identify authors, publishers, series titles, place names and many other desired elements of the record in some cases allows the possibility for an intelligent cataloguer to produce an accurate transcription even in the absence of any knowledge of the language of the text. The same cannot be said for subject analysis which nearly always requires an ability to read the text of the item described. (Possible exceptions are such items as dictionaries where format is obvious and the languages involved easy to identify or guessed from the title page, publications with an abstract or publisher's insert in a known language, etc.) While records for publications from outside the Euro-American universe often reveal outrageous misunderstandings, numerous examples can be found among descriptions for standardized publications in European languages. A look at a few examples reveals just how mechanically the description is produced.

The first example was provided by the largest commercial vendor of bibliographical records in the United States. The title below is for a Russian book which the cataloguer apparently transliterated basing the transliteration of the cyrillic letters on their topographic similarity to Latin letters:

Example I.
Actual title: День Ленина: сборник для пионерских лубов
Transliteration provided: Dehi rehuha; cdophuk dra nuohepckux krydob
(Proper transliteration: Den' Lenina: sbornik dlia pionerskikh klubov)

Clearly, someone was given a job to do, and did it, even in the absence of any comprehension, and without any thought to the usefulness of the description provided.

Example II.
Senni dende / Jiiri Jina and Jiiri Hinkanto.
Author: Jina, Jiiri

Author: Hinkanto, Jiiri

One trouble is that although the 'and' recorded above is a good translation, it is an incorrect transcription – the title page has 'nda'. More importantly, the 'authors' are not authors, but in fact this phrase means 'First Year and Second Year'. Even in a library which specializes in African imprints such as the library which provided this record, one cannot expect cataloguers who can read all of the languages which appear in print in Africa. The intended readership of the book was mistaken for the authorship, and the result is both absurd (especially reversing the order to match English onomastic structure) and useless for the library user. This may be an instance of dedication to access (the book is available by title, which is really the only way anyone would look for it) but the 'authors' identified in the record were clearly cranked out without any understanding.

Example III.
Title: Johannis Jessenii a Jessen, Anatomiae, Pragae, anno M.D.C. abs se solenniter administratae historia: accessit eiusdem de ossibus tractatus.
Added title: Anatomiae, Pragae.

In this case the cataloguer identified the author correctly and thought that the real title of the book must follow the author's name which appears at the beginning. (According to the current rule in the Anglo-American Cataloguing Rules, when a name is grammatically linked to the title which follows – as in this case – the Name + Title is given as it appears, and an additional title (called a Uniform title) is added, this title being that by which the book would be cited.) However, the cataloguer who provided this record clearly did not understand the meaning of the Latin title and provided not the title by which one might expect the user to know the book, but two words describing the author: "A doctor, from Prague". Again, a useless title, evidently provided simply as a matter of following the rules with no understanding of the meaning of the title. A similar case involved the provision of the original Latin title for a Russian translation of a portion of a work by Orosius:

Example IV.
Author: Orosius, Paulus
Uniform title: Historiarum adversus paganos libri IV–V.
Title: Istoriia protiv iazychnikov: knigi IV–V
Title on facing page: Historiae adversum paganos libri IV–V

The authorized Uniform title for the complete original text of Orosius appears in the Library of Congress database and is the standardized form used by American libraries, including the commercial vendor which provided this record and the authority heading to match it. That title is: Historiarum adversus paganos libri VII. The vendor which supplied the amusing version of Orosius' original title as the Uniform Title clearly did not understand the difference between the Latin title found in the Library of Congress file (from which it was clearly derived) and the Russian and Latin titles found on the book. The Russian title was probably understood, but not either of the Latin titles. Yet since the record was created to satisfy a particular quality assurance program (PCC), an authorized heading for the Uniform title for this item had to be created and added to the database, leading to the curious result that in the Library of Congress file of authorized headings it appeared that Orosius wrote a history in seven books (Historiarum adversus paganos libri VII) and another one in four to five books (Historiarum adversus paganos libri IV–V).

In each of these examples the product of bibliographical description is a well-formed technically perfect "information object" which unfortunately must be judged to be a "misinformation object". The problem at this level is not actually as severe as it may seem, for, with the exception of Example I, all of these books could easily be located by anyone searching for the title (Examples II–IV) or author (Examples III–IV). (My discovery of Example I is a long story which is irrelevant here.) The problems become severe when the subject analysis and classification are produced in the absence of any understanding.

Example V.
Title: Bezopasnost v regione tsentral'noi i vostochnoi Evropy: rol' Rossii i NATO
Classification: U413 (Army War College, Carlisle Barracks, Pennsylvania)
Subject heading: North Atlantic Treaty Organization–Russia (Federation)

Even without any understanding of the title, the reader will immediately note the discrepancy between the classification and the description of the subject. If we translate only the title we get a fair idea of the topic of this volume: Security in the region of Central and Eastern Europe: the role of Russia and NATO. The subject heading used is a perfectly good subject heading, and according to the syntax of LCSH this subject heading indicates that the item so described should discuss Russia's participation in or relations with NATO. But the book is no more about Russia's participation in NATO than it is about the US Army War College in Carlisle Pennsylvania.

While it is impossible to determine exactly how this description was produced, it is possible to suggest the probable manner of arriving at such inappropriate description and classification since the work often follows common heuristic procedures and the telltale marks of that process are evident in this record. First, the subjects are assumed to be in the title itself and the task becomes one of determining which of these words to select and search for the authorized form in the authorized headings file. In this case the subtitle was apparently mistakenly identified as the significant element of the title and the words simply combined without realizing how the system of subject headings prescribes the meaning of such concatenation. The classification number was probably assigned by the common method of looking up the subject heading assigned and using the same number which was assigned for any other book with that subject heading. Of course, a book about nuclear disarmament treaties, Ronald Reagan, China or the Army War College could have as one of its subjects the same subject assigned for this book (whether this topic is also discussed therein or was also mistakenly assigned as it was in this example), and therefore the existence of the same subject in any record is no guarantee that the two items ought to be classified together. This kind of error is often referred to as similarity matching in the literature on human error: the assumption of similarity, for better or worse, determines the description and ends the work of interpretation. Past interpretations arising in different contexts are wrongly assumed to fit the present context, a matter of significance not only for bibliographical description but for a general theory of semantic interpretation.

Example VI.
Title: Rezistenţa - prima condiţie a victoriei: articole politice apărute în "Dreptatea" (1944-1947) / N. Carandino.
Subjects: Carandino, Nicolae
    Dreptatea (Timisoara, Romania)
    World War, 1939–1945 – Romania
    Critics – Romania – Biography
    Resistance movements, War (Another library has
    replaced this heading with ''Peace movements'' in its
    catalogue.)

This description, perhaps even more clearly than that in Example V, demonstrates a complete incomprehension of the meaning of the title, as well as the contents of the book. The book is not about Carandino nor about *Dreptatea*, rather it is a collection of articles by Carandino published in the journal *Dreptatea* encouraging resistance to the communists after the departure of the German army, i.e. neither 'Resistance movements, War', nor 'Peace movements' but 'Anticommunist movements'. Although the record appears to have an impressively thorough list of subject descriptors, *not one of them is appropriate to the contents of the book*. Again, the general method of assigning these subject headings is fairly easy to guess: word in title, it must be the subject, so therefore 'Rezistenţa' and 'Dreptatea', while 'World War' was perhaps suggested by the dates, and Carandino was assumed to be the subject as well as the author.

Example VII.
Title: Bitva na Kalke : 31 maia 1223 g.
Subject: Khalkha (Mongolian people) – History.
Class no.: DS793.M7 (Mongolia – Ethnic groups – Khalkha)

This example perfectly exemplifies how language would work if human beings searched a mental lexicon for vocabulary items, for that was almost certainly how the description of this book was produced. The entry 'Khalkha (Mongolian people)' in the Library of Congress authority file has cross-references to alternative terms for most items, and for the Khalkha there is a cross-reference 'Kalka (Mongolian people) – See Khalkha (Mongolian people)'. The cataloguer apparently searched the authority file, found the cross-reference above and used it without looking a little further where one finds ''Kalka River, Battle of, Ukraine, 1223''. It is hard to imagine that the cataloguer tried to make any sense of the title: Battle at/on the Khalkha (Mongolian people), 31st May 1223 is absurd. The heading was chosen simply by selecting the first available match in an alphabetical list in a thesaurus with no understanding or interpretation involved (and probably no examination of the contents of the volume either).

From an integrationist perspective these examples are especially revealing, particularly if my reconstruction of the processes of the production of Examples V and VII are correct, because they demonstrate a reliance on past interpretive acts, assumptions of identity of reference or meaning between forms without regard for context, and the generation of linguistic artifacts in the absence of any communicative situation or intent. In fact Example V is known by this author to have been produced in an organization in which the cataloguers are specifically instructed not to provide an intelligent record but simply to produce 'a record' with 'a subject heading' and 'a classification number' and move the book onto the shelf; the useful description which the library does admit to needing is expected to be provided by someone else somewhere else and only later downloaded from a shared database. Mindless labour provides 'more, faster, cheaper' the administration insists – which it does – but the additional claim of 'better' is contradicted by all the evidence and matters stand as Ellul described them in 1981: Le parler pour ne rien dire a cancérisé la parole. (p. 172)

5. Descriptions correct/incorrect, appropriate/inappropriate and useful/useless

In this section a variety of topics relating to variation in bibliographical records are discussed. Remarks on the determination of what is an acceptable variant versus an error, problems of multilingual collections and users, and inconsistent analyses are followed by brief discussions of the implications of the uniqueness of each description, the treatment of errors and the interpretation of error in libraries and in error research in ergonomics.

5.1. Evaluating quality and identifying errors

In the literature of library and information science, there has been a modest number of publications devoted to problems of bibliographic quality, of errors and misinformation in bibliographies, library catalogues and shared databases.[6] Most of that literature has focused on the simplest of matters, for example identifying typographical errors in the bibliographical records which are not also found on the item described. In matters such

---

[6] See Bade (2002, 2003, 2004) for references and discussions of that literature.

as typographical errors, the issue of useful/useless is not addressed so much as assumed: typographical errors are not useful for any searcher. The issue of appropriate/inappropriate is irrelevant, and the issue of correct/incorrect is easily decided on the basis of what actually appears on the item being described.

Another aspect which has received considerable attention is the correct assignment of coding in the record. In this case, the usefulness is determined by the nature of the online catalogue and is therefore simply a technical necessity: there can be no specific searches unless the metadata identifying the nature of the various elements of the record is supplied. Correct/incorrect in matters of coding, however, depends entirely upon their appropriateness which can only be decided by an act of interpretive judgement concerning the item described. In Example II above the record was perfectly coded for the 'authors' identified, but the identification of those particular black marks on the page (Jiiri Jina, Jiiri Hinkanto) as authors was inappropriate and hence the coding which appears to be correct to anyone who does not understand Songhai must be judged as useless and incorrect by anyone who can understand the information recorded (even without having the item itself to examine) because the entire field containing those 'authors' should not be in the record at all.

The chief defect of most of the literature on the correctness of bibliographical records has been that qualitative evaluation of these matters has been performed strictly on the basis of the records in the database – formal characteristics, completeness, conformity to standards – with no attempts to evaluate these records in terms of their appropriateness in respect of the actual item being described and their usefulness for the potential and future users.[7] An evaluation of the appropriateness and hence usefulness and correctness of these records can only be made with a knowledge of what is being described and for

---

[7] Mann (1997) and Hjørland (1997, and other works) discuss these matters in detail.

whom the description is being prepared. In some published evaluations, if a record contained no indication that the record had been corrected, then the record was assumed to be correct; in other studies if the classification and subject headings matched, then they were both assumed to be correct (even though they could just as well both be incorrect); and in yet other studies no attempt was made to evaluate anything other than the formal structure: for such evaluators, 'Colorless green ideas sleep furiously' is indeed a wellformed syntactic structure.

Any evaluation of the language of bibliographic description which would focus upon appropriateness and usefulness must necessarily consider both the item described and for whom the description is created: who might be interested in this item and how might they go about looking for it. In such a situation, judgements of correctness, appropriateness and usefulness cease to be matters of counting departures from previously determined rules and standards. Instead, the task of evaluation as of description itself becomes a complex art of understanding and interpretation, of considering the subject of a publication, the indexing language of the thesaurus used in light of a specific publication which did not exist for the compilers of that thesaurus, and an unknown group of potential users searching for this item for various practical reasons and thinking according to any number of disciplinary and theoretical approaches.

The rules for cataloguing, however, cannot specify what ought to appear in the record beyond the most abstract formal description. The form of the rules are in fact like those found in a generative grammar: a well-formed sentence must have the structure (NP) V (NP), etc. The cataloguing rules stipulate that a well-formed bibliographical record should have the form (Author) – Title -(Publisher) – Subject – Class number and so on. If the cataloguer is asked to create 'a record' (with 'a subject heading' and 'a classification number') and that work is evaluated solely on the presence of 'a subject' and 'a class number', then there simply are no errors other than the lack of 'a record', 'a subject' or 'a class number'. Any record is as good as any other, questions of appropriateness and usefulness are considered inappropriate and useless while evaluation is simply quantitative: is there a record (subject, class number), yes or no, for each item to be evaluated. The expectations and evaluations of quality differ among many kinds of libraries with varied expectations, all the way from this practice in which there are no errors, to those music libraries which demand that every composition must be established in a uniform manner, every performer, conductor, composer, arranger must be identified and established in a uniform manner, and every piece on every sound recording described and available for searching by all parties involved, and titles in the language on the label as well as according to their authorized standard forms.

The practice and evaluation of subject analysis is a crucial and much debated aspect of bibliographic description.[8]

---

[8] Subject analysis is one aspect of cataloguing which distinguishes it from traditional bibliography as defined for example by Greg (1966), for whom it was the first step in literary criticism. 'The study of books as material objects' (p. 241) is 'in no way particularly or primarily concerned with the enumeration or description of books...bibliography has nothing to do with the subject matter of books, but only with their formal aspect.' (p. 240). Greg insisted that 'what the bibliographer is concerned with is pieces of paper or parchment covered with certain written or printed signs. With these signs he is concerned merely as arbitrary marks; their meaning is no business of his... the study of textual transmission involves no knowledge of the sense of a document but only of its form; the document may theoretically be devoid of meaning or the critic ignorant of its language' (p. 247) but did not acknowledge that in order to distinguish between an apostrophe and a meaningless speck of ink – one of his prime examples – one must know what an apostrophe is and why it is used. He does admit that in practice the ideal is not followed: 'Of course, in practice, we should hardly follow this severely ideal method of textual research. Nobody would think of editing a text that had no meaning, and nobody would choose to edit a text in a language he did not understand – though it might be a very interesting exercise. We all involuntarily pay attention to the sense of the texts we are studying; and the sense often enables us to arrive by a short cut at results that could only be laboriously achieved by strictly bibliographical methods, and may lead us to results that could not be reached by those methods at all.' (p. 248). I would say that a text that one cannot understand is a text that has no meaning for the reader/

There are those who believe that in the era of the Internet no subject description is necessary because today's students and younger scholars use Google and do not, will not and in fact cannot use a more complicated searching system, least of all one which requires searching terms according to a controlled vocabulary. There are others who insist that natural language keyword searching is all that is ever needed; at the very least, they insist, the current systems of subject headings need to be totally revised to reflect 'natural language' (meaning, presumably, their own preferred vocabulary or some vocabulary common at the date of their writing). Finally, there are those who advocate and develop the various restricted indexing languages including thesauri such as LCSH, the terms of which must be pre-coordinated with stringent restrictions on cooccurrence.

Most of the discussion of these matters has been informed by a reading of the library literature, not so much of it by actual use or observance of subject searching by library users, and few writers on the topic appear to have studied the immense literature in linguistics and philosophy devoted to natural or ordinary language.[9] While there is a growing interest in cross-language information retrieval, no one has yet focused on the problems arising from the multilingual character of most library catalogues and the large databases upon which they rely and how natural language will work in that context: the model of the library and its users is always monolingual. Furthermore, awareness and discussion of the temporal aspects of subject thesauri has been limited to proposals and policies for incorporating new terms; obsolescence and historical changes in meanings are matters which information scientists and librarians have not attempted to address.

---

indexer, and it is in just such an activity that one finds librarians everywhere engaging, according to Greg's ideals but without any of Greg's scruples.
[9] Blair (1990, 2003) being an important exception discussed below.

5.2. Using and evaluating the multilingual catalogue

Since the advent of electronic catalogues the multilingual nature of any large library catalogue (and those of many small libraries as well) has been a seriously neglected issue. Previously wherever libraries had publications printed in scripts other than the Latin alphabet, these often had their own separate catalogues, e.g. one catalogue for publications in the Cyrillic alphabet, another for Burmese publications, another for Chinese and so on. With the conversion to electronic catalogues in the 1960–1970s, everything had to be transliterated and entered into the catalogue in the Latin alphabet, with a set number of diacritics. This move was itself an extreme impoverishment of the catalogue, whatever the benefits may have been. Even now with the possibility of displaying scores of different scripts including Chinese characters, searching for most of these scripts in most available systems must be done using the transliterated forms.

The other side of the multilingual nature of the library catalogue is the language of bibliographical description: no matter what the language of the title and text, in American bibliographical databases the language of description (e.g. pagination, subject headings, notes) was for decades assumed to be – and often required to be – English. In the past decade some of the large shared bibliographical databases have sought to expand into the international library market, inviting libraries and vendors from all over the world to input records into these databases according to any language of description and any set of standards or even none at all. One such database, OCLC, intends eventually to provide parallel records for each item in all of the languages of description used by its members and clients. That sounds good, but it is far from a reality, and the current practice is that many records are input in one language of description (e.g. French, German, English) and then other libraries using other languages of description add their own subject headings to the record or make a 'parallel' record in another language. This again is not necessarily a problem other than the multiplicity of records for the same item, except for one practice which became prevalent after the introduction of those internationally supplied records. That was the translation of headings supplied – in whatever language – into English by persons who could not understand (1) the non-English headings, or (2) how those headings ought to be stated according to the local system (e.g. LCSH) and usage, or (3) the topic of the item described. The result has often been word-for-word translation, followed by an attempt to match that with something in the local subject thesaurus. The use of this 'dictionary' approach based on something in the record but not upon an understanding of the contents of the book leads to all the misunderstandings and misrepresentations which this form of twice-removed translation predictably entails.

In the absence of the promised catalogue of multilingual records searchable by multilingual search strategies, the problems which different languages of description produce are problems directly related to communication with the users: either an international user group uses an international language (which, the reader will have already suspected, will be English if American librarians get their way) or every user has to work with records in every language and according to a multitude of standards for representing names and subjects. That is the dilemma of the large databases. For individual libraries, the problems are otherwise.

In the United States there are many public libraries that serve a non-English using community (e.g. Chinatowns, Latino barrios, settlements of refugees from Somalia, Afghanistan), or a bilingual or even multilingual community, and here multiple languages of description may be desired, just as they are in South Africa, Israel and Canada. There are also many colleges and universities with large populations of students and faculty from outside the Anglophone world. These students and faculty are nevertheless assumed to be learning English, and the language of instruction is English, so there should be no necessity for a multilingual catalogue and the extraordinary expense which that entails. What is needed is a catalogue in English, with materials in all languages described according to that language. Purchasing records from a library abroad or an international vender with description and subject analysis in any language other than English fragments the results of any subject search. Instead of finding all the books on Mongolian literature under one heading, the searcher will get only a partial set of responses for any search such as 'Mongolian literature'. For additional records the user must search 'Menggu wenxue', 'Mongolische Literatur', 'Letteratura mongola' and so on for eternity. No one search will suffice, and the number of searches required for an exhaustive search is both unknown and unknowable. Where English is the language of the library user community, English needs to be the language of the description, just as an Arabic community requires an Arabic description and libraries in South Africa need descriptions for each item in all of the national languages.

5.3. Indexer inconsistency: valuable variation or errant behaviour?

One of the most contested issues in the area of subject description of the past 20 years has been the problem of 'indexer inconsistency', i.e. the problem that different persons given the task of determining the subject of any given item will, between 20% and 80% of the time (depending upon which study you read), differ on which subjects are assigned.[10] On the one side are those who argue that it is such a subjective practice that objective evaluation is impossible and any description is as good as any other, some even suggesting that automated indexing is just as good and should replace human indexers.[11] On the other hand are those who insist that the extent of agreement on subject analysis can be very high when those doing the subject analysis are

---

[10] Discussions of this literature may be found in Hjørland (1997) and Mann (1997). See also Bade (2003).

[11] One of the clearest results of my research is that indexing produced by persons who apparently cannot (or at least who do not) read is often accomplished in the same manner as a computer and is indeed no better than automated indexing.

familiar not only with the rules and tools (e.g. LCSH) but with the subject matter itself and the associated discipline(s). The crux of the matter involves linguistic matters of long standing: problems of unlimited semiosis (Pierce) and reocentric semantics (Harris).[12]

Subject analysis is an attempt to state in a specific language – in many cases in a severely restricted and artificial construct based upon that language – and in as few words as possible what a particular item (book, film, journal) is about for the specific purpose of enabling persons to browse the collection by subject. When this activity is carried out in the belief that indexer consistency is both impossible and unnecessary, any description may (but need not be) regarded as being as good as any other; when this activity is undertaken by a cataloguer with reocentric convictions, there is only one correct description; in both of these cases there is a strong likelihood that the manner in which the description provided fits into the existing catalogue, its appropriateness for local users, and its potential use by persons distant in place and time will be left out of consideration.

There is never only one possible useful description; Blair has argued 'that the number of different descriptions that can represent the intellectual content of even a relatively short document may have no upper bound' (Blair, 2003, p. 5). Not only may a particular document be of interest for many different reasons, but 'opposing views arise as to how a particular literature should be described' (Blair, 2003, p. 4): what one regards as physics another regards as metaphysics. The language of bibliographic description is, like all language, 'a continuously ongoing, creative activity . . . socially contested, differentially valued, variable, and inseparable from its participants' purposes, prejudices, and desires. It is, in short, the creature of its integration into cultural circumstances' (Taylor, 1997, pp. 24–25).

---

[12] For a discussion of Pierce's notion of unlimited semiosis in information retrieval, see Blair (1990); for reocentric semantics and the language of science see Harris (2005).

Subject description will always be contested terrain – exactly like scholarship – and it always should be. This revisioning and reinterpretation gives rise to variation which should be understood as an increase of knowledge and approaches to the collection rather than error understood as a departure from a norm or the one and only correct description. Description and understanding change through time, as they ought to if the world is not static. Stating the problem in terms of indexer consistency is to misplace the emphasis on conformity rather than usefulness. Library users need useful headings and these will be as varied as the potential uses of the users. The real issue is that some descriptions are useful to many and some are not useful at all.

5.4. Words and babies

The problem of locking description and therefore the catalogue into past understandings exists with the use of any preestablished thesaurus of subject terms. The problem is solved one item at a time every time a cataloguer succeeds in providing a useful description in terms drawn from that thesaurus or establishes a new heading. No set of subject descriptors can be successfully used if it is assumed that their meanings are invariant, identical reproductions no matter what the context. Words are not like that; they are like babies.

Babies are the same and always have been the same if we think of them only as the identical and predictable products of exactly the same course of events following upon the accident of boy meets girl, and this has been the case since there were boys and girls of any species. Yet if this were the only way in which someone understood babies, then that someone would know nothing about babies at all. For no two babies are ever alike; just ask mom and dad. Nor is any baby ever the same from one moment to the next. A baby is indeed a baby, but no baby is ever just a baby in the abstract way in which they are 'babies.' Babies can be and must be understood in terms of what all babies are like (they need the nipple, they cry, they make messes, they shed their clothes and their teeth) but no matter how much each baby is like every other baby, in every way and in everything it does, each baby is unique. Born into a particular family, they shape it as it shapes them. Such are those creatures we call babies, and so are words, and subject headings in a thesaurus: every individual use is a brand spanking new creation, a unique message offered to the world.

Blair insisted that 'when we describe what we want [for information retrieval], we must mean something by that description'. Only if the cataloguer understands something about the unique item, and something about the culture of its potential readers, their engagements, commitments and intentions, only then can the cataloguer offer something meaningful for their use. For Wittgenstein, Blair noted, 'meaning is intimately linked to the activities and practices that we have in common with others. If we do not have any activities in common, then there is nothing that we can talk about.' (Blair, 2003, p. 16. The notion of shared practices/activities is not problematic in the way that shared meanings or shared concepts and ideas are, cf. Weick, 1995.)

5.5. The treatment of errors

When inappropriate or incorrect bibliographical records such as those in the examples above are detected in library catalogues, the range of responses are as varied as the kinds of errors found. The treatment of errors in libraries cannot be considered to be the same thing as correcting errors, since the identification of an error may just as easily be followed by ignoring it or by introducing yet more errors; it depends on the significance of the error and the policies concerning what is to be regarded as an error in need of correction. For purposes of exposition, bibliographical errors may be classified into three broad categories corresponding to the taxonomy developed by Jens Rasmussen in ergonomics: skill-based (biomechanical), rule-based (misapplication of rules), and knowledge-based (misinterpretation of the item described). Active responses to error (as opposed to ignoring the problems) depend upon the skills and knowledge required for satisfactory performance but the kind of response which follows detection is generally determined by policy. Responses to error may also be classified into three categories: automated correction (quality control software for verification or validation at the time of input or regular scanning of the database for particular kinds of known problems, or tapeloading of records from external sources which have been marked as new or improved), human correction in the shared database, and correction limited to the record in the local catalogue.

All automated programs for quality control suffer from being limited to just those elements which can be entirely specified within an invariant environment or which are invariable in any environment, where 'everything that needs to be known is known, [. . .] behaviors not prescribed are proscribed.'(Landau and Stout, 1979, p. 149) Only in these conditions can automated correction unfailingly correct. Consequently, entirely automated correction is never possible in any element of the record which is determined by the unique item being described. Such simple elements as typographical errors cannot be automatically corrected since these may be errors on the item described, orthographical variants or words in other languages. An inappropriate subject can be matched with an authorized heading but cannot be determined to be appropriate, the only determination which matters.

One of the most troubling forms of mechanical correction is the replacement of an existing record by that of another institution if the later record is coded as being better or was created by a more prestigious institution (e.g. the Library of Congress). As a mongolist specialising in Czech and Polish historiography on the Mongols, I created the record below:

Example VIII.
Title: Tataři na Moravě
Subjects: Moravia (Czech Republic) – History-Mongol
        Invasion, 1242
        Olomouc, Battle of, Olomouc, Czech Republic, 1242.

Mongols – History
Mongols – In literature.
Jaroslav ze Šternberka, d. ca. 1290.
Hostýn Hills (Czech Republic) – History, Military.

The entire book concerns the Mongol invasion of Moravia in 1242 as recorded in Czech literature and historiography. This record was subsequently replaced by a record in which the only subjects were the following:

Moravia (Czech Republic) – History
Tatars – Czech Republic – Moravia

A rather drastic decrease in information, a substitution of the term Tatars which is both broader (according to LCSH it refers to Turkic tribes from Manchuria to the Ukraine) and narrower (in practice it is usually used to refer specifically to the peoples of modern day Tatarstan), and the elimination of the Mongols, the battle sites and the hero.

When human agents are responsible for identifying and correcting errors the fundamental problem is that they cannot correct any errors which they cannot detect. Detection of errors in transcription requires inspection of the item, detection of misapplication of the rules requires both a knowledge of the rules and how they should be interpreted and applied in each specific case, and errors in subject analysis require both a knowledge of the authorized headings and how these relate to the content described. My own studies of corrections made in shared databases (Bade, 2003) revealed that most corrections were of trivial elements affecting neither comprehension nor retrieval and attempts to correct and add to incomplete records often only substituted one misinterpretation for another, or actually increased the number of erroneous elements in the record. Example IX illustrates a typical case of 'correction'.

Example IX.
Title: W Rzymie zwyciężonym Rzym niezwyciężony. Spory o
   Wieczne Miasto (1575-1630)
Subjects: Rome – Civilization
Rome – History
Rome – Description and travel
Rome – Antiquities
(N.b. The heading Rome refers to the Roman Empire in LCSH; for the city, the heading is Rome (Italy))

The book is actually a study of 16th century Polish poetry about the city of the Pope written by Jesuit priests. The subjects are all wrong. However, when a second library attempted to fix this record, everything remained as it was except that two additional elements were added to the record – a code indicating that the geographical subject area was the Roman Empire, and a classification number for the Roman Empire, both of which constitute an increase of misinformation rather than correction.

The third manner of error correction is the most common and occurs at the local level, and the situation is similar to correctional activity in shared databases. The chief difference is that this manner of correcting records is usually performed by non-professional staff who are instructed to trust the records imported from the shared databases since these were presumably created by professionals and must therefore be correct. Often the only corrections allowed are those involving errors in transcription evident on the item, typographical errors in name headings or other easily identifiable problems.

5.6. The interpretation of failure: mismatches, accidents and mindlessness
The reference librarian encounters library users face-to-face; not so the cataloguer for whom the chief medium of communication with library users is the bibliographic record, a linguistic artifact integrated into a technical system as much by its users as by its creator. One frequent reason for the failure of that communica-

tion between cataloguer and library user is the inadequacies of the bibliographical record, whether from errors or incompleteness.

From one perspective errors in the record can be identified and counted based solely on the information in the record and its correspondence with the item it represents, an interpretation of error much like the notion of 'grammaticality' in linguistics, where that is defined by the linguist's or pedagogue's grammar and not by the communication situation. This is also the same kind of approach to 'human error'–the 'engineering' approach– common through the 1970s in ergonomics and industrial psychology. Of this approach Woods et al. (1994, pp. 199–200) remarked that any approach to error which sees hu-man error 'as a distinct category that can be counted and tabulated' will 'generate a huge volume of error statistics' but can provide no understanding of errors in context.

The ergonomic interpretation of human error changed radically in the 1980s, building upon Rasmussen's view that it was impossible to understand human error in the same manner as mechanical faults. He insisted that what had been called human error must be understood as a mismatch in specific person-task situations. Human error for Rasmussen was 'basically the effect of human variability in an unfriendly environment. [. . .] There are no such things as 'human error' data characterized only with reference to human functions or mechanisms. Human errors are man-task mismatch situations.'[13] Hollnagel pushed this view further, arguing that human error and failure 'depends on the working conditions rather than on the propensity of humans to screw up' and that in order to understand accidents and errors it will be necessary to look at 'what is really important– the natural contexts in which people have to work.'[14] Drawing on Hollnagel's work, Woods et al. (1994) summarized an un-

---

[13] Rasmussen (1987), p. 296, 300.
[14] Hollnagel (2001), p. KN7–KN8.

derstanding of error towards which various approaches had converged in the early 1990s:

> System failures can be viewed as a form of information about the system in which people are embedded. . . . [S]ystem failures indicate the need for an analysis of the decisions and actions of individuals and groups embedded in the larger system that provides resources and imposes constraints. To study human performance and system failure requires studying the function of the system in which practitioners are embedded. In general, failures tell us about situations where knowledge is not brought to bear effectively, where the attentional demands are extreme, or where the n-tuple bind is created.[15]

Taylor (1987) focused on the notion of accidents as unintended events, while Langer (1989) discussed the importance of mindfullness in action and the role of mindlessness in accidents. If meaningful events are intentional events, then the accident is a meaningless event. This interpretation of accident seems particularly relevant for the study of errors in language, including the language of bibliographic description. The mindless, unintentional nature of many of the absurdities in bibliographical description is striking. The only intention that can be attributed to these descriptions is solely to create 'a bibliographic record', to fill in the blanks, and therefore the result is an 'information accident', because what was entered into the record is irrelevant, meaningless, and often absurd.

6. Learnability of the language of bibliographic description
An early writer on information systems noted that many people believe that the technical system by itself 'performs selections, analysis, indexing, sorting and retrieval' but he insisted that 'in

---

[15] Woods et al. (1994, p. 206) n-tuple bind = a collection of factors that occur simultaneously within a large range of dimensions.

reality the decisions that determine the response to an enquiry are made primarily by the user himself' (Weeks, 1963, p. 9). Blair considered information retrieval to be 'a kind of conversation between the searchers and those who designed the system or represented the documents' and remarked that 'the quality of retrieval is in some sense related to the quality of this conversation.'[16] In spite of nearly 30 years of studies focusing on sensemaking in libraries, user feedback and the social contexts of information seeking, Blair could still claim in 2003 that no major systems are based on user feedback and there is no consensus regarding which techniques are useful (Blair, 2003, p. 39). In the matter of bibliographical description many have found problems in the language and style and have made proposals to fix those problems or have advocated the abandonment of catalogues in favour of Google searching for everything. Research on sense making complements research on error in acknowledging that what is needed is a detailed study of how library users succeed, of how the language of bibliographic description communicates enough to enable library users to find what they want.[17] Not all of the time, but much of the time. My own work for the past seven years has been devoted to understanding the nonsense which I encounter in my efforts to find and provide useful description, but one fact which became clear to me as I sought materials for my own publications was how well I succeeded in spite of countless mistakes, typos, missing or inappropriate subjects and other inadequacies in the items for which I searched. How does an intelligent user make sense of a library catalogue that is deficient in so many ways?

The linguistics of Chomsky and his followers requires an innate language since it would be absolutely impossible for any

---

[16] Blair (2003, p. 38). For a review of the literature on user studies and approaches to information seeking focusing on the context of that engagement, see Solomon (2002).

[17] Efforts in this direction have been reported in a number of recent publications by Brenda Dervin, Carol Kuhlthau and Paul Solomon, many of which are cited in Solomon (2002).

child or adult to make sense of a rule-governed language the products of which never appear in real speech, or of a language engaged solely with the production of well-formed sequences of sound with no communicational intent. The language of bibliographic description, on the other hand, is not only not innate and must be learned but in addition it requires unlearning much of the supposedly innate language upon which it is based. It must be learnable or it is of no use; if it is to be learnable it must have a normative character, i.e. cataloguers cannot, like Humpty Dumpty, make the headings mean whatever they want, but the very nature of their work compels them to construct headings for new and unique items which have never been described before, many of which will require the creation of new terms to be added to the thesaurus. Artificial indexing languages are not simple artifacts found and used like hammers or shoes. Each use of these languages for describing a previously undescribed item determines the scope of the headings as much as past usage. The usage of the established headings for these languages varies with every item described, while the headings themselves change constantly, although the changes usually occur only a considerable while after the changes adopted have appeared in popular and scholarly literature. The LCSH subject heading for the phenomenon of pause in language, for example, remains *Juncture (Linguistics)*, a theoretical fiction long ago exposed by linguists of an integrationist inspiration. Rather like the Oxford English Dictionary, changes to LCSH require justification by citation in reference sources.

Juncture is nevertheless a good point of departure for investigating how library users may adapt their search strategies to the exigencies of the catalogue. As a subject heading, *Juncture (Linguistics)* has cross-references to *Pause* and *Transition*, each of which refer the user to *Juncture (Linguistics)*. The user who searches *Pause* or *Transition* gets to *Juncture (Linguistics)* and presumably will get there again if need be, whether or not the heading *Juncture (Linguistics)* is remembered. Thus the system of cross-references ameliorate some of the problems of a restricted artificial subject vocabulary, even in the case where the established headings are obsolete in a particular disciplinary sublanguage.[18]

The existence of cross-references is a feature built into most technical systems because it was for decades the backbone of the functionality of those card catalogues organized by subjects. Another technical feature provides a measure of relief for the searcher who searches for a known author or person as subject, but cannot find the desired book because the author's name was entered incorrectly (e.g. genitive case or nominative plural instead of nominative singular: Havla instead of Havel, or Pellarovi instead of Pellar). If a search is made on the full correct form of the name, only those items with that form will appear, whereas any item with the incorrect form will not. However a persistent searcher may also search by a browse command which arranges the names in alphabetical order. It is possible that with such a search the incorrect form will appear sufficiently near the correct form to be noticed by the searcher, although there is no guarantee of that nor of the searcher's looking beyond the sought after name.

Redundancies, keyword searches, truncation commands, browsing online or in the shelves in the desired call number ranges, discovery in other databases which link to the local catalogue: all of these characteristics of the bibliographic record and the technical system into which it is incorporated can be combined by the intelligent and persistent searcher to find items inadequately described. Yet Blair has argued that 'The information retrieval problem will probably not be addressed satisfactorily if it is seen as a purely technical problem' (Blair, 2003, p. 39) since the usefulness of the description provided is not only constrained by the technical possibilities of the searching system but by the cataloguer's knowledge. The most important factor in

---

[18] But not all of them. The user who wants to locate books on *Pause* in the sense of *Hesitation* must search for *Hesitation* where she will find a reference to *Hesitation form (Linguistics)*; you cannot get to *Hesitation form (Linguistics)* from *Pause*.

the successful use of the catalogue is the intelligence and persistence of the user. Alternatively, we could state that the catalogue remains useful because people persist in using it, accepting its limitations in stride and creatively working with and around them to achieve their purposes. If they wish to use the library at all, they do not have much choice.

It is not just the local library catalogues which continue to serve the users but the international shared databases as well. In the absence of a shared language of description, with conflicting and contradictory standards, no oversight, little or no attention to error and the interpretive work performed as often as not by persons having no knowledge of, engagement with or commitment to the cultural and linguistic practices of the multitude of scholarly activities which produce these millions of publications, how can these international databases continue to satisfy their users? For they do appear to work remarkably well, so much so that many library users prefer using these databases over the local catalogue. The answer is the same as that suggested for local library catalogues: the expectations of the users, a reliance on a very limited number of searches for keywords or browsing (chiefly title, author, subject), knowledge of the limitations and diversity of the information that may be found, and most importantly searching for known items, often with a citation (in the case of the reader) or the item (in the case of the librarian) in hand. The shared international databases provide an overview of what is available not just in the local library but in thousands of libraries. The local catalogue is only searched after the desired items are known to exist and then with a citation in hand the local database can be effectively and exhaustively searched.

Under current conditions, 'a record' is often all the librarian hopes to find, a record which can be purchased and adapted to local needs as necessary. When librarians or other users use these databases to locate items known to exist and base their search on a citation (in reference work or interlibrary loan), an advertisement (the acquisitions librarian) or the item in hand (the cataloguer), these databases can be used effectively and efficiently by almost everyone. Not because of the quality of the information in the databases, but because of the limitations of the search imposed by the existence of a citation or the actual item. Every particular search is itself the most stringent restriction of possibilities for the system and more than any other factor that constraint imposed by the user determines the success of the search. It is only in the search for items unknown but hoped for that failure can be severe and invisible: when the user does not know what is being missed, its absence is not noticed. And this failure is identical in both the local catalogue and in the shared databases.

7. Responsible language

> If language has form, it is precisely because it is a normative activity, an activity that matters to its participants because they make it do so. (Taylor, 1997, pp. 139–140)

> It is because language is normative that it matters to us, that it can be used to mean, that it has a communicational and a psychological instrumentality. (ibid., p.161)

The question remains: if the shared databases and local library catalogues are increasingly constructed according to purely economic and technical considerations with no effort to supply appropriate and useful description at the start, how much longer can library users continue to make sense of the library catalogue? When the linguistic variation of the community over time is combined with a continually increasing number of absurdities in the catalogue, at what point does the catalogue become uninterpretable and unlearnable? How much longer can it continue to be a locus of communication for users if it is no longer being constructed for them but only for the computers and the librarians who sit in control of the information they are being paid to find and deliver? Hannele Dufva (1992) insisted that 'to speak is to be able to evaluate things, to make choices, to mean' (p. 216) and that linguistic cooperation 'simply means the acknowledgement of the fact that persons who talk . . . are doing it for a reason. The situation is thus ontologically meaningful, not arbitrary' (p. 115). If the next generation of library users discover at the very beginning of their library experiences that one finds Mircea Eliade's essays on oriental religions classified and analyzed as the history of Romanian literature, a world almanac classified and analyzed as an encyclopedia of mathematical statistics, a congress on the languages of Buddhism in Central Asia classified and analyzed as a study of Indo-Aryan languages of Southeast Asia, and authors with names like 'From the lectures of, School' and 'Osman Mister and his students, H.H.' (these examples are all taken from actual recent instances and are discussed in Bade (2004)), what are they likely to learn? Most likely: do not waste your time, ask the librarian. Which is exactly the situation that those librarians obsessed with their own status and power want.

Today's libraries work largely because they have been constructed over decades (and sometimes centuries) by responsible persons dedicated to serving library users, users among whom one finds mothers with their children, students in schools and colleges, avid readers, book lovers, university faculty and other librarians. In the past the work of bibliographical description was only a part of the work carried out in libraries, and this work, as all of the work, was done in the name of service to the users. The changes which have occurred in the past 25 years have led many professional librarians to rethink librarianship, a rethinking which has advocated dislocating the library into cyberspace and abandoning the work of bibliographical description in favour of current and hoped for technologies of electronic document storage and retrieval. The library is no longer considered to be a finite collection in a particular place serving a particular community of users but only a function, and the function of the librarian is no longer considered to be a servant of the users of a particular collection but rather to be an information provider in a global market. The creation of bibliographic information is now considered beneath the dignity of professional librarians, work suitable only for clerks or software; instead the librarian is imagined to be a knowledge worker, an information broker, an Oh so important element in the information economy who ought to expect a corresponding salary and status (unlike the interchangeable and disposable lower level staff who will actually produce the bibliographical information on which the librarians rely).[19]

For the product of bibliographical description to have a serviceable future it must be an intentional, mindful object, the work of persons sufficiently engaged in the same intellectual

---

[19] Princeton University's University Librarian Karin Trainer (1989, pp. 368–369) offered the following remarks:
'There is no sign that the amount of technical information falling under the purview of the catalog department will decrease with passing time. On the contrary, the growing number of formats [. . .] are adding to the complexity of daily work [. . .] It is reasonable to assume that, as in the past, libraries will continue to look to their catalogers for mastery over the technical procedures and detail necessary to keep collections organized and accessible.
'While expected to possess these technical skills, catalogers in the future will be using them in a different way than their predecessors did. The change is already underway. More and more libraries are discovering that they can no longer afford to have professional catalogers be mostly catalogers. With the decrease in the amount of original cataloging to be done locally, and because of economic pressures, cataloging is being turned into an activity for non-professionals – and someone must train them in the technical aspects of cataloging and supervise them. This responsibility typically is falling to the professional cataloger, who is becoming a cataloging manager, whether formally called that or not.'
Ms. Trainer's conception of cataloguing is of a purely technical skill, with no recognition of the importance of an engagement with the cultural activities which produce and give meaning to the materials which libraries acquire, nor of the relationship between the cataloguer and the reader. If cataloguing can become a non-professional activity 'because of economic pressures' why was it not always a non-professional activity? Should we not reverse the question and ask how a professional activity can suddenly become non-professional 'because of economic pressure'?

activities as the users to have something to say to tomorrow. If something like Grice's Principle of Cooperation – or more simply trust – is the necessary foundation of any communication, then this mutual commitment must underwrite each description created and entered into a library catalogue. Eugen Rosenstock-Huessy insisted that every genuine act of speech establishes relationships and creates a new language and this is exactly what is needed for successful communication in the library, particularly in a technologically mediated context such as the user working with the catalogue.[20] It is in the generational relationships among authors and readers that knowledge lives and it is precisely such relationships which the work of bibliographical description should create and foster. Without it we have nothing but warehouses full of ink and paper.

When the work of bibliographical description has been removed from the library – as it has been in many American 'research' libraries – the librarians will no longer be directly in touch with that description upon which both the users and the technologies depend. The language of bibliographical description will be developed by persons watching the clock in an information factory rather than persons engaged in the cultural activities giving rise to the works described, divorced from the libraries and their users, neither of which will have much influence upon the production and distribution of those information objects which will of necessity be abstract general objects for mass consumption and not directed to any particular community. Or, more probably, those bibliographical records will be created by and for an Anglo-American managerial elite, in the

---

[20] *Die Sprache des Menschengeschlechts* (1963–1964) is a collection of most of Rosenstock-Huessy's writings on language. Not included in that collection are three lectures published under the title '*The lingo of linguistics*' (1966) in which Rosenstock-Huessy discussed marriage as a relationship rooted in language that holds the speaker responsible: 'I do.' Like Michael Toolan a few years later, he insisted that what linguists forget is that people sometimes fall in love. The linguists in the audience in 1966 admitted that the object of their linguistics had nothing to do with relationships, and certainly not marriage.

English language, and according to all the presuppositions, prejudices and ignorance which that insular situation fosters.

There is nothing wrong with English, of course, unless among librarians responsible for a multilingual collection it is the only language known and valued. Should that descent into monolingual devaluation of the world's cultural legacy continue to overtake our libraries, the language of bibliographical description will become both tyrannical and productive of innumerable absurdities. Responsible language requires responsible people and can never be the result of mindless incomprehending production of well-formed but meaningless descriptions intended not for a reader but solely for computer validation, filling a quota, and generating statistics.

> [P]er gli uomini dell'età della tecnica la vita e il mondo sono privi di senso perché, in un universo di mezzi, la tecnica non se ne propone alcuno (Galimberti, 1999, p. 689).

8. Conclusion: Making sense and the indeterminacy of the sign

In spite of the elaborate and detailed classification schedules and indexing languages, the increased searching capabilities in libraries through the application of information technologies and the enlargement of the universe of collections searchable in a networked library system and international databases, the basic problem of library users confronted with a library of unknown materials has not fundamentally altered during the past century. That problem is to query the library, whether in the person of a librarian or through the medium of a catalogue, concerning materials desired but of unknown availability. The language of bibliographical description has been treated as a fixed code (rules for cataloguing and restricted subject vocabulary) ideally used by a professional (or a software program) inhabiting the homogeneous world of Science and knowing that language perfectly. Whether the language of the searcher is natural language or a restricted set of subject terms, the language of the descriptions provided work seamlessly with the technologies enabling the users to successfully navigate the catalogue. The success of the users proves the validity of the system *in toto* – not the intelligence and persistence of the library users. This is the view of librarians, both those who argue for particular systems of description and those who argue against description and assume that everything can be built into the search engine technologies.

Even a cursory look at the absurdities, the failures and the technical limitations indicates that this story cannot be the whole story, and perhaps not the real story at all. What the evidence indicates is that many librarians follow Hilary Putnam's 'Principle of Reasonable Ignorance', of which Harris (2003, p. 62) wrote:

> What it amounts to is that, in the scientist's view of the universe, you are allowed to use a word sensibly and reasonably even if you do not fully comprehend what it stands for. . . All that remains is that the word must somehow be 'tied to' something. What that something is does not matter.

The reader will recall that this is precisely the policy of some of the libraries mentioned above in regard to the assignment of classification numbers and subject terms to a bibliographic record. It is not because the language of bibliographic description is a rule-governed, severely restricted descriptive tool used by professionals that it sometimes works (and sometimes does not). In his remarks on the language of Wittgenstein's builder and his assistant Harris insisted that 'only as long as we refrain from inquiring too closely into what might go wrong' can we maintain our illusions that it is the code which enables communication.

> Once we grasp this, it becomes obvious that the indeterminacy which pervades the whole communicational en-

terprise is being masked by its pragmatically effective operation . . . the successful integration of activities is attributed to determinacy of the signs involved. Whereas, on the contrary, what is happening is that the indeterminacy of the signs is being obscured by their apparently effective application. (Harris, 2003, p. 78)

A related phenomenon was described by Weick in his studies of high-reliability organizations. He found that mutual dependability is a key factor in these organizations and provides a constant successful outcome. He illustrated the reliable organization with a stable family and alcohol rehabilitation programs, noting that these situations 'collapse when people stop doing whatever produced the stable outcome. And often what produced the stable outcome was continuous change, not continuous repetition' (Weick, 1987,p. 119). It is not rules and constraints (or government and binding) which permits communication and common action in those organizations noted for their constant successes, but flexible, knowledgable and responsible actors.

Finally, this leads to an understanding that the rules and tools, techniques and technologies of libraries and librarianship are not what make sense in libraries at all:

> The integrationist alternative to fixed codes construes communication as a continuum of creative activities in which the participants strive to integrate their own actions and objectives with those of others, as best they may, in particular circumstances. The communicational continuum is open-ended and that is why there is no determinacy of meaning. Nor is there any guarantee in advance that a satisfactory integration is possible. In integrational semiology, signs are not prerequisites of communication, but its products. (Harris, 2005, p. 110)

If this be true, then everything depends on me and you.

References

Bade, D., 2002. *The creation and persistence of misinformation in shared library catalogs.* Graduate School of Library and Information Science, Urbana.

Bade, D., 2003. *Misinformation and Meaning in Library Catalogs.* The author, Chicago.

Bade, D., 2004. *The Theory and Practice of Bibliographic Failure, or, Misinformation in the Information Society.* Chuluunbat, Ulaanbaatar.

Blair, D.C., 1990. *Language and Representation in Information Retrieval.* Elsevier, Amsterdam.

Blair, D.C., 2003. Information retrieval and the philosophy of language. *Annual Review of Information Science and Technology* 37, 3–50.

Dufva, H., 1992. *Slipshod Utterances: a Study of Mislanguage.* University of Jyväskylä, Jyväskylä.

Ellul, J., 1981. *La parole humiliée.* Seuil, Paris.

Galimberti, U., 1999. *Psiche e techne: l'uomo nell'età della tecnica.* Feltrinelli, Milano.

Greg, W.W., 1966. Bibliography – an apologia. In: Greg, W.W., Maxwell, J.C. (Eds.), *Collected Papers.* Clarendon Press, Oxford, pp. 239–266 (Originally published in *The Library*, September 1932, vol. 13, pp. 113–143.).

Harris, R., 1990. *The Foundations of Linguistic Theory: Selected Writings of Roy Harris.* Routledge, London.

Harris, R., 2003. *History, Science and the Limits of Language: An Integrationist Approach.* Indian Institute of Advanced Study, Shimla.

Harris, R., 2005. *The Semantics of Science.* Continuum, London.

Hjørland, B., 1997. *Information Seeking and Subject Representation: An Activity-theoretical Approach to Information Science.* Greenwood Press, Westport, CO.

Hollnagel, E., 2001. Anticipating failures: what should predictions be about? In: *Human factor in system reliability – Is human performance predictable? Papers presented at the Human Factors and Medicine Panel (HFM)*

Workshop held in Siena Italy from 1–2 December 1999. NATO Research and Technology Organization, Neuilly-sur-Seine, pp. KN1–KN9.

Landau, M., Stout, R., 1979. To manage is not to control, or the folly of type II errors. *Public Administration Review* 39 (2), 148–156.

Langer, E.J., 1989. Minding matters: the consequences of mindlessness–mindfulness. *Advances in Experimental Social Psychology* 22, 137–173.

Mann, T., 1997. Cataloging must change! and indexer consistency studies: misreading the evidence at our peril. *Cataloging and Classification Quarterly* 22 (3–4), 3–45.

Morel, C., 2003. *Les décisions absurdes: sociologie des erreurs radicales et persistantes.* NRF Gallimard, Paris.

Rasmussen, J., 1987. Reasons, causes, and human error. In: Rasmussen, J., Duncan, K., Leplat, J. (Eds.), *New Technology and Human Error.* Wiley, New York, pp. 293–301.

Rosenstock-Huessy, E., 1963–1964. *Die Sprache des Menschengeschlechts: eine leibhaftige Grammatik in vier Teilen.* Lambert Schneider, Heidelberg.

Rosenstock-Huessy, E., 1966. *Lingo of Linguistics.* Argo Books, Essex, Vermont (Eugen Rosenstock-Huessy Lectures, vol. 29).

Solomon, P., 2002. Discovering information in context. *Annual Review of Information Science and Technology* 36, 229–264.

Svenonius, E., 2000. *The Intellectual Foundation of Information Organization.* MIT, Cambridge, MA.

Taylor, D.H., 1987. The hermeneutics of accidents and safety. In: Rasmussen, J., Duncan, K., Leplat, J. (Eds.), *New Technology and Human Error.* Wiley, New York, pp. 31–41.

Taylor, T.J., 1997. *Theorizing Language: Analysis, Normativity, Rhetoric, History.* Pergamon, Oxford.

Trainer, K.A., 1989. Dollars and sense: training catalogers. In:

Intner, S., Hill, J.S. (Eds.), *Recruiting, Educating, and Training Cataloging Librarians*. Greenwood Press, New York, pp. 367–374.

Weeks, D.C., 1963. Information system theory as the foundation of practical design. In: Howerton, P.W. (Ed.), *Information Handling: First Principles*. Spartan Books, Washington, DC, pp. 1–17.

Weick, K.E., 1987. Organizational culture as a source of high reliability. *California Management Review* 29 (2), 112–127.

Weick, K.E., 1995. *Sensemaking in Organizations*. Sage, London.

Woods, D.D., Johannsen, L.J., Cook, R.I., Sarter, N.B., 1994. *Behind Human Error: Cognitive Systems, Computers, and Hindsight*. CSERIAC, Wright Patterson AFB, OH.

IV

Rapid Cataloging
Three Models for Addressing Timeliness as an Issue of Quality in Library Catalogs

Abstract
This paper analyses the presuppositions, goals and implementations of policies for rapid cataloging in three large academic libraries in the United States. In the first model (The University of Chicago's W-Collection), there was no attempt to catalog materials, using the order record alone and shelving the items in a publicly accessible area by accession number. The second model (Princeton's ATA Procedure) made cataloging the initial activity upon receipt, the purpose of which was "to give the future librarians enough information to know if the item is already in the collection or not" and also to serve (with subject headings and classification) the library's users. Finally, Cornell's COR Procedure in which all information in the records is assumed to be temporary and therefore unimportant; the necessary information is expected to be acquired later from commercial sources.

This paper is an expanded version of part of chapter III of my *Politics and policies for database qualities* (privately printed, 2006). My thanks to James Weinheimer for bringing the Princeton documents to my attention and correspondence concerning them.

I. Institutional Policies, Organizational Structures and Catalog Quality

The discussion of information quality in libraries has followed two predominant orientations: a positivistic orientation which identifies the qualities intrinsic to a product or service, and a user-focused orientation. The first orientation is concerned with a product and its characteristics, this latter being understood to be objective elements which can be identified and quantified. Discussions of quality arising from such presuppositions regularly identify a number of qualities or determinants of quality such as accuracy, completeness, appropriateness and timeliness, detect their presence or absence in a product or service, count these and then judge the results on some scale of acceptability. At the opposite pole are those approaches predicated on the notion that the user determines quality. Total Quality Management programs are usually oriented in this latter direction.

Both pragmatically and theoretically, neither orientation alone is adequate. Paim, Nehmy and Guimarães stated the problem succinctly:

> Absolutizing the user can lead to the renunciation of the search for rigor and exactitude of information, and in the end to the renunciation of intrinsic attributes resulting in an exacerbated and chaotic relativism which, taken to the extreme implies attention to every desire of the user. On the other hand, attending exclusively to intrinsic attributes can lead to the growth of information systems or services alienated from the interests of the users, compromising its efficacy. ... In the current situation the information professional adopts the pretense of a neutral stance between these two poles: the truth of the information and the desire of the user.[1]

---

[1] Isis Paim; Rosa Maria Quadros Nehmy and César Geraldo Guimarães, César Geraldo, "Problematização do conceito "Qualidade" da informação" *Perspectivas em ciência da informação*, v.1 n.1 (Jan.-June 1996): 117-118.

The problem may be theoretically resolved by understanding quality as a social judgement which may follow individual and idiosyncratic criteria, the goals of a larger social practice or institution (such as religion, science, law, markets) or technological requirements, with any or all of these factors shaping goals and needs, and therefore the determinants of quality in any given situation. In any goal-directed activity, the goals may conflict. In the railroad industry, for example, measures taken for railroad safety may very well create difficulties for the timely departure and arrival of trains. In such cases, theory does not decide the issue; rather, decisions are made by railroad executives, lawmakers, stockholders and passengers, decisions which taken together over the course of events and changing circumstances produce a continual adjustment of attention to these two factors, neither of which can be ignored.

Similar conflicts among goals arise in every other social activity, including library operations. A one-sided focus on timeliness (for example) may and often does lead to insufficient, inaccurate or useless misinformation which vacates all value from the achievement of timeliness, whereas the opposite focus can and often does lead to inaccessible backlogs of many decades standing. One example to be discussed below—the University of Chicago library's W-Collection—was initiated to make materials accessible before cataloging but left 10s of thousands of items (as many as 140,000 items at a time were in the collection) without subject access, some of these remaining without subject access for two decades and perhaps longer. On the other hand, portions of the University of Chicago's Berlin Collection (acquired a century ago) remain in remote storage, uncataloged, inaccessible and the contents unknown.

The simple fact is that providing 'a' bibliographic record for an item in a 'timely' fashion does not mean providing 'access' to that item: it means nothing more nor less than providing 'a' bibliographic record. Whether and how that record provides access, whether and to whom it is useful and to what degree it is useful are questions that can only be answered by enquiring about the users and investigating what useful information that record makes available. A record designed for inventory control can serve that purpose well, but may fail if it is expected to serve researchers' needs. Inaccuracies and missing elements can render a 'timely' record absolutely worthless.

Faced with a library backlog many library administrators blame catalogers for being too slow, wasting time on accuracy, error checking and correction, confirming interpretations, ensuring consistency and in general being human when machines can do something much quicker. Faced with typos, incorrect or missing subjects or other varieties of nonsense, many library administrators blame the problems on inevitable human error or ignore them, regarding them as the expected and acceptable products of the information industry.

In both cases the problems reveal the perennial conflict between the need to have up-to-date information and the need to have accurate and sufficient information. These conflicts are not unique to librarians—journalists, businessmen and military intelligence analysts have identical difficulties—but the seriousness of the conflict has been largely ignored or simply denied in the library literature. For some librarians (typically administrators) timeliness is the only thing that matters, while for others (typically catalogers) accuracy, completeness and consistency trump timeliness. In every library the balance between these two conflicting orientations is established by policies and embodied in organizational structures. The results of those policies and structures are revealed in the nature of the libraries' collections, whether they are backlogs closed or open to the public, collections (whether backlogs or open stacks) classified by subject or shelved by accession number, materials accessible by subject or only by author/title, and so on.

II. Three Historical Models of Rapid Cataloging

Because the nature of library collections is always the result of institutional policies and organizational structures, different policies and structures lead to different collections and different possibilities for using those collections. This paper examines rapid cataloging policies in three large private university libraries in the United States: the W-Collections in the University of Chicago libraries, Princeton's procedure for handling items acquired from the book vendor ATA, and Cornell library's Cataloging on Receipt (LTS Procedure #53). The three policies, their presuppositions and effects on access, will be briefly described and discussed, after which they will be compared and their merits—and demerits—evaluated.

The W-Collections in the Libraries of the University of Chicago

Description[2]

The W-Collection was formed in the early 1970's as an attempt to make materials in the University of Chicago libraries' backlogs available to patrons without having to request a librarian to catalog them before check out. The W-Collection in time came to comprise several collections dispersed throughout a small number of locations according to subject and format.

When the W-Collection began, OCLC did not exist, and there was no way to share cataloging copy among libraries. The library used only LC copy, cataloging everything else originally. The Acquisition Dept. sent to Cataloging any book that had MARC copy available right away on the MARC tapes. They

---

[2] The following description of the W-Collection is based on my own work with the collection, the library's annual reports from the early 1990's to the present, and what I have learned in converations and discussions with others. I did not have access to any documents concerning the collection written prior the the early 1990's and therefore the reasoning behind the decision to initiate the collection, the discussions concerning how to implement it and all decisions regarding the W-Collection prior to my arrival are not matters which I am competent or indeed able to discuss at all. The description here as well as the interpretation which follows represent the author's understanding of the collection and should not be understood as the viewpoint of the Joseph Regenstein Library administration, past, present or future.

also searched the National Union Catalog (NUC) for copy for older titles, and staff keyed those records into the local database from the photocopied NUC cards. Almost everything else that did not have copy was sent to W, except for some things that were sent to the Original Cataloging Section because the physical pieces were too flimsy to stand up on the shelves, or were so old that we could not expect them to be cataloged by anyone else. Brief acquisitions records were made for all materials received in the acquisitions section and those not selected for immediate cataloging were routinely sent directly to the W-Collections in the various libraries with an accession number and the record created in the acquisitions department.

The idea of putting the books into W was that eventually LC would catalog them, the copy would appear on the MARC tapes, and the book would be retrieved from W for processing. In the meantime, the books were available for use, instead of in restricted storage. Yet prior to about 1986 there was no OPAC and other than the W shelflist in the card catalog only librarians had access to the W records. All materials in the W Collection were available for public browsing in the stacks, but since there was no order on the shelves other than accession order, browsing was meaningless. If the library's patrons asked a librarian about an item and the librarian could locate it in the catalog, then and only then would the patron have any real access to the items in the collection. With the advent of the OPAC all of these records were available to all users within the library, and when the webpac was inaugurated all users with Internet access could search the W Collection.

Over time, staff time limitations led to an increasing number of bibliographic records for items in the W collections being overlain by the MARC tape records but not pulled from the W collections and integrated with the rest of the collection. The Library began using OCLC copy in 1989, but even after that, many things went to W if the copy was not identified at the time of acquisitions processing. The number of volumes in the W collections grew steadily, remaining in the 120,000 range in the early 1990's after peaking at about 140,000 volumes. The library's records for items in the W collections were sent only once to OCLC (sometime about 1995). The part with copy from the MARC tapes (46,000 records) was sent in order to post holdings to Worldcat, while the other part (55,000 records) was sent in the hopes that OCLC would be able to match the short records with full records. Of this latter group, copy was identified and loaded into the catalog for about 29,000 records. The existing short records were overlaid with the fuller ones and coded so as to enable identification later when the library began pulling books from W on a regular basis. Processing items from the W-Collection which had OCLC copy was begun on a regular basis in 1996/1997 and became a high priority in January 2003 at which time copy-catalogers began systematically checking all items in the W Collections, searching OCLC for those which had no copy in the local catalog and processing those for which records were found in OCLC. At the end of the 2005-2006 fiscal year (June 2006), there were just over 10,000 titles remaining in the W collections, including about 3000 volumes of print materials. The W-Collection remains an option during times of critical backlogs in the Cataloging Department, but items have been added only rarely during the past six years.

Sample records from the current W-Collection without MARC or OCLC copy overlain:

Example 1:
```
000      00501nam 2200145   4500
008      900130n     xx |||| |   u||||||und u
009      b30
020      __$c0.10rub
035      __$a(ICU)BID12532088
245      00$aFehristi majallahoi sharq /$cmurattib M. Kholov.
260      _0$aDushanbe :$bKitobkhonai davlatii RSS Tojikiston ba nomi A. Firdavsī shūbai dastnavishoi sharkī,$c1986.
300      __$a42 p.
900      __$aICU:90228590$bOST:70$cHST:160$dCopy:new
```

Example 2:
000	00515nam 2200157c 4500
008	741204n xx |||| | u||||||und u
009	b30
035	__$a(ICU)BID187895
130	0_$aAnuario.
245	00$aEstadístico de las Corporaciones Locales.
260	__$a-Madrid,$bInstituto de Estudios de Administración Local,$c1973.
300	__$a390 págs.
350	__$a350ptas.
900	__$aICU:74110265$bOST:70$cHST:160$dCopy:new
921	$a19000000$b2-6-80-Sent to Serial Record

Example 3:
000	00383nam 2200133 4500
008	760317n xx |||| | u||||||und u
009	b30
035	$a(ICU)BID1543938
100	1_$aRyan, Kevin.
245	_0$aKaleidoskope.
260	0_$aBoston :$bHoughton Mifflin Co.,$c[1975].
300	__$a272 p.
900	__$aICU:75208330$bOST:70$cHST:160$dCopy:new

Example 4:
000	00469nam 2200145 4500
008	900723n xx |||| | u||||||und u
035	__$a(ICU)BID13108199
100	1_$aKruus, Hans,$d1891-
245	0_$aPersonaalnimestik.
260	0_$aTallinn :$bEesti NSV Teaduste Akadeemia Teaduslik Raamatukogu,$c1988.
300	__$a213 p.
490	__$aNõukogude Eesti teadlased
900	__$aICU:91212564$bOST:70$cHST:160$dCopy:new

Example 5:
```
000       00405nam 2200133  4500
008       900718n    xx |||| |   u||||||und u
009       b30
035       __$a(ICU)BID13093515
245       0_$aSela meniaiushiĭsia oblik :$bsbornik.
250       __$a2-e izd., dop.
260       0_$aL'vov :$bKameniar,$c1986.
300       $a136 p.
900       $aICU:91212325$bOST:70$cHST:160$dCopy:new
```

Discussion

The W-Collection was formed in order to make these uncataloged materials available for use rather than remaining unknown and unavailable to anyone in an inaccessible staff arrearage. Relying on the unexamined order record meant that any significant errors or omissions would effectively relegate the item to an arrearage inaccessible to everyone, including librarians. Some of these problems are evident in the examples above: Example 1 describes a catalog of serials in Arabic, Persian and Tajik published in Afghanistan, Iran and the Arab countries. If one knows what this is and its exact title in Tajik (according to the LC romanization of the cyrillic form), it can be located in the library; no other search strategies will succeed. Searching the author or the exact title according to the romanization of the Arabic script Tajik title will not be successful because neither the author nor that title were entered into the record, nor will keyword searching in Arabic and Persian be of any use. In Example 2, the title is split into two fields, the first word given as the uniform title (Anuario) while the rest of the title—meaningless by itself since grammatically inseparable from Anuario—is offered as the title proper. Example 2 is in fact an old record which was not replaced by the later serial record—which is also in the catalog now—because it was never located. It clearly reveals some of the most troublesome problems which historically plagued the W-Collection: the record was not deleted, suppressed from display or merged because the librarians could not find it, and if the librarians cannot find their own records, there is little likelihood that any other patrons will. Example 3 is for an early edition of a book published in many editions, but the title offers no subject information at all. Example 4 gives the title as the author, while the author's name does not appear anywhere in the record (the correct title is: Hans Kruus: personaalnimestik). The Russian parallel title is not given, and subject access cannot be gained from either title since these titles mean only 'personal bibliography'—whose personal bibliography is not given in the title, because that long dead 'who' was mistaken for the author. The fifth example has a correct title which unfortunately gives no useful subject information, while neither editors nor subjects are included in the record.

The information in W-Collection records is *usually* sufficient to match orders and to identify duplicates, since they were in fact input as order records. The records are perfectly adequate for circulation, if the patron can find them. The existence of author and title information in these records makes it possible for users to search known authors and titles in most cases (exceptions exist, such as Examples 2 and 4 above), but because these records lack subject headings, subject access is limited to what can be gleaned from title keyword searching. The examples above demonstrate that keyword searching using English terms is often useless as a subject searching strategy even for items with English titles (which were a minority in the W-Collection in any case). Furthermore, because the books are shelved by accession numbers, adjacency on the shelves has no meaning and thus browsing by subject is not available in any form. The records utilize a very basic level of description provided to support inventory control—ordering, receiving and circulation—but do not offer the library users enough information in the record or in the arrangement on the shelves to permit anything more than known item searches—and sometimes not even that (Examples 2 and 4).

Because the W-Collection was intended to be a holding area, neither it nor the records in the catalog were ever intended to be permanent. The records were not loaded into OCLC so neither inadequate records nor misinformation were distributed to other institutions and databases. Unfortunately this also meant that for those items not already in OCLC, the library's holdings were not reflected in OCLC nor were these items known to be available for interlibrary loan unless a librarian elsewhere sent a request with the hope that the Regenstein Library might own the desired item. (Since the implementation of a webpac all items in the W-Collection are now searchable to anyone with Internet access.)

The W-Collection did not constrain catalogers in any way nor did it require of them unprofessional or hasty work: it required nothing of them at all. It was a policy of doing as little as possible to make the items available to library users, leaving the burden of finding out what the library held on any particular topic almost entirely on those users. It was in effect a third-rate library policy in the most surprising of places. The object of concerted efforts for the past few years, the W-Collection has almost been eliminated through a combination of using OCLC copy without professional review, vendor records, machine matching using the Marcadia service (a bibliographic service which searches a shared utility for full or enhanced versions of the records sent to them and sends these records back to the client), shifting staff resources and special projects involving catalogers. The drastic reduction of the W-Collection by using all available means has been a major accomplishment of the past decade, and it is hoped that its elimination in the near future will put it away for good.

ATA Cataloging Procedures, Princeton University Library

Description
In the late 1990's Princeton University Library encountered significant difficulties in processing materials received from the

book vendor ATA and a special policy was developed to deal with these materials. A description of Princeton's ATA procedures may be found in the report on ATA producedures *New Trends in Slavic Cataloging at Princeton University: ATA Procedures* listed on Princeton University Library's Cataloging Documentation web page for the Slavic Cataloging Manual: ATA Cataloging Procedures.[3] A second report, *Report on ATA Procedure (March 2000)* is also available on the same website. The discussion that follows is based on these two documents and all quotations are taken from them.

A history of the ATA service and its peculiarities (e.g. no order records, invoices sent separately from the book packages) begins the report, which notes that the 'Order Division became overwhelmed with the workload and fell behind' at the same time as the number of staff decreased. With a reorganization of Technical Services, the Department decided to 'redesign the workflow and rethink the purpose and function of the catalog record. ... There was also a major push to ensure that each person in the workflow would handle the item only once.' Princeton's solution was 'to catalog the item before checking it off of the receipt. The inescapable conclusion was that cataloging had to be done at the time of receipt. The invoice would then be compared to the catalog record, and the acquisitions information added to the record at that time.'

The report continues with a description of the decisions concerning what would be included in the catalog record, the purpose of which would 'be to give the future librarians enough information to know if the item is already in the collection or not,' including

---

[3] Princeton University Library. New Trends in Slavic Cataloging at Princeton University: ATA Procedures.
http://library.princeton.edu/departments/tsd/katmandu/sgman/ATAhistory.html (accessed 28 Nov. 2006) For the Report on ATA Procedure (March 2000), see: http://library.princeton.edu/departments/tsd/katmandu/sgman/ata.pdf (accessed 28 Nov. 2006)

Names (1XX, 7XX)
Title, subtitle (245 ‡a, ‡b)
Edition (250)
Publication (260 first ‡a and first ‡b, ‡c)
Paging (300 ‡a)
Series (490)
Subject (6XX) kept to one if possible
Call number
Acquisitions number (037)

Sample ATA record (copied from the March 2000 report, in which diacritics and special characters are not evident other than as spaces):

Example 6:

TS FMT B RT a BL m T/C DT 08/10/99 R/DT 01/28/00 STAT nn E/L 5 DCF a D/S D
SRC d PLACE ru LANG rus MOD o T/AUD REPRO D/CODE s DT/1 1998 DT/2
CONT b ILLUS GOVT BIOG FEST 0 CONF 0 FICT 0 INDX 0
037/1: : $a ATA 1998 340-100
040: : $a NjP $c NjP
245:00 : $a Pravda o Ekaterinburgskoi tragedii : $b sbornik statei / $c pod redaktsiei IU. A. Buranova.
260: : $a Moskva : $b [s.n], $c 1998.
300/1: : $a 241 p. ; $c 20 cm.
504/1: : $a Includes bibliographical references.
600/1:00: $a Nicholas ‡b II, $c Emperor of Russia, ‡d 1868-1918 $xAssassination.
700/1:1 : $a Buranov, IU. A. $q (IUrii Alekseevich)

The treatment of names differed little from previous practice except that authority work was diminished, and the number of subjects was limited to two. The records were either upgraded by the catalogers or tagged for later Marcadia searching. Support staff would create a preliminary record '(...100,

245, 250, 260, 300, 490, 700, adding 246's or 500's if they encountered a problem) and send it on to a cataloger for updating, subjects and call number.' The purpose of this was 'to take as much of the typing from the cataloger as possible, to save their time for updating and subject work.'

In the old workflow items were ordered, received, the invoice checked and the bibliographer made his/her decision. For books to be added to the collection, someone searches RLIN for copy and if copy is found the item went to cataloging. Otherwise the book was put into a holding area for 1-2 years after which it is cataloged. The new workflow for ATA materials is presented in the *New trends...* report:

> No orders >> Item received >> Selection >> Item is cataloged: >> Skeleton record by non-professional staff, Cataloger upgrades record, gives single subject and call number >> Invoice checked against catalog record. Marcadia upgrades record automatically (1-2 years).

The report mentions some of the advantages of this new workflow:

> 1) 'Creating the catalog record at the beginning of the process allowed for a searchable database and made check-in much easier: the invoice could be checked against the catalog record--not against the item.'
> 2) 'Each staff member handles the book only once, and books are available immediately to the user with basic name/title/subject access.'
> 3) 'The possibility of using Marcadia to automatically upgrade the records makes the need to wait for LC/PCC copy less necessary: the records will be upgraded automatically.'

The purpose of new procedures was stated in the *Report on ATA Procedure (March 2000)*: 'To provide an adequate description of the item both for users and for a later Marcadia overlay. *'Adequate'* in this sense is defined by the cataloger using his/her own discretion.' A significant element in the new procedure involved the division of labor between students, support staff and professionals in order 'to decrease the amount of repetitive work for the professional cataloger, e.g. transcription of title information, adding item records, writing gutter notes, etc.'

In the March 2000 report a number of significant procedures are highlighted. The following instructions are taken verbatim from that report:

>--Copy records are selected by the support staff according to a list of preferred libraries.
>--All books are reviewed by a professional, including LC full-level copy.
>--Some LC practices have been set aside. Primarily, tracing the corporate body that is at the head of the title is ignored. If the cataloger feels that a corporate body is a useful access point, he/she is free to add it, but the number of corporate body headings added to the catalog is much fewer than before.
>--All fields are checked and updated by the cataloger. Additional information from the t.p is often added, along with any notes that are deemed necessary by the cataloger *for identification of the item*. Again, the cataloger checks and edits every portion of the record created by the student/support staff member.
>--*Subjects* are left to cataloger's discretion. All items (aside from belle-lettre) get at least one subject, but the cataloger is free to add any additional subjects he/she sees fit to add. It may be easier to have two or more subjects instead of choosing one. Or, if the cataloger feels that the item is exceptionally important, he/she may do deeper subject analysis. The focus is on *adequate* access as determined by the cataloger.

> --*Call numbers* are added quickly, depending on the book's final destination. If it is headed for the stacks, the cataloger may spend more time on the number, while if the item is headed for the Annex where browsing is impossible, the call number takes less time.

And finally, the March 2000 report notes some 'other considerations' (again, quoted from that document):

> --While catching up with the backlog, the professionals have placed themselves on a quota of 15 items per day. To reach this goal, LC and PCC copy must be included in the mix, but even so, such a rate is unsustainable in the long run.
> --Professionals feel that a rate of 10-12 per day is more reasonable as a sustainable number.
> --Professionals prefer doing a higher number of books with some easier copy included to having a lower number with no copy. Professionals can also keep current with LC practice.

Discussion

The procedure was developed as a response to a specific situation: ATA packages without invoices. This in itself appears to me to be a matter of great importance: instead of attempting to develop a new policy which would affect all incoming materials equally, the policy was developed to address the particular conditions pertaining to a special class of materials. The manner of their packaging, invoicing and arrival in the library permitted treating them in a manner different from other materials.

The understanding that the record must serve three very different use situations from the moment of its creation is also a crucial presupposition. The purposes of the procedure are threefold: to facilitate librarians, users and technologies in using or handling these records. The *New trends* document mentions that the record needs to provide enough information to enable future librarians to identify what is and is not in the collection, while the March 2000 *Report* describes the purpose as 'To provide an adequate description of the item both for users' and for machine overlay.

The procedures specify at least one subject and no corporate bodies, but the cataloger is free to add either in the number required depending on what is deemed important in the specific case. The example found in the documentation—and reproduced above—demonstrates the value of adding subject headings, as well as the need to go beyond the title for subject analysis. The title of the sample record (Example 6) could suggest its possible subject to a reader knowledgeable of Russian revolutionary history, but for all others and especially for automated systems and keyword searching strategies, the subject heading is necessary: without it there would be no subject access for the vast majority of searche(r)s.

The numerous problems which frequently arise and escape detection in systems involving the division of labor are largely prevented by having catalogers look at everything, including copy. Error checking and correcting are expected at each step.

The importance for catalogers to examine copy, especially LC copy, as a means of continuing education is noted.

The single most salient characteristic of these documents is that at every point the cataloger, not the policy or the technical system, is expected to be in control. The professional is given a great deal of latitude in determining what is needed and what may be left out. It is characteristic of both of the documents examined above that they focus not only on efficiency or technical possibilities, but on adequacy, sustainability and professional development, and at every point in the process the cataloger is expected to consider the individual item and make decisions in accordance with the main tasks of the librarian in pursuing the purposes of the library: to enable *future* (this word is key) librarians to utilize a complex technical system for the benefit of the library's users.

Compare Princeton's ATA Procedures with Weick and Sutcliffe's 'hallmarks of High Reliability':

—Preoccupation with failure
—Reluctance to simplify interpretations
—Sensitivity to operations
—Commitment to resilience
—Deference to expertise[4]

The preoccupation with failure is implicit in the procedural insistence on catalogers checking every field in every record, no matter who created the original information. Reluctance to simplify interpretations is evident in the repeated call on cataloger's judgement to determine what is useful, adequate and necessary for the various users (librarians, patrons, technologies). The policy itself is an example of sensitivity to operations: the particulars of ATA invoicing and shipping. A commitment to resilience is not particularly noticeable in a fashion other than the checking required of catalogers, but deference to expertise is, as mentioned, the most salient characteristic of the procedure.

Classification on Receipt

Description
In January 2003 Cornell University Library implemented a set of procedures called Classification on Receipt (hereafter, COR). The scope of the policy is concisely stated in the first paragraph of the online documentation Classification on Receipt (COR) (LTS Procedure #53):

> ***Scope (Policy):*** This procedure applies to printed monographic materials that, upon receipt, are ineligible for

---

[4] Karl E. Weick and Kathleen M. Stucliffe, *Managing the unexpected: assuring high performance in an age of complexity.* (San Francisco: Jossey-Bass, 2001), 10.

fast or copy cataloging and that are not immediately selected for original cataloging. Such items are handled in the manner outlined below, assigned full call numbers, and sent to the stacks to await overlay by Marcadia. This process is called classification-on-receipt, or COR. This procedure does not apply to non-book formats (serials, microforms, videos, scores, maps, or electronic resources). There are special guidelines for some kinds of printed materials. The first volume or volumes received in a multi-vol set should be searched for full copy. If copy is not found, the volume (regardless of whether or not it is vol.1) is still eligible for class-on-receipt. Each time a new vol. is added to a mutli-vol. record, the item should be searched for fuller copy, and if not found, added to the encoding level 3 record. Books with accompanying materials should be excluded from class-on-receipt and instead handled by original or copy catalogers as appropriate. Because of their unique workflow, CJK materials are also excluded from classification-on-receipt. Complete multi-vols are eligible for classification-on-receipt. Considerations: Remember that COR records are, like input or vendor records, designed to be temporary. Do not fuss over them extensively. The primary consideration is that they be sufficiently accurate for Marcadia processing and that they correctly represent the item until a better record becomes available. The need for processing materials using classification-on-receipt varies from collection to collection. For those collections or areas that are likely to have copy available over 24 months, classification-on-receipt can be applied more liberally; for those collections where the proportion of unique items is greater, fewer items will be given COR.[5]

---

[5] http://lts.library.cornell.edu/lts/pp/cat/53cor.cfm (accessed 28 Nov. 2006)

The Abbreviated Level Records which are produced in accordance with this procedure are short records that do 'not meet the National Level Bibliographic Record minimal level cataloging specifications.' If established headings are available, they may be used, but this is not required. Inputters are instructed to 'retain data elements that are already present in the record you are modifying unless they are clearly in error' while the fixed fields—with the exception of Type, Lang, and Dates—are to be left with the default codes, including COR defaults (Enc Lvl: 3; Desc: a; Srce: d). For variable fields, the following 'guiding principles' are offered:

> Focus on the data elements spelled out in this procedure as mandatory or mandatory if applicable.
> Accept what is present to the extent possible, making sure that the input record matches the piece in hand.
> Do not delete or change information unless it is clearly inaccurate or egregiously misleading.
> Limit changes.
> Finally, do not agonize over existing data elements in a record. Make a quick decision.
> Name and series headings that are included in the input record should be examined for accuracy, but not added if absent from the input record.

Classification numbers are to be assigned not strictly by the LC schedules, but using "ClassWeb, LTS COR Manual, and Voyager catalog as appropriate."

The COR procedures instruct the cataloger to use uncontrolled subject terms (653s) rather than subject strings formed according to LCSH or some other thesaurus. The specific instructions are as follows:

> Add English words, translated generally from the title, to items written in foreign languages and to English-language books with titles that do not reflect their subjects.

For example, the English title *The high road and the low road*, which is about bookmobiles, does not reflect the subject of the work, so you would assign a 653 field.

However, do **not** apply these instructions to works of the imagination (novels, stories, poetry, plays).

General rule: If item meets criteria for assignment of 653 field as outlined above, assign only one 653 field. Multiple terms may be assigned in some instances if appropriate. If you use a subject phrase, keep it brief.

...

When selecting subject words, follow these guidelines:
1) Use the title of the work, translated into English, as the primary source for words or phrases.
2) If the title field does not contain words about the subject of the work, quickly examine the covers, tables of contents, and preface to select appropriate words.
3) If it is not possible to determine useful words quickly, omit the 653. Do not analyze the book in depth nor agonize over selection of terms.
4) Do not duplicate a term that appears in another keyword-searchable field of the record. ...
5) Use natural word order, and concentrate on words that are rich in meaning...
6) Use foreign words that have no English equivalent, if they would provide useful keyword access (e.g., if the work is about glasnost, assign 653 Glasnost).
7) If the work is about a person, place or corporate body, give the name in direct order in the 653 field. For corporate names, make a quick judgment whether an English translation would provide useful keyword access (if not, omit it).

Sample COR record found in OCLC (copied November 1st, 2006; left and right ligatures removed for technical reasons):

Example 7:
008 __060607s2006 ru 000 0 rusod
020 __$a5860074697
035 __$a(OCoLC)70072618
040 __$aCOO$cCOO
049 __$aCGUA
050 _4$aDX241$b.I29 2006
245 00$aIAzyk tsyganskiĭ ves´ v zagadkakh :$bnarodnye aforizmy russkikh tsygan iz arkhiva I.M. Andronikovoĭ /$csost., podg. S.V. Kuchepatovoĭ.
260 __$aSankt-Peterburg :$bDmitriĭ Bulanin,$c2006.
300 __$a647 p.
653 __$aRomanies$aSocial life and customs$aAphorisms
700 1_$aKuchepatova, S. V.

Discussion

The procedures outlined in COR are to be used for 'printed monographic materials that, upon receipt, are ineligible for fast or copy cataloging and that are not immediately selected for original cataloging.' Original catalogers examine all incoming materials and select only non-monographic and high-priority monographic items for full original cataloging; everything else goes through the COR procedure. It is a local procedure that requires a complex network of external organizations all operating according to a more traditional model. Error correction, subject analysis and detailed, accurate description are all outsourced to commercial vendors. The vendors in turn do no evaluation of the information which they provide Cornell; their procedure is simply to search a database for bibliographic records containing coding indicating a certain level of completeness, or check the data in certain fields against a file of authorized forms, and pass on what they find to their clients. (Nota bene: no automated system and no human being without the item cataloged can determine the level of completeness of a bibliographic record without the item in hand; what can be checked is the fixed field indicating cataloging level. Without the item in hand, that code cannot be evaluated for appropriateness but must be accepted at face value.) Those bibliographical records and authorized headings may or may not have been created by persons capable of intelligently and accurately creating appropriate bibliographic information; the only real requirement for entering this information into bibliographic and authority files is institutional participation in certain cooperative databases and programs. In this network of working relationships it is clear that Cornell has relinquished all responsibility for the accuracy and completeness of their bibliographic information in the pursuit of faster and cheaper production. If everything everywhere beyond the boundaries of Cornell libraries were perfect, this system would work as long as Cornell never received any materials that were not available and cataloged elsewhere; if Cornell produces COR records for unique items or if anything goes wrong anywhere, Cornell suffers the results and has no mechanism for discovering much less correcting the problems.

COR has a few significant but mostly unstated premises underwriting its implementation. These can be discovered by a careful reading of the COR procedures, asking at each point what assumptions the particular procedure requires or implies. We can begin with a statement found in the introductory paragraph: 'The primary consideration is that they be sufficiently accurate for Marcadia processing and that they correctly represent the item until a better record becomes available.' The reference to the need to correctly represent the item may be charitably interpreted as an acknowledgment of user needs, but the remainder of the document contradicts this assumption: no error correction (unless egregious), no subjects if not easily ascertainable, no authorized headings required, default fields are entered because they are required by the technical system rather than because 'they correctly represent the item', etc. The second half of this conjunction must rather be interpreted in terms of the first half: without an accurate representation of the document no other libraries would be able to find the record and upgrade it, which would mean that Marcadia would never find an upgraded record but only the original record. Since other libraries do not search by subjects, added entries or fixed fields when looking for copy in the shared utilities nor are they required by the technical system, these elements are unnecessary for the Marcadia process to work properly. Not being technically necessary, they are ignored in COR regardless of user needs. Regarding subjects and all added entries, an additional assumption is that general keyword searching is the only search strategy which users will use, and therefore any information in one field should not be duplicated in any other.

If there is to be an upgraded record for Marcadia to supply, someone other than Cornell must do that work; furthermore, since this work is all done by machine without human review any COR record coded as having been upgraded in the shared utility will be delivered to Cornell where the record will be coded as finished with no evaluation of what improvements were made nor of what desirable improvements (from the users' perspective) were not made. Whatever changes and additions have been made, by whomever, the result is assumed to be both adequate and appropriate for the library.

The document clearly states that these records are temporary and therefore do not merit time and attention. Since call numbers will not be changed and since Cornell has no plans to retrieve COR records from the stacks if no upgrade is supplied within two years, these records with all of their deficiencies will be the permanent records in the catalog. Furthermore, for all unique items these will also be the permanent record in the shared databases as well. If this is acceptable it can only be because misinformation and the lack of information are of no importance, and that error correction and prevention are deemed unimportant.

Finally, the salient characteristic of the policy is its insistence upon doing things quickly, to the point that if one cannot determine particular elements quickly, they should be omitted.

In the interest of clarity we can state these presuppositions in a list, beginning with that factor which is the only consistent goal of the policy, proceeding to the presuppositions concerning the external information environment:

1) rapid processing is the only goal;
2) quick decisions are better than intelligent decisions because they are quicker;
3) 'COR records are, like input or vendor records, designed to be temporary';
4) the records are not intended for user access but for machine matching at a later date;
5) general keyword searches are the only searches used by library patrons;
6) error correction and prevention are unimportant;
7) misinformation and the lack of information for an indefinite period of time are of no consequence or at least of less importance than shelving immediately;
8) others external to the institution will provide the necessary completion and corrections;
9) any additions and changes made by anyone anywhere will be both appropriate and adequate for local needs;
10) all other institutions will continue to operate in a more intelligent and responsible manner.

What is wrong with these assumptions? Hélène Denis offered a list of five reasons that catastrophes seem to come out of nowhere:

—Ignorance of the dangers that surround us;
—An incomplete analysis of the risks;
—A lax definition of acceptable risk;
—The complexity of major sociotechnical risk
—Inadequate measures of attention and preparation[6]

---

[6] Hélène Denis, 'Les risques et les catastrophes,' in Minguet and Thuderoz (eds.), *Travail, entreprise et société: manuel de sociologie pour ingénieurs et scientifiques.* (Paris: PUF, 2005), 70.

The COR policy represents a spectacular example of all of these reasons for catastrophe in the building of an information system. Denis suggested that in the absence of actual catastrophes and evident risks, 'prevention is often the impoverished parent' in governments and business alike, concluding her essay with the remark that it is 'cooperation between professionals that defines the technologies and their reliability, these being not any pre-existing reality but a provisional achievement,'[7] a conclusion that one can find in diverse formulations in numerous publications on high-reliability organizations.

Compare COR with the "hallmarks of High Reliability"[8]:

—Preoccupation with failure: nonexistent in COR
—Reluctance to simplify interpretations: exactly the opposite in COR
—Sensitivity to operations: none in COR
—Commitment to resilience: reliance on others in COR
—Deference to expertise: professionalism and expertise disvalued and discouraged in COR

'The chief danger of modern media consists in subordinating our thought to its speed and brevity' Večerník suggested, and his interviewer responded that this is due 'in every case to the failure of science and intelligence.'[9] The COR procedures certainly lend credence to the opinions of Večerník and Hvížďala. The stress on speed and specific directives to limit thinking ('agonizing' as the Cornell administrators describe it four times), changing and correcting are present throughout the document and deserve some discussion.

---

[7] Ibid., p. 78.
[8] Op cit.
[9] Jiří Večerník and Karel Hvížďala, "O rychlosti, kvalitě a ceně informací," in K. Hvížďala, *Moc a nemoc médií: rozhovory, eseje a články 2000-2003.* (Praha: Máj; Dokořán, 2003): 46-47.

'Do not fuss over them [i.e. COR records] *extensively.'* The interpretation of 'extensively' is implied in the remainder of the document: any activity that takes time (i.e. understanding, interpretation, considering the potential users, making judgements, correction) is too much fussing.

'retain data elements that are already present in the record you are modifying unless they are clearly in error.' 'Do not delete or change information unless it is clearly inaccurate or egregiously misleading.' In order to ascertain that something is 'clearly in error' one must have a different understanding of what the correct information should be, an understanding that can only come from an examination of the item itself. While COR catalogers are instructed to pay attention to errors only if they are 'clearly inaccurate or egregiously misleading,' Marty noted that 'Tracking down and correcting even the simplest error helped them improve and evolve their information systems overall.'[10] His final paragraphs present conclusions similar to that arrived at by philosophers of science and researchers on high reliability organizations:

> As this article has demonstrated, information systems encouraging error recovery have a much greater potential value than merely helping employees to correct the odd, unexpected error that sneaks through already existing error prevention mechanisms. By supporting and encouraging error recovery in collections databases, employers are actually supporting and encouraging a culture in which employees are rewarded for taking an active role in improving the quality of data across the entire organization. The attitude that there is no reason to bother correcting a small number of errors can breed an envi-

---

[10] Paul F. Marty, 'Factors influencing error recovery in collections databases: a museum case study,' *Library Quarterly* 75:3 (2005), 318.

ronment in which employees are more likely to look the other way when errors occur, even if they were in a position to correct those errors and regardless of the severity of the error or their desire to fix it. In contrast, the attitude that one should not let an opportunity to correct mistakes slide by, even knowing full well that correcting all mistakes is impossible, can encourage employees to improve data quality in collections databases and to believe that developing more robust information systems is a worthwhile goal to pursue.

The implications of this article, therefore, are generalizable for all information organizations at multiple levels of implementation. First, they demonstrate how error recovery procedures, if properly implemented and encouraged in collections databases, can help the users of these systems play a role in detecting and correcting unexpected errors, which would solve a variety of problems for libraries, museums, and archives. Second, they document how collections databases that are flexible, open, and designed to work with errors tend to be more robust and more likely to encourage error recovery than systems that are rigid, closed, and designed to prevent errors. Finally, they illustrate how information organizations concerned with finding the best error management techniques for their collections databases will reap rewards that go beyond a simple ability to correct errors.[11]

'Accept what is present to the extent possible...' The ultimate mark of conservatism. Given the emphasis on speed and the prohibition of thinking (fussing), the quickest and most efficient solution for the staff member is to accept everything just as it is.

'Limit changes.' This, from the advocates of 'radical change' in catalog departments. A broad proscription such as this can only

---

[11] Ibid., p.323-324.

have an inhibiting effect on any desire to make sense of the record and the library catalog.

'Do not agonize over which call number to choose if the series has been classed in more than one call number; make a quick judgment to select one that is appropriate for the item.' Instead of using this conflict as an opportunity to learn why more than one class number has been assigned (and perhaps correcting a serious error), one simply makes a quick decision, thereby prohibiting both learning and error correction.

'Add English words, translated generally from the title, to items written in foreign languages... If the title field does not contain words about the subject of the work, quickly examine the covers, tables of contents, and preface to select appropriate words.' The assumption here is that the title will usually indicate clearly and unambiguously the subject, i.e. that no investigation, analysis or interpretation is needed, only selecting a few words from a prominent source which will be combined in no meaningful way in an uncontrolled subject field (653). In order to determine whether or not the title contains words descriptive of the contents, one must first have an understanding of what the contents are, i.e. one must look beyond the title *in every case*.

'If it is not possible to determine useful words quickly, omit the 653. **Do not analyze the book in depth nor agonize over selection of terms.***'* [Bold type in the original.] Note the use of the word 'agonize' to describe the work of information seeking, interpretation and judgement. If you cannot do the work mindlessly and quickly, then you should not do it for not doing it does not matter. Subject analysis is eliminated for precisely those items which are not readily amenable to title or table of contents keyword access.

'Do not duplicate a term that appears in another keyword-searchable field of the record.' The assumption here is that a

general keyword search is what the user will use, since any intelligent search will fail in this impoverished information environment. The effect of basing description upon this assumption is that the record created can *only* be retrieved on a general keyword search; all intelligent search strategies are defeated and rendered useless by this limitation of description. While LC's decision to cease the creation of controlled series headings resulted in rendering intelligent series searching counterproductive, COR renders all intelligent searching useless.

'If the work is about a person, place or corporate body, give the name in direct order in the 653 field. For corporate names, make a quick judgment whether an English translation would provide useful keyword access (if not, omit it).' Again, general keyword searching is assumed to be the sole manner of information seeking among the users, and intelligent searching (e.g. according to authorized forms) is rendered counter-productive. In one of the examples given in the COR document, the title *Historia del Sindicato de Culinarias* is given the 653 Culinary Syndicate, a heading which is presumably useful for subject access but which matches nothing which anyone would know to search for, it being not a variant name of the Sindicato but a literal translation made locally and, of course, quickly.

'Add a 948 field for statistics tracking.' The only really crucial information needed, and which must be added with absolute accuracy, is the information required by the management tools.

The result of this organization of the work of cataloging has been an extraordinary increase in productivity but increased productivity is not the only result. The results not only affect Cornell's library, but the catalogers who do the work, the international databases to which Cornell distributes its records, the libraries worldwide that use those databases, workflows within those libraries, and users everywhere of all kinds, not just librarians. Without pretending to be exhaustive, the following results have become clearly evident:

Classification too general
When the classification is not based on a clear understanding of the contents and how the item fits into the system of relationships expressed in the classification system used, the place assigned to it will be appropriately specific only by accident. The strong tendency towards general classification numbers evident in the COR records examined by this author and discussed in two earlier papers leads to congestion in these numbers and poverty in the specific numbers.[12] The larger the collection, the greater the problem. The objection may be made that these criticisms do not apply since the records are not intended to be permanent, but the classification *is* permanent for all of these materials ('classification numbers will not be changed'[13]).

Example 7 given above illustrates this problem. The subject information given lacks one of the most important elements —Romani language—as well as the place, northern Russia. The classification number given is for Romanies—Russia. The book is a collection of Romani proverbs, riddles and sayings from northern Russia collected by Ms Andronikova but never published during her lifetime. The LC classification schedule has a number for Proverbs, Modern, Other special, A-Z under which .R65 is for Romani proverbs, but the note under the main number (PN6519) says 'Prefer classification under language.' The number for Romani language, dialects, Russia is PK2899 .Z9R8. (The record also contains no indication that the proverbs are in the Romani language with Russian translations, nor is there an entry for the person responsible for collecting these proverbs, Andronikova.)

---

[12] David Bade, *Misinformation and meaning in library catalogs*, (Chicago: the Author, 2003); *The theory and practice of bibliographic failure, or, Misinformation in the information society* (Ulaanbaatar: Chuluunbat, 2004).
[13] David Banush, posting to PCCLIST, 21 July 2003.

Classification/shelf browsing becomes increasingly useless.
Even more problematic than general classification is improper classification, and these arise from exactly the same operating conditions as too general classifications: insufficient attention and the insistence upon simplification of interpretations. The use of sources other than the current LC class schedules for the determination of classification numbers is evident in the repeated use of obsolete numbers. Worst of all, these numbers, incorrect or obsolete, are frequently retained in the upgraded records in the shared utilities and reproduced in many or even all holding libraries.

Precise searching is counterproductive.
Sawyer and Davis' conclusion remains sound: 'Sophisticated search and retrieval capabilities are worthless if the data on which the searches depend are inaccurate.'[14] The combination of broad subject terms rather than precise terms, uncontrolled subject data that for non-English materials is largely restricted to translation of elements found in the title, the prohibition of duplicating information found in one field in another and the non-provision of subjects in many cases, particularly where interpretation and judgement are required, severely reduces the value of all precise, intelligent searching, leaving the general keyword search as the only possibility when comprehensive retrieval is desired, that being in many cases impossible due to the lack of any information input for many items. This goes not only for users of Cornell libraries but for users of the shared databases as well, since these records are sent to the shared bibliographical utilities.

---

[14] Jeanne C. Sawyer and Jinnie Y. Davis, 'Automated error detection in library systems,' in M. Gorman, ed., *Crossroads: proceedings of the First National Conference of the Library and Information Technology Association, September 17-21, 1983, Baltimore, Maryland.* (Chicago: ALA, 1984): 217.

Creation and dissemination of misinformation
Records are created using defaults in the fixed fields and catalogers are instructed to leave the defaults, changing only the Type, Lang, and Dates fields. I have examined and discussed many COR records in an earlier report and the vast majority of those records had identical information in most of the fixed fields, regardless of their applicability to the items themselves.[15] As noted above, classification and subject headings are, when present, frequently much too general to be useful or are in fact incorrect, but these, rather than an analysis of the item, nonetheless serve as the basis of much of the enhancing done to COR records by other libraries, including LC (for an example, see the following section). The combination of using defaults and title keywords as subjects in order to save time with a policy of 'Do not correct' results in the deliberate creation of misinformation which is then distributed globally via tapeload to the shared databases. In 'Observations on fraud and scientific integrity in a digital environment' LaFollette made the following remarks on the ethical relationship between publishers, editors and authors:

> First, as researchers, we want to be able to trust what we read in the journals in our field. With so much information published, in so many diverse and mutable forms, some type of certification or sifting—trustworthy and reliable certification or sifting—will become paramount. There must be increased attention, therefore, to ethical standards for validation and evaluation. ... Hapless readers subjected to an explosion of sloppy scholarship, multiple misspellings, and similar avoidable errors will soon demand that authors—and journals—pay more attention to such details. Authors have an ethical responsibility to be especially careful and conscientious in an electronic context, where errors can take on a life of their own. Even the mundane issue of citation takes on new impor-

---

[15] David Bade, *Misinformation and meaning in library catalogs*.

tance in a world where seemingly unlimited amounts of 'useful' information is present on the Web in one week and moved to another address or changed altogether the next.[16]

Should not the same ethical attitudes be expected of librarians?

Errors persist and propagate, 'temporary' misinformation becomes permanent.
Catalog management and all corrective activity are removed from the library, and therefore all capacity for quality control and evaluation. No one can observe the decline of access because no one is looking at the obstacles to access. Again, Weick and Sutcliffe noted that being 'preoccupied with failures, large and mostly small' was a primary characteristic of HROs:

> HROs encourage reporting of errors, they elaborate experiences of a near miss for what can be learned, and they are wary of the potential liabilities of success, including complacency, the temptation to reduce margins of safety, and the drift into automatic processing.[17]

According to COR documentation, these records are not intended to be permanent, but Banush stated 'We currently have no plans to retrieve items from the stacks and upgrade them should they lack better copy after the 2-year Marcadia cycle', so these records in their entirety *are* effectively intended to be permanent unless something better is provided by someone else from another institution within 2 years.[18] And of course the records for all unique items will be permanent. Finally, many of the upgrades performed in OCLC on the basis of these Cornell COR records

---

[16] Marcel C. LaFollette, "Observations on fraud and scientific integrity in a digital environment" *Journal of the American Society for Information Science* v.51:14 (2000): 1336.
[17] Op cit., p. 10-11.
[18] David Banush, posting to PCCLIST, 21 July 2003.

treat them as essentially correct and simply add trivia and change the 653 tags into the appropriate 600, 610, 630, 650 or 651 without investigating the item or correcting the call numbers and subjects supplied by Cornell. Ironically, when Cornell subsequently downloads these 'enhanced' records into its catalog, it frequently gets little more than what it entered into the shared databases in the first place.

We can see this in OCLC 70140053, where the COR record originally had a call number for Hebrew language—History—General works (PJ4545) and for subject, a single 653: Hebrew language $a History $a Shapiro F.L. This record was 'upgraded' from Level 3 to Level I by Syracuse University Library and this enhanced version may be seen in that library's catalog (viewed 28 November 2006). The record was slightly altered: the 653 changed to 650 0 Hebrew language $x History.; Shapiro dropped as subject; and probably fixed fields corrected, giving the following (left and right ligatures removed for technical reasons):

Example 8:
000   00613cam a2200205Ia 450
001   2451305
005   20060710110912.0
008   060522s2005 bw af 000 0 rus d
035   __ $a (OCoLC)ocm70140053
040   __ $a COO $c COO $d SYB
020   __ $a 985436500X
050   _4 $a PJ4545 $b .P744 2005
049   __ $a SYBB
100   1_ $a Prestina, Liia.
245   10 $a Slovar´ zapreshchennogo iazyka : $b 125-letiiu F.L. Shapiro / |c L. Prestina.
260   __ $a Minsk : $b MET, $c 2005.
300   __ $a 316 p., [16] p. of plates : $b ill. ; $c 20 cm.
440   _0 $a Sto let sionizma
650   _0 $a Hebrew language $x History.

This Syracuse version was subsequently upgraded again by Columbia University Library. In this enhancement (viewed in that library's catalog 28 November 2006) the first subject and classification remain the same, but the 653 has been reintroduced and an additional subject heading for Shapiro added. This name heading was taken from the erroneous authority heading created earlier by University of Pittsburgh (the miagkii znak appears in the main entry, cross-references and 670 as an apostrophe). This record was then imported into the University of California-Berkeley Library catalog (viewed 28 November 2006) where the order of subjects was altered, putting the still erroneous name heading for Shapiro first, but leaving the classification as it originally was. It is this record which was then retrieved by Marcadia for Cornell and appears in the Olin Library catalog (viewed 28 November 2006: left and right ligatures removed for technical reasons):

Example 9:
000   01017cam a2200313 a 450
001   5813609
005   20060927133850.0
008   060613s2005 bw af 010 0drusod
020   __ $a 985436500X
035   __ $a CUBGGLAD152060419-B
035   __ $a (CU)GLAD152060419
035   __ $a 5813609
040   __ $a COO $c COO $d SYB $d ZCU $d CUY
050   _4 $a PJ4545 $b .P744 2005
090   __ $a PJ4545 $b .P744 2005
100   1_ $a Prestina, Liia.
245   00 $aSlovar' zapreshchennogo iazyka : $b 125-letiiu F.L. Shapiro / $c avtor-sostavitel' Liia Prestina
260   __ $a Minsk : $b MET, $c 2005.
300   __ $a 316 p., [16] p. of plates : $b ill. ; $c 20 cm.
490   1_ $a Sto let sionizma
600   10 $a Shapiro, F. L. $q (Feliks L'vovich), $d 1879-1961.

650	_0	$a Hebrew language $x History.
830	_0	$a Sto let sionizma.
852	__	$a CU $b MAIN $h PJ4545 $i .P744 2005
948	3_	$ 20060927 $h marcadia $i 060912A.M
948	1_	$a 20060616 $b z $d ysk2 $e cts
948	0_	$a 20060613 $b i $d nk31 $e cts $h appr
988	__	$a Marcadia
950	__	$l olin

The Library of Congress also took the Syracuse-Columbia revision of the COR record (Example 8) and sent it through its copy-cataloging section, changing the classification to properly reflect the subject (Shapiro), adding an entry for Shapiro as author since the work includes selections of his writings, but still using the erroneous form of name in both the 600 and 700. The subject for Hebrew language—History remains in the LC record as well as the main entry for Prestina, who was only one of dozens of contributors (viewed 28 November 2006).

The final transformation (so far) is the result of my own emendations and is the record currently in OCLC (28 November 2006: left and right ligatures removed for technical reasons):

Example 10:

010   2006371502
040   COO $c COO $d DLC $d SYB $d ZCU $d NLGGC $d CGU
066    $c (N
020   __$a985436500X
020   __$a9789854365008
029 1_ $aNLGGC $b 293018731
042   __$alccopycat
050   _4$aPJ4534.S53 $b S56 2005
084   __$a18.77 $2 bcl
049   CGUA
245   00$aСловарь запрещенного языка : $b 125-летию Ф.Л. Шапиро / $c автор-составитель Лия Престина.

245 00$aSlovar´ zapreshchennogo iazyka : $b 125-letiiu F.L. Shapiro / $c avtor-sostavitel´ Liia Prestina.
260 __$aМинск : $b МЕТ, $c 2005.
260 __$aMinsk : $b МЕТ, $c 2005.
300 __$a316 p., [16] p. of plates : $b ill. ; $c 20 cm.
440 0_$aСто лет сионизма
440 0_$aSto let sionizma
500 __$aIncludes selections by Shapiro.
600 10$aШапиро, Ф. Л. $q (Феликс Львович), $d 1879-1961.
600 10$aShapiro, F. L. $q (Feliks L´vovich), $d 1879-1961.
600 10$aШапиро, Ф. Л.$q (Феликс Львович),$d 1879-1961.$t Иврит-русский словарь.
600 10$aShapiro, F. L.$q (Feliks L´vovich),$d 1879-1961. $t Ivrit-russkiĭ slovar´.
650 _0$aJewish linguists $z Belarus $v Biography.
650 _0$aHebrew language $x Lexicography $x History.
650 17$aHebreeuws. $2 gtt
700 1_$aПрестина, Лия.
700 1_$aPrestina, Liia.
700 1_$aШапиро, Ф. Л. $q (Феликс Львович), $d 1879-1961.
700 1_$aShapiro, F. L. $q (Feliks L´vovich), $d 1879-1961.

From this record it can be seen that the book is about a linguist and his dictionary, that it is not about the history of the Hebrew language but about the history of Hebrew lexicography. Yet this specific information can be found in none of the catalogs of the holding libraries (including a Japanese library that used LC copy) other than the Joseph Regenstein Library and the Bibliotheekcatalogi van de Universiteit Leiden. In none of the other holding libraries were the erroneous name and subject heading detected or corrected.

The money that Cornell is paying for someone to change the encoding level and the MARC tagging without getting any real improvements in information quality or user value is simply money wasted. Copy cataloging sections in other libraries including the Library of Congress are neither detecting nor correcting these problems and the problems in this record are not nearly as far off the mark as can be found in many other COR records. Similar problems with LC preliminary records were reported in Preece and Fox, who noted that 'continuing technical difficulties in matching them with existing member copy' led to LC's decision to stop contributing these records to OCLC.[19]

Encourages poor working habits, prohibits the exercise of scholarly values, destroys professionalism.
Serbian librarians are asking 'How to build a culture of quality into an organization's culture?'[20] while American librarians are priding themselves on destroying organizational culture altogether. Catalogers are treated essentially like unskilled laborers and temporary workers, and Guerrini's remarks on outsourcing are appropriate in this context as well:

> An adequate number of qualified persons ensures a minimum of work time with optimal results. Libraries resort more and more to temporary personnel recruited through competitive and cooperative contracts. While the solution can be positive by favoring the introduction of younger persons to the world of work and by solving cataloging problems otherwise unsolvable, it becomes pernicious the moment when the library (or the body which oversees it) uses as the only criteria of selection the lowest price. The inevitable consequence is an unsatisfactory catalog and inadequate economic treatment of the cataloger that is humiliating for the workers. The result of lower quality arises almost always from the need

---

[19] Barbara G. Preece and Mary Anne Fox, 'Preliminary LC records for monographs in OCLC' *Information technology and libraries* v.11 (March 1992): 3-9.
[20] Гордана Стокић, "Библиотеке и управљање укупним квалитетом," *Глас библиотеке*, nr.11 (2004): 46. Available at: http://eprints.rclis.org/archive/00003928/ (accessed 28 Nov. 2006)

to reduce cataloging time ... a temporal restriction that results in frustration, because it prevents the expression of the cataloger's professional values.[21]

Increased burden on other libraries
David Woods' First Law of Cooperative Systems: 'It's not cooperation, if either you do it all or I do it all.'[22] Cooperative cataloging depends entirely upon the contributions of the cooperating libraries. COR records represent the refusal to contribute the institution's fair share, thus requiring other libraries to do Cornell's work for them, work that many libraries cannot afford to do. That other libraries cannot afford to correct and complete the work of Cornell and others leads to the result that all libraries continue to find the original deficient record rather than the enhanced record they hope or believe they should find.

Kills the goose that lays the golden eggs.
Denis' remark quoted above identifies the principal problem, namely that it is 'cooperation between professionals that defines the technologies and their reliability, these being not any preexisting reality but a provisional achievement'.[23] It is mutual dependability—not the technologies in themselves—that provides a constant successful outcome, a matter stressed by Weick and one which he illustrated with the examples of stable families and alcohol rehabilitation programs. Situations and systems founded upon mutual dependability 'collapse when people stop doing whatever produced the stable outcome.'[24] Writing of joint human-computer systems Hollnagel noted that 'In any situation where humans use artefacts to accomplish something, the dependability of the artefact is essential. Quite simply, if we can-

---

[21] Mauro Guerrini, *Il catalogo di qualità.* (Firenze: Pagnini, 2002): 39-40.
[22] David D. Woods and Erik Hollnagel, *Joint cognitive systems: patterns in cognitive systems engineering.* (Boca Raton: CRC Press, 2006): 117.
[23] Op cit., p. 78.
[24] Karl E. Weick, 'Organizational culture as a source of high reliability,' *California management review*, 29: 2 (1987):119.

not rely or depend on the artefact, we cannot really use it'.[25] COR already presents great problems for many libraries; should other libraries adopt COR or similarly organize and instruct their cataloging departments, there will soon be no bibliographic information created, completed or corrected, much less shared, among libraries: the system in its entirety will collapse.

A comparison of the COR(nell) vision of the library with the vision outlined in Di Domenico is a sobering exercise indeed:

1) to create the opportunity for continued learning;
2) promote research and dialogue;
3) encourage overcoming the "defensive routine" of all towards collaboration and group learning;
4) activate systems of acquiring, sharing and elaborating knowledge;
5) favoring processes of transfer and diffusion of knowledge and powers of decision...
6) spreading a vision orientated toward learning;
7) to bring the library as closely as possible to its proper state[26]

In the final analysis, the evaluation of COR must be even more damning than Preece and Fox's evaluation of LC's preliminary records: 'An experiment designed to foster resource sharing had foundered because of its incompatibility with the needs of network members for a standardized and reliable cataloging source'.[27] COR is not an experiment but a deliberately planned

---

[25] Erik Hollnagel, 'Dependability of joint human-computer systems,' in S. Anderson et al., eds., *Computer safety, reliability and security: 21st International Conference, SAFECOMP 2002, Catania, Italy, September 10-13*. (Berlin: Springer, 2002; Lecture notes in computer science, v.2434): 4.

[26] Giovanni di Domenico, 'La biblioteca apprende: qualità organizzativa e qualità di servizio nella società cognitiva,' in O. Foglieni, ed., *La qualità nel sistema biblioteca*, Milano: Editrice bibliografica, 2001: 45.

[27] Op cit., p.8.

procedure that fails as a reliable method for information provision and undermines resource sharing: no information in a COR record can be accepted by anyone as being accurate or adequate, i.e. COR records are neither trustworthy nor reliable. COR records are certainly timely but they are useless and deceptive.

III. Orientations and Results: The Three Policies Compared

All three of the policies examined were implemented mainly as attempts to make materials available to the public in the most timely fashion possible—without increasing staff or labour costs—rather than relegating them to an inaccessible backlog hidden away in a staff only area of the library. All three policies succeeded in getting the volumes physically out of a staff only area and into a publicly accessible space within the library, even though that space may itself be available to library patrons only via the catalog, as in that subset of Princeton's ATA materials which are available for online searching and borrowing but shelved in a remote storage facility not physically browsable by library patrons.

The questions which must be asked of each of these policies are: Are these items 'really' available to users? Does 'a' record in the online catalog actually make items usable? If so, in what manner? What search strategies may/must the library patron/librarian use to find these materials? What kind of searches are not supported by the records created according to these policies? The answer to these questions varies considerably from one policy to another.

As noted above, the W-Collection records permitted known item searches by librarians prior to 1986 and to all users thereafter for those items which had been correctly analyzed at the time that the order record was created; any significant problem in those records remained when the item was sent to the W-Collection. As the examples revealed, this meant the loss of shelf browsing for all W-Collection materials, and additionally there could be a lack of author, title and subject access, even without considering the effects of typographical or MARC encoding errors.

The loss of browsability, whether in the stacks or in the OPAC via subjects, was probably the most serious limitation these materials imposed upon users. Classification systems for libraries were designed for the express purpose of shelving library materials by design rather than simply by order of their arrival. Classification systems allow for the shelf order to impart information to the browser in the bookstacks about the contents of items on the shelf, much as subject headings do for the catalog browser. The classification numbers, like subject headings, serve not merely as position indicators for finding a particular item, but also as a subject searching system. In a library using such a classified system for the spatial ordering of material the classification number is therefore a crucial component of the information system considered in its totality.

The importance of all forms of browsing in library research was discussed by Abbott, who offered the following remarks:

> Library research is, then, a fairly simple net computing system. Like most such net systems and indeed like most current optimization routines, library research relies heavily on browsing, which can be defined somewhat formally as random inspection of a local knowledge vicinity for items with a high probability of payoff, particularly in terms of taking one to productive new localities. It is crucial to recognize that this happens at many different levels in library research, not just at one: within books as one turns pages, on shelves as one searches for a book, in the stacks as one walks by unknown call numbers, in bibliographic indexes and other research tools as one glances through topics, and so on. In all these cases, the power of browsing is great. Note

that this means that browsing is a constant concomitant of library research, not an occasional activity within it. Browsing is always going on and gaining knowledge from browsing is not a rare, serendipitous event but rather a constant, routine one.

Browsing has two requirements. First, the materials being browsed must already themselves be highly ordered either by virtue of their internal structure or by their places in an indexing or cataloguing or classification system. Otherwise, adjacency has no meaning and browsing can't work. Second, the browsers must have broad knowledge that primes them to recognize likely connections. ...

Browsing in this extremely broad sense and at all these many levels is thus one thing that absolutely must be protected in the research libraries of the future. It means keeping materials ordered and in a setting where they can be effectively scanned in the random fashion that browsing demands. Since, as we have noted, browsing involves many levels of organization, all of these levels need to be preserved, not just the order of books on shelves.[28]

The assignment of classification numbers requires an analysis of the subject of the material; to assign such a classification number without basing it upon that analysis would render the system itself of no use, a waste of effort, time and money. This is what we find in COR classifications, which are intended simply to be place markers on the shelf. Collocation would require analysis and interpretation, and COR policies

---

[28] Abbott, Andrew (2006). The university library.
http://www.lib.uchicago.edu/staffweb/groups/space/abbott-report.html#VIA (accessed 28 Nov. 2006)

severely restrict these activities. In contrast to both W (accession number shelving) and COR (too general, obsolete and incorrect numbers understood primarily as shelving locators), the ATA procedure demonstrates a sensitivity to operations (one of Weick and Sutcliffe's hallmarks of high reliability), specifically instructing the catalogers to produce an appropriate classification number for items going to the open stacks, but not to worry too much about those numbers for items in a closed stacks since browsing there is not an available strategy.

The W-Collection made no pretense to information provision; the intent was simply to put the books in a publicly accessible area and have a record attached to them which would serve inventory contol in the various library-internal tasks. There was no lapse in reliability, nor any removal of thought, judgement and responsibility from the catalogers, since they were never involved. The W-Collection was what it was and no attempt was ever made to present it otherwise; other than matching MARC tapes and on one occasion sending these records to OCLC in hopes of obtaining member copy, neither subject access nor authority control was attempted or claimed for this collection. Nor were these records shared with any other databases.

COR policies produce a completely different situation, involving a lapse in reliability, the removal of thought, judgement and responsibility from the persons creating, manipulating and maintaining the database, and hence from the library as a whole. The records appear to be fully analyzed with subjects, call numbers and name entries. They are widely distributed to shared databases. They are integrated into the open classified stacks at Cornell as though they belong there. Because it is assumed that the required information will be created elsewhere later, the quality, value and responsibility for the information is located externally. Because the work performed in the library is by policy not to be concerned with any of these issues of quality, complete trust has been placed in the technical system and all sources from which information may be acquired at any point in the process. The result is that the library no longer has any possibility of maintaining a mindful awareness of what is happening and loses the internal variety required to deal with the complexity of the system in its entirety.

Records created according to Princeton's ATA Procedure, unlike the other two policies examined, are created to serve all users: librarians, patrons and technologies. Responsibility for creating a record which serves those three uses is kept within the library and under the control of professional catalogers to whom all judgements concerning adequacy, accuracy, completeness, appropriateness *and* timeliness are referred. In contrast, the W-Collection was created for inventory control, offering very little for other users and machine manipulation, while the work and all judgements were left in the hands of nonprofessional staff and student workers, with no cataloger involvement at all. No attempt was made to address any concerns other than timeliness, payment processing and circulation.

The COR policy created the worst results of the three, for three principal reasons: 1) all the work was assumed to be temporary and *therefore* unimportant; 2) all responsibility was removed from the library, both professionals and nonprofessionals forbidden to think and act responsibly; and 3) as required by the data mining techniques implemented, these irresponsible records were (and continue to be) loaded into shared databases from which the misinformation created at Cornell has been copied and distributed globally ever since.

IV. Conclusion

Policies for creating bibliographic records must take account of a number of users and uses and their conflicting goals, not just one goal. In a cooperative environment, the impact on all parties involved must be considered and not simply a particular institution's goals viewed in isolation. Both the technical system and the systems of social relationships within which it is embedded must be understood as systems in all their complexity rather than simply as tools to be used or resources to be exploited. Most importantly, the communication purposes of bibliographic information must be the primary consideration in the creation of the record. It is in this matter that both the W Collection and COR failed. Records created according to those procedures were created for inventory control (W Collection) and for machine matching (COR) rather than for patron use.

Whether or not the ATA procedures at Princeton could be adapted and expanded to apply to other classes of materials, the simple fact that the goal of these procedures is to create records serving all of the various users and uses within a socio-technical system of given possibilities and constraints strongly suggests that these policies will have a much higher likelihood of producing reliably useful bibliographical records for users across the entire range of use situations. My own experience with Princeton's ATA records in OCLC has convinced me that this is indeed the case. And Princeton's ATA records have been timely as well.

REFERENCES

Abbott, Andrew (2006). The university library. http://www.lib.uchicago.edu/staffweb/groups/space/abbott-report.html#VIA (accessed 28 Nov. 2006)

Bade, David. (2003). *Misinformation and meaning in library catalogs*. Chicago: the Author.

Bade, David. (2004). *The theory and practice of bibliographic failure, or, Misinformation in the information society.* Ulaanbaatar: Chuluunbat.

Denis, Hélène. (2005). 'Les risques et les catastrophes,' in Minguet and Thuderoz (eds.), *Travail, entreprise et société: manuel de sociologie pour ingénieurs et scientifiques.* Paris: PUF, 68-80.

Domenico, Giovanni di. (2001). 'La biblioteca apprende: qualità organizzativa e qualità di servizio nella società cognitiva,' in O. Foglieni, ed., *La qualità nel sistema biblioteca*, Milano: Editrice bibliografica, 32-48.

Guerrini, Mauro. (2002). *Il catalogo di qualità.* Firenze: Pagnini.

Hollnagel, Erik. (2002). 'Dependability of joint human-computer systems,' in S. Anderson et al., eds., *Computer safety, reliability and security: 21st International Conference, SAFECOMP 2002, Catania, Italy, September 10-13*. Berlin: Springer (Lecture notes in computer science, v.2434): 4-9.

LaFollette, Marcel C. (2000). "Observations on fraud and scientific integrity in a digital environment" *Journal of the American Society for Information Science* v.51 nr.14: 1334-1337.

Marty, Paul F. (2005). 'Factors influencing error recovery in collections databases: a museum case study,' *Library Quarterly* 75 nr.3: 295-328.

Paim, Isis; Rosa Maria Quadros Nehmy and César Geraldo Guimarães, César Geraldo. (1996). "Problematização do conceito "Qualidade" da informação" *Perspectivas em ciência da informação*, v.1 n.1 (Jan.-June): 111-119.

Preece, Barbara G. and Mary Anne Fox, (1992). 'Preliminary

LC records for monographs in OCLC' *Information technology and libraries* v.11 (March): 3-9.

Sawyer, Jeanne C.; Jinnie Y. Davis. (1984). 'Automated error detection in library systems,' in M. Gorman, ed., *Crossroads: proceedings of the First National Conference of the Library and Information Technology Association, September 17-21, 1983, Baltimore, Maryland.* Chicago: ALA, 213-217.

Stokić. Gordana. Стокић, Гордана (2004). "Библиотеке и управљање укупним квалитетом," *Глас библиотеке*, nr.11: 41-50.

Večerník, Jiří and Karel Hvížďala. (2003). "O rychlosti, kvalitě a ceně informací," in K. Hvížďala, *Moc a nemoc médií: rozhovory, eseje a články 2000-2003.* Praha: Máj; Dokořán, 45-49.

Weick, Karl E. (1987). 'Organizational culture as a source of high reliability,' *California management review*, 29 nr.2: 112-127.

Weick, Karl E. and Kathleen M.Stucliffe. (2001) *Managing the unexpected: assuring high performance in an age of complexity.* San Francisco: Jossey-Bass.

Woods, David D. Woods and Erik Hollnagel. (2006). *Joint cognitive systems: patterns in cognitive systems engineering.* Boca Raton: CRC Press.

V

The Perfect Bibliographic Record: Platonic Ideal, Rhetorical Strategy or Nonsense?

Abstract

Discussions of quality in library catalogs and bibliographic databases often refer to "the perfect record." This paper examines the usage of that phrase in the library literature, finding that its predominant use is as a rhetorical strategy for reducing the complex and context dependent issue of quality to an absurdity, thus permitting the author to ignore or dismiss all issues of quality. Five documents in which the phrase is not used in this fashion are examined and their value for understanding the inextricably intertwined values of quantity and quality are discussed. The author recommends rejecting both the rhetoric of "the perfect record" and satisfaction with "the imperfect record."

The Perfect Record

Last year Charles Blair, the co-director of the Digital Library Development Center of the University of Chicago Library, remarked to me that at an interview a cataloger had protested that he was not dedicated to the pursuit of "the perfect record." He asked me what do catalogers mean when they speak of the "perfect record"? It was such a simple sounding question, but I was unable to answer. I was aware that there had been references to the "perfect record" in the library literature, but I had never seriously thought about what that might mean. More recently, in his summary of my talk at the May 9th meeting of the Library of Congress Working Group on the Future of Bibliographic Control, Clifford Lynch made remarks to the effect that we need to move away from thinking about perfect records to thinking about resource allocation (variously reported without reference to "the perfect record" in Lindner and Hillmann's blogs).[1]

Where did "the perfect record" come from? When did it appear? I first encountered "the perfect record" in Intner's (1990) essay "Copy cataloging and the perfect record mentality."[2] Responding to that article in a 2002 publication, I wrote

---

[1] The talk itself ("Structures, standards and the people who make them meaningful", available at: http://www.loc.gov/bibliographic-future/meetings/docs/bade-may9-2007.pdf) was not about quality, much less perfection, but rather about communication, the activity which gives meaning to the act of cataloging, the activity for which structures and standards were created to facilitate and support. A videocast of both my talk and Lynch's summary is available at http://www.loc.gov/bibliographic-future/meetings/webcasts-may9.html accessed June 18, 2007). Mark Lindner reported Lynch's remark as "Perfect quality is easy to talk about and advocate for – is a moral position, and few human systems can provide this." (http://marklindner.info/blog/2007/05/ 13/ lc-working-group-structures-and-standards-part-6-public-testimony-and-wrap-up/)For another report, see Diane Hillmann's report "Structures and Standards for Bibliographic Data" (pt. 2) May 9th, 2007: http://litablog.org/
[2] Sheila S. Intner, "Copy Cataloging and the Perfect Record Mentality." *Technicalities*, 10: 7 (July 1990): 12-15.

> Intner sets up the impossible goal of the "perfect catalog," one that requires catalogers with language and subject expertise. Having asserted that this is economically impossible, she then asks: "Who cares if the perfect catalog is doomed?" Her response: "Not I."[3]

adding in a footnote "Perfect is impossible because humans are imperfect; as a goal toward which we strive it is essential."[4]

When the phrase "the perfect record" or a variant thereof first appeared in the library literature I do not know. Steinhagen and Moynahan claimed that "For at least one hundred years, catalogers have been committed to creating perfect bibliographic records"[5], while Mason[6] dates the origins of the debate "between cataloguing quickly for user access, versus striving for a perfect record" in the rise of library automation and the sharing of catalog copy.

The earliest instance of the phrase which I was able to locate was in a brief note in *Library Journal* in 1978:

> And Cornell gave its definition of the "perfect record"—one in which the 049 field, cutter number, and series tags are the only changes necessary.[7]

---

[3] David Bade, *The Creation and Persistence of Misinformation in Shared Library Catalogs: Language and Subject Knowledge in a Technological Era* (Urbana: Graduate School of Library and Information Science, University of Illinois at Urbana=Champaign, 2002. *Occasional Papers*, no. 211 (April 2002)): 19.

[4] Ibid., p. 33.

[5] Elizabeth N. Steinhagen and Sharon A. Moynahan, "Catalogers Must Change! Surviving Between the Rock and the Hard Place," *Cataloging & Classification Quarterly,* v.26:3 (1998): 3.

[6] Moya K. Mason, Copy Cataloguing: Where is it Taking Us On Our Quest for the Perfect Copy?
http://www.moyak.com/researcher/resume/papers/clog4mkm.html

[7] "Costs of upgrading cataloging," *Library Journal,* 103: 11 (June 1, 1978): 1124.

but the use of quotations marks in this note suggests that already the phrase raised eyebrows and therefore quotation marks.

That note from 1978 is an interesting note, not only because it is the earliest mention of the phrase that I could find and it is in scare quotes, but for several other reasons. It is one of only three matches in EBSCO's Library, Information Science & Technology Abstracts with Full Text (it does not appear in EBSCO's Library Literature and Information Science database). It claims that Cornell offered a definition of "the perfect record" and reproduces that definition. Most of all, the published version of the presentation which this note discusses appeared the following year and in that paper there is no mention of "the perfect record." That paper deserves our full attention.

The Perfect Record or the Authoritative Record?

"The Quality of OCLC Bibliographic Records: The Cornell Law Library Experience" by Christian M. Boissonnas was published in 1979, "an expanded version of a presentation made on 6 October 1977".[8] It is one of the most perceptive, theoretically sound and carefully written papers on bibliographic quality that I have ever read. The second paragraph makes it clear that the author is concerned not with some objective abstract ideal but a practical goal which is consistently achieved at Cornell.

> There is not even common agreement on what quality is when applied to a bibliographic record. The purpose of this paper is to explain what it means in the Cornell Law Library and to show what it costs for this particular library to achieve the quality which it deems necessary.[9]

The author elaborates on general aspects of quality in bibliographic records in the next section, noting specifically issues regar-

---

[8] Christian Boissonnas, "The Quality of OCLC Bibliographic Records: The Cornell Law Library Experience," *Law Library Journal*, 72:1 (1979): 80-85.
[9] Ibid., p. 80.

161

ding standards and the varying significance and importance of data elements across types of libraries, as well as over time:

> Quality is a concept which means different things to different institutions. When applied to a bibliographic record, it means that what is of high quality for one, because each data element has been verified somewhere, is unacceptable to another because the record is not in the ISBD format or does not have all the added entries it could have. It is only by examining these records against predetermined standards that one can say that one record is of higher (or lower) quality than another. Lacking these standards, it is difficult to argue that one institution's definition of quality is better or worse than another's.
> When dealing with the OCLC database, the problem of definition is compounded because not all data elements in a record are equally important to all members. Moreover, it is difficult to anticipate whether certain data elements, which are important now, will still be as important in the future.[10]

The section closes with remarks on the cost of quality control:

> Given the great pressure to input as quickly and therefore as cheaply as possible, there is a real tendency to follow the minimum available standards. This may have rather unfortunate consequences in the future on the ability of users of the OCLC database to retrieve bibliographic data. The current standards are loose enough to almost guarantee that, for many, the conflict between quality and quantity of input will be resolved in favor of quantity. ... the question which each library must resolve is: "Given our resources and the current standards, how

---

[10] Ibid.

much quality can we afford to provide?" ... As will be seen, quality control costs a great deal.[11]

Following these general remarks Boissonnas offers Cornell Law Library's definition of quality—not a definition of the perfect record—a definition which "as applied to the OCLC database assumes that there is something which, for lack of a better term, can be called an authoritative bibliographic record." He then defines "authoritative bibliographic record" as

> any record for which no modification needs to be made except in the following:
> —The 049 field
> —The cutter number
> —The series tags [since] information in these fields is essentially local in character.[12]

What is the difference between an authoritative bibliographic record (without scare quotes and with an indefinite article) and "the perfect record" (within quotation marks and with a definite article)? According to Boissonnas, an authoritative record is a record that is acceptable to a particular institution in all of those elements that are not locally determined. This implies that what is there is correct, and that the elements required by the particular standards which the institution embraces are all present, insofar as they can be determined from the item in hand.

Without knowing whether or not Boissonnas actually used the phrase "perfect record" in the original presentation, it is impossible to do anything more than guess at the connotations which the author of the note in *Library Journal* intended to convey by means of the quotation marks, but the use of the definite article is definitely inappropriate, a twisting of the carefully stated context in which Boissonnas situated his

---

[11] Ibid.
[12] Ibid., p. 81.

authoritative record: the goals of one library, which will differ from the goals of other libraries. What the *Library Journal* note appears to convey, is exactly the same connotations as the phrase "the perfect record" (and its variants: perfect catalog, single most perfect record, etc.) suggests in the statements by Lynch and Intner mentioned above as well as a host of other writers using that phrase since then. "The perfect record" is introduced in order to discredit and dismiss discussions of qualitative aspects of cataloging in which originally there were no references to perfection.

The Ideology of the Perfect Record

Searching the literature for the "perfect record" revealed no advocates of "the perfect record" but many denouncers. If no one is advocating perfect records, why are so many people denouncing them? Here are a few of the remarks which I found, mostly from material located via Google since only four items could be located by searching "perfect record" in the EBSCO databases:

> Many contributors to library literature assume as a given that catalogers are concerned with a Platonic vision of a perfect record and an almost obsessive regard for how they are ranked by their peers.[13]

> Current trends in information service won't permit catalogers to continue keeping faith with the ideal of producing perfect catalogs made up of perfect catalog records. Remaining faithful to our ideals in the face of what is happening in the field is worse than quixotic, it spells doom to the essence of cataloging and discredits what catalogers can and should be doing instead of creating perfect records.[14]

---

[13] Ruth Hafter, *Academic Librarians and Cataloging Networks : Visibility, Quality Control, and Professional Status*. (New York: Greenwood Press, 1986): 44-45.
[14] Intner, op. cit.: 13.

Catalogers had become too focussed on creating the perfect record according to LC standards.[15]

Cataloging should be defined in terms of function and access rather than in terms of conformity to rules and achievement of the "perfect record"[16]

[A] less than perfect record is better than no record.[17]
There are many options for creating or obtaining records for electronic content. With basic tools like those described in this article, even the largest of databases can be handled in some way, even if it does not mean creating the perfect record. Perhaps there is no perfect record.[18]

We need to go beyond the perfect record if we were [sic] to save the eminent decline of our catalogs.[19]

... I suggest that readers spread their focus more broadly and pay attention to a theme that emerges in everything else I discuss here: the idea that the single perfect record is just not enough... that we need to focus on discovery as a discipline. ... in the end both our users and our profession will be better served if we rethink how we are

---

[15] Barbara B. Tillett, "Catalog It Once for All: A History of Cooperative Cataloging in the United States Prior to 1967 (Before MARC)," *Cataloging & Classification Quarterly* 17:3/4 (1993): 28.
[16] Remark made by Joan Swanekamp at the 1994 OLAC/MOUG Conference, October 5-8, 1994, Oak Brook, Illinois. Taken from the report by Richard A. Stewart http://ublib.buffalo.edu/libraries/units/cts/olac/conferences/1994.html
[17] Ed O'Neill, "Matching and Validating Personal Names Authority Records" *Cataloging & Classification Quarterly* 22:1 (1996): 100.
[18] Chuck Hamaker, "Creating Record Sets For E-content in OPACs" *Charleston Advisor* 2:3 (January 2001). (Accessed 31 May 2007 at: http://www.charlestonco.com/features.cfm?id=52&type+fr)
[19]] Nelia C. Wurangian, "Dressing the Part..." *OLA Quarterly* 9:1 (Spring 2003) http://www.olaweb.org/quarterly/quar9-1/wurangian.shtml

doing things and focus on providing the best aggregate user experience versus the most perfect single record.[20]

In these and many other texts "the perfect record" is simply a rhetorical strategy for dismissing all issues concerning quality by reducing the very complex and context dependent notion of quality to what is implied in the phrase "the perfect record." It is a phrase used almost entirely by those who categorically reject it in the context of demands for or questions concerning quality.

One good example of this reduction can be found in Deeken's report on the January 2005 discussion group meeting of the ALCTS Heads of Technical Services at Medium Sized Libraries.[21] One of the eight topics discussed at this meeting was "The myth of the perfect cataloging record". The report of the discussion of this topic begins with the statement (in quotation marks) "There is no such thing as a perfect cataloging record and people should get over trying to create one." Fair enough. But what followed that assertion? Another quote from the meeting: "Nobody's willing to pay for highest level cataloging in a Google environment. Maintaining systems and technology that are now out-dated—it's like spending money on building the ideal buggy." The "perfect record" is equated with the ideal buggy; neither goal nor ideal, but a useless out of date relic from the past. The report continues:

> A major shift in emphasis from catalog perfection to patron need is taking place. Suggestions for ways to ap-

---

[20] From: K.G. Schneider. Subject: Re: "Third Order"--was Libraries & the Web. Newsgroups: gmane.culture.libraries.ngc4lib Date: 2007-05-19 12:32:46 GMT http://article.gmane.org/gmane.culture.libraries.ngc4lib/2121 (accessed 31 May 2007)

[21] JoAnne Deeken, "Quicker, Cheaper, Better: Pick Two. A Report on the ALCTS Heads of Technical Services at Medium Sized Libraries discussion group meeting. American Library Association Midwinter Meetings, Boston, January 2005" *Technical Services Quarterly*, 23:3 (2006): 81-89.

proach cataloging include not spending lots of time on precise call numbers; examining the priority of assigning subject headings; investing less time during cataloging process and anticipate an acceptable error rate; weighing precision versus recall; cataloging based on access as opposed to cataloging expertise; and adding a culture of a value-added focus.[22]

The quality of information is deemed to have no direct relation to patron need—a curious disjunction which leads one to ask what patron needs are being discussed. Smith argued that

If excellence has any relation to customer satisfaction (and it should), then in terms of cataloging the seeming contradictions between quantity and quality, and between production and development vanish under the higher rubric of the constant purpose of service (i.e., customer satisfaction demands both a qualitative and quantitative focus).[23]

but he was not arguing for "the perfect record."

Perhaps because "the perfect record" is almost always used to indicate an impossibility or absurdity, among the many publications on bibliographical record, catalog and database quality there appear to be only two articles which directly address "the perfect record" in their title. The first, quoted and briefly discussed above, was Intner (1990). In her article she offered three reasons why "the perfect catalog" is a waste of our time and money:

1) the continuing information explosion;
2) computerization of bibliographic services;
3) the real cost of perfect catalogers[24]

---

[22] Ibid., p.83.
[23] Stephen J. Smith, "Cataloging With Copy: Methods for Increasing Productivity" *Technical Services Quarterly* v.11:4 (1994), p.4-5.
[24] Intner (1990), op. cit.: 13.

Because of the first development, collection development is hopeless, she claims, and cataloguing even more so. Of the second development, she states

> I believe the fullness and accuracy in records produced by machines will far outstrip those in records produced by humans in most library cataloging departments ... If cataloging were removed from the hands of well-meaning but unschooled library staff and put into the realm of automatic computerized production, it would improve immediately. Between trusting a host of different humans with different educations, backgrounds, biases, and capabilities or a host of different computers all running the same expertly-programmed system to do the best job of cataloging, I'll bet on the computer every time.[25]

Her economic argument rests on the assumption that intelligent people will not work in the library for less than professors and managers, the proof against which I offer my own 30 years in libraries and the even longer careers of many of my colleagues. On all three counts, then, Intner is ill-informed, perhaps most of all in her estimation of what computers do. Since we cannot have perfect catalogers (too expensive), we cannot hope to get perfect records, and thus no perfect catalog, therefore she claims that she is and we all should be happy with faulty records.

The only other article specifically focusing on "the perfect record" that I was able to locate was an undated paper by Moya Mason available on her website.[26] The title suggests that Mason is indeed looking for "the perfect record", but the text informs us otherwise. She makes some rather curious claims,

---

[25] Ibid.: 14. Her high hopes for expert systems in cataloging have presumably vanished in the wake of the actual results as discussed by Šauperl and others. That "host of different humans" whom she so disdains produces remarkably useful metadata when brought into the cataloging process in the practice of what we now know as "social tagging."

[26] Op. cit.

asserting that "Original cataloguing is seen as the ultimate in the library world, and by many, to be practically free of mistakes because librarians with their MLS degrees do the lion's share of the work." She rightly suggests that this is unrealistic and that human inequalities, the type of training and character traits such as diligence, dependability, precision and commitment are the real causes of discrepancies in the quality of records found in our databases. She states that "there has been a definite move away from the ideology of the perfect database, to an emphasis on meeting the needs of users," but when she describes "what catalogers are looking for" she does not write of "the perfect record" but "the most appropriate record." Yet she continues one sentence later with the remark "What every library wants are perfect records, but they often settle for a compromise of sorts." She sheds no light on what are the virtues, vices and differences between appropriate and perfect records, but her reference to the move away from the ideology of the perfect record to meeting the needs of users does direct us to the real source of the perfect record rhetoric.

When "the perfect record" appears in the library literature, it is most often (in fact, almost always) associated with discussions of "quality" cataloging as a retrograde insistence on the retention of arcane and expensive practices that had demonstrated insufficient benefit (e.g. Thomas[27] and Deeken's report discussed above). Harris and Marshall (1998) quoted one library director's remarks on "the perfect record" as "I think we worry far too much about that sort of thing" following that with another quote "To build a collection for the researcher of the future? We simply cannot do that." They described library directors' attitudes towards catalogers thus:

> Denigrating those who have applied 'excessively high' standards in cataloging ... The work of cataloging is not skilled work, their comments suggest, rather an activity

---

[27] Sarah E. Thomas, "Quality in Bibliographic Control," *Library Trends* 44:3 (Winter 1996): 491-505.

over-rated and over-controlled by the people who performed it. In this fashion, professional catalogers are held up to be somehow silly, small-minded or, at the very least, off base.[28]

The administrators surveyed by Hafter (1986) were not the same ones surveyed by Harris and Marshall, but the attitudes were the same. While I have not seen the questionnaire used by Harris and Marshall, neither of Hafter's questionnaires—the one for catalogers and the one for administrators—mention "the perfect record" but the discussion of the findings of her survey is full of such references. (Did this come from the interviewees or from Hafter? I do not know, but Hafter did inaccurately indicate that the quest for the perfect record was part of Boissonnas' article published in 1979.)

What are these unbeneficial overrated arcane and expensive practices pursued by silly, small-minded, retrograde, obsessive and isolated librarians called catalogers? Boissonnas (1979) spelled out exactly what these were at Cornell in 1979, and the two assumptions underlying them:

> Each record used must be in the ISBD format, it must be cataloged according to the AACR code and Library of Congress practice, and it must be as complete as possible. In this framework, there is no such thing as an optional field. All fields are either mandatory or required if available. ... The cataloger does not go to undue lengths to find this information but provides it if it is available anywhere on the item being catalogued ...
>
> The assumptions underlying this procedure are two. First, CLL believes that the more complete a record is at the input stage, the greater its chances of being retrieved under any number of search algorithms that will be available in the future. Second, CLL believes that it

---

[28] Roma M. Harris and Victoria Marshall, "Reorganizing Canadian Libraries: a Giant Step Back from the Front?" *Library Trends* 46:3 (Winter 1998).

has an obligation as a member of the OCLC network to input the most complete and accurate records possible.[29]

Boissonnas' language is not that of "the perfect record" nor of any such ideology. It is rooted in a sound understanding of what socio-technical information systems require, and the expectation that future systems will offer more search strategies and therefore users will demand more. His assumptions are not only pragmatic and technologically sound, but ethical as well, as he recognized that in networked and shared databases no one catalogs for themselves and their institution alone, and that the product of our labours will be used by future generations of users and technical systems.

Responsibility beyond ideology

Like Boissonnas, De Gennaro never mentioned the perfect record. He understood that future users and systems will demand more, not less: more standards, more accuracy, more expense, more information, more capabilities and more benefits. All of Intner's (1990) arguments against the perfect cataloger, the perfect record, and the perfect catalog were refuted by De Gennaro in 1981 without him mentioning "the perfect record." Why? Perhaps because he was focusing on the realities facing a research library desirous of providing excellent rather than faulty bibliographic service. "Computer-based systems" he noted, "impose much higher standards of accuracy on cataloging and catalog maintenance." The demanding scholars we serve will make us "pay dearly to input, maintain, and search the detailed records required" because "We are no longer merely automating ... we are multiplying our capabilities and raising the level of expectations of library staff and users alike." Information, he declared, is "an increasingly valuable and expensive resource. ... Cheap

---

[29] Boissonnas, op. cit.: 81.

information and cheap research libraries are going the way of cheap energy."[30]

There were only five mentions of "the perfect record" which I found to be responsible, informed and beyond ideology. Those five documents, like Boissonnas' paper, deserve attention not only for their remarks on "the perfect record" but for discussing the very real problems of database quality in an era of shared data without transforming that into a simple problem of quantity. The first of those which I want to discuss—Campbell's report on retroconversion of a map collection[31]—openly discusses quality as a problem rather than an (impossible) ideal, an approach I found refreshingly honest. The second—Mowat on the future of Edinburgh University Library[32]—sets the not-doing of perfect records in the wider context of not doing a lot of other things; again, a wonderful contrast to those who describe imperfect (faulty, below minimal level) cataloging as the answer to all our library woes. The third paper is a perfectly (if I may) frank discussion of the relationship between a library's goals and their achievement, issued by the National Library of Australia.[33] The fourth contribution is also one of the most recent: a 2006 address by Martha Yee at the seminar

---

[30] Richard De Gennaro, "Libraries & Networks in Transition: Problems and Prospects for the 1980's" *Library Journal* 106 (May 15, 1981): 1045-1049.

[31] Tony Campbell, "Retroconversion of the British Library's Map Catalogue - The Art of the Possible." *Liber Quarterly* 3:1 (1992): 1-6, http://liber-maps.kb.nl/articles/campbell.htm

[32] Ian R.M. Mowat, "Edinburgh University Library: A Vision For the Immediate Future. Paper presented to Library Committee, 21st October 1998." Available at: http://www.lib.ed.ac.uk/about/vision.shtml

[33] National Library of Australia. Libraries Australia. Cataloguing Workflows Options for Australian Libraries. Available at: http://www.nla.gov.au/librariesaustralia/workflowoptions.html

"Beyond the OPAC".[34] And finally, Robertson's short essay on what metadata quality means for the LIS community.[35]

Campbell: retrospective conversion of a special collection
Campbell's article on retrospective conversion of the British Library's map catalogs discusses a number of problems associated with catalogs as historical objects, leading this reader to think about the online catalog and databases as historical artefacts as well.

> Treating mapping as a continuum from the earliest times to the present is logical. But it immediately brings you face to face with 'quality', because the catalogue descriptions also represent a long date-span. Inevitably, this means records of different style, completeness and accuracy. ... How could we sacrifice the quality of the current records by mixing them up with the old?[36]

He goes on to identify four kinds of deficiencies in the catalogs to be converted to electronic form: "omitted information, inaccuracy, data expressed in the wrong way, and structural problems." The first of these if unaddressed will simply mean that "the converted catalogue will be no worse than its printed predecessor." The second will be partially corrected when the geographical and authority headings are edited as a whole in the converted form. Finally, data expressed in the wrong way and structural problems (e.g. variant typography) should be dealt with in the specifications for those keyboarding the catalogs.

Campbell then insists on making a distinction between a bibliography and a library catalogue—a distinction stressed by

---

[34] Martha Yee, "Beyond the OPAC: Future Directions For Web-Based Catalogues." http://www.nla.gov.au/lis/stndrds/grps/acoc/documents/Yee_Keynote.doc
[35] R. John Robertson, "Metadata Quality: Implications for Library and Information Science Professionals" *Library Review*, 54:5 (2005): 295-300.
[36] Campbell, op. cit.

Osborne in 1936[37]—and how these serve library users in different ways.

> We expect from a cartobibliography to be able to distinguish similar maps, and we look for a full and clear statement of the bibliographical relationship of one variant to another. A library catalogue, on the other hand, should be judged firstly by how well it provides access to the geographical content of the listed material. ... We see it as our task to lead the user, quickly and helpfully, to anything that might be of relevance. Thereafter, it is up to them to examine the items for themselves.[38]

What the conversion process is focusing on is "headings and indexed elements rather than unsearchable factors." In accepting certain compromises rather than striving for an "impossible perfection" Campbell insisted that the library was not acting irresponsibly.

> It seems unarguable to me that it is more important to have some kind of record for every map than a perfect record for some of them. This does not rule out further improvement. Retroconversion should not be seen as a 'once and for all' operation... The most serious defect of some of our own earlier records is the lack of a date. Since date will probably be used to refine most searches, this means that the records concerned would simply not appear. This is perhaps the most urgent of the future editing tasks.[39]

---

[37] Andrew Osborn, "Cataloging Costs and a Changing Conception of Cataloging," *Catalogers' and Classifiers' Yearbook* 5 (1936): 48.
[38] Campbell, op. cit.: 3-4.
[39] Ibid.: 5.

Assuming at the start that the project will be ongoing and involve future editing tasks that may not even be imagined today is an attitude that bodes well for the project.

Campbell mentions yet another factor that deserves special mention. The British Library had never cataloged the contents of its pre-1800 maps bound into atlases. These are the greater part of most historical map collections, he noted, and therefore of great interest to cartographers. These would not have been part of the retrospective conversion project at all except for a blessed event:

> Rodney Shirley, the well known cartobibliographer, volunteered to describe the contents of our pre-1800 atlases. These will be published in the form of collations, and the entries will also be added to a later edition of the CD-ROM. The records have not been created by a librarian and they do not fully conform to the complex AACR-2 cataloguing rules. What matters is that we shall be able, for the first time in our history, to provide a full answer to questions such as: 'how many pre-1800 maps of Catalonia are there in the British Library?'[40]

To my thinking, having a scholar describe material in his or her field for the use of others in that field is likely to produce a more valuable catalog than any produced by anyone else not involved in that scholarship, AACR or no. I can think of no more perfect solution to the British Library's pre-1800 atlas problem than the solution it found.

Mowat: the future of Edinburgh University Library
Mowat's article includes a number of disturbing remarks about librarians, the culture of libraries, and the future of library employees of all sorts. Having noted that, I want to pass over that and look at some of his more surprising and provocative state-

---

[40] Ibid.

ments. After discussing financial matters and at the end of the section on the library's response to them, Mowat states

> It is accepted that the library may have attempted too much in promising to deliver services in the past. A willingness to agree to do something on paper and then not deliver has not been uncommon and the consequential discrepancy between intention and performance may be increasing as resources diminish. ... Promising less and fulfilling more should be one of the Library's top priorities.[41]

It should be understood that offering users a catalog or database which promises to be able to search by series, genre, publisher, date, language, subject and so on which is nevertheless populated with bibliographical records which lack this information (imperfect, faulty, minimal level records) is a perfect case of Mowat's discrepancy between promise and performance.

The next section is *Priorities*, and this begins with the blunt statement "Priorities must include stopping doing things." As part of this approach to priorities Mowat notes "the continued pursuit of the most cost-effective way of data creation. Quality in cataloguing does not mean producing the theoretically perfect record but in getting a useable record out in a time suitable for the greatest demand—usually closest to the time of acquisition." This is a familiar enough refrain in the American library literature, but Mowat does not stop there. External users will be charged to use the library (a change to be introduced in 1999, according to the paper). Furthermore, he argues, "the cost of holding largely unused collections is no longer acceptable and it is necessary to examine critically what is collected, why it is collected and how it is collected," an approach quite the contrary of Intner's claim that collection development is impossible.[42]

---

[41] Mowat, op. cit.

[42] Intner, op cit.: 14: "there is no hope of success in collection development."

From the American perspective, that seems to be a dismal, terrible future. And I agree. But Mowat sees the problems and faces them by telling the story straight: no money, no honey. American librarians prefer to bury the truth behind false statements such as "more, cheaper, faster, better." On this side of the Atlantic, we do exactly what Mowat refuses to do: promise more and deliver less.

National Library of Australia: Cataloging workflows[43]
This document addresses two concerns related to the distinction made in Campbell (1992): the difference between bibliography and library catalogs. Many Australian libraries do not only catalog for their library or a consortium, but for the Australian National Bibliographical Database (ANBD). Section 5 of the paper (Best Practice Workflows) addresses issues of library objectives, policies, priorities, conflicts among goals, types of libraries, size of staff, quality standards, contributing to the ANBD, cost and much more. It is a brief but excellent description of what needs to be taken into account in library workflows. Some of the statements most relevant to this paper are the following:

> There is no single definition of best practice that would apply absolutely to every library. For example, a library that does not need to deliver material to users promptly but is subject to an imperative to catalogue to the highest standard (e.g. where data is destined for a National Bibliography), will have one definition of best practice. Another library with users waiting for ordered material to be available as soon as possible will have another definition of best practice. Each must define what its cataloguing operation should achieve and then set about developing best practice within that definition.

---

[43] National Library of Australia., op. cit.

Therefore, best practice for most libraries can be defined as achieving the quickest flow through of material at the lowest cost without sacrificing a specified level of quality.

Models of best practice will vary in different library environments. However, the one essential starting point is that the requirements for cataloguing have to be clear and well documented.

Clarity as to what any operation should achieve is a critical factor underpinning best practice. The balance between efficiency and quality needs to be addressed and priorities clarified. Cataloguing and technical services staff must have a clear understanding of what they are expected to achieve and be committed to that outcome. Formal statements are important but the crucial factor is open and consistent communication. Without a clear, library held understanding of what is required of cataloguing; it is not possible to aspire to any notion of best practice.

If a library has not thought through exactly what it requires of its cataloguing operation, the result may be that cataloguing staff are faced with conflicting requirements. They may have to work towards specified throughput targets while also working to time-consuming quality requirements and may end up meeting neither requirement or sacrificing one for the other.

Cataloguing and technical services staff and managers need to have a clear and shared understanding of expectations. Time consuming requirements such as correcting every error in a copy record, extensive checking, local customisation, locally maintained manuals, extensive record keeping etc should only be undertaken if they are required to support the goals of the cataloguing operation as defined by the library.

Cataloguing best practice includes reference to quality where this is of relevance to the library's objectives. However, the pursuit of the "perfect" record can create complexities in workflow and absorb considerable resources in the process. It also begs the question of a definition of the "perfect" record.

Timeliness of contributions and maintenance of data, particularly holdings information, are important considerations for all libraries that use the ANBD. Timely data contribution, data quality and ANBD coverage directly influence the effectiveness of the ANBD as a source of copy cataloguing and enhance the efficiency of resource sharing activities between libraries.

The conclusion is spectacular, as it leaves all of these matters to be determined by what the individual institution wants to achieve:

> All Australian libraries are encouraged to determine what their cataloguing operation should achieve and then set about ensuring that desired outcome.

Yee and the user[44]

Martha Yee's remarks at the Australian Committee on Cataloging's seminar "Beyond the OPAC : future directions for Web-based catalogues" included a section entitled Current misconceptions. The first of these involves the perfect record.

> Misconception 1: All users need to find a single perfect bibliographic record that fulfils their information need.

---

[44] Yee, op. cit.

> Correction to misconception 1: Most users are looking for one of the following entities: a) a particular work of which the author and/or the title is known; b) works on a particular subject; c) the works of a particular author. Each of these entitities will be represented in a catalog of any size by many records of many different kinds, including authority records which contain variant terms for the works, subjects and authors users seek, multiple bibliographic records for all of the expression-manifestations of a sought work, or a work on a sought subject, and holdings records. The user will not achieve optimal results unless the catalog software can deal with complex indexing and with the assemblage of all of these types of records into complex, readily scannable and well organized displays.[45]

Like so many other discussions of "the perfect record", Yee's remarks pull us away from the catalog record to considering the user, but unlike every other discussion, rather than dismissing quality issues in the bibliographic record, she argues that patrons are not looking for any bibliographical record at all, rather they are looking for the information contained in them, including relationships among works. In her list of "what needs to change" are indexing, display, MARC21 and some items relating to cataloging practice:

> Cataloguing practice: follow uniform title rules; make it mandatory, not optional, to create an authority-controlled work identifier for any work that exists in more than one manifestation or expression. This is the most neglected area in cataloguing practice, despite the fact that catalogue use studies have shown over and over again that the most common search in research libraries is for a known work of which both author and title are known. It

---

[45] Ibid.

reflects very poorly on our profession that we have neglected the infrastructure necessary to ensure that the most common search done by our users is efficient and effective.[46]

Users of the library do not need bibliographic records at all, perfect or not. What they want is to find what they are looking for. It is necessary to add that both libraries and existing library catalogs do need bibliographic records because of the work that they do. With that (rather large) caveat, Yee's argument ought to lead to a radical revision of our OPACs, which is the point of her paper, not some "perfect record."

Robertson: Metadata quality.[47]
The author refers to a 2002 paper by Greenberg and Robertson in which quality metadata is understood to be accurate, consistent and sufficient, continuing with the remark that "the primary and overriding definition for quality in any setting: fitness for purpose—as true for metadata as it is for designing a car or boiling an egg." (p. 296). The future success of digital repositories, he states, is intimately related to "an awareness of how to address the aforementioned aspects of quality ... [and an] understanding of the implications of making compromises in metadata quality within large systems" (ibid.). Discussing rules of metadata creation (AACR, etc.) Robertson notes that

> within any given library the implementation of these rules and the completeness of a record will be interpreted through local priorities and resource constraints, there is an acknowledgement that a, nearly, perfect record is possible. There are also mechanisms which allow libraries to buy or exchange this agreed "perfect" minimal record from external sources to reduce the volume and cost of

---
[46] Ibid.
[47] Robertson, op. cit.

in-house cataloguing. Mechanisms such as this can exist because the library community has shared purpose and conception of metadata quality, which allows an agreed "level" for exchange.[48]

In this context it is "local priorities and resource constraints" that determine what a "perfect record" will be, but it would probably have been much more accurate to describe those as determining what an "acceptable record" would be. After all, "a, nearly, perfect record" and an "agreed 'perfect' minimal record" effectively vacate all meaning from the adjective *perfect*.

This is followed by a section entitled "Implications of defining metadata quality outside the library." I balk at his statement "within the library community the purpose [of metadata quality?] is understood and the context is clearly limited" as it seems to me that the purpose of metadata is anything but understood and the contexts envisioned among librarians anything but limited! We have the death of the OPAC and library catalogs that search every imaginable resource through a Google style box in which both metadata and limitations are ignored by all but a few. While it is true that "different settings and purposes require different types of metadata quality" and that "there are already other domains of knowledge management which have very different standards and purposes," it seems strange to follow this recognition with the statement "The metadata record for the same book will look very different in each setting and no one option is objectively better."

"Objectively" makes no sense at all if one is referring to different types of institutions, with different user needs and different purposes. The metadata record for an individual item created in one type of institution will not be acceptable in another because it was created to serve different purposes. We should therefore turn the discussion of "the perfect record" completely on its head and state that there are as many "perfect

---

[48] Ibid.: 297.

records" as there are user needs, search strategies and administrators: whenever the user is happy, whenever the search succeeds, whenever the administrator is happy, the record is "perfectly" adequate. The problem is that in a shared database, no record serves just one user, just one search strategy, or just one purpose.

The final two paragraphs of this section of Robertson's paper reach out into the unknown, again much like three of the papers previously discussed. In the first of these he discusses the requirements for metadata records using IEEE LOM standard.

> [A] record using the IEEE LOM standard (IEEE, 2002) is as complex as a MARC record but has a smaller bibliographic description and supports extensive educational description of the nature and use of the resource. By implication, such a record requires different skills to create its different parts. The use and life expectancy of such learning resources is however, a very unknown quantity and it remains to be seen how justifiable an investment in extensive and precise cataloguing is.[49]

That last sentence mirrors the debate over cataloging the "long tail", the books which catalogers are accused of cataloging only for themselves. Mowat suggested that this is a matter first of all of collection development: if it is not worth the time and money to catalog it, should we acquire it in the first place? Should we be locating and cataloging *any* Internet resources of unknown life expectancy?

In his summary Robertson offers a list of observations coupled with their implications. Let me repeat three of those:

> 1) The metadata required to support such multiple purposes, will require the use of new or multiple standards, and may demand compromising on library metadata guidelines.

---

[49] Ibid.

2) The granularity required for a given purpose and the scale of the digital repository may influence what metadata can be provided and how it is created.

3) The nature of the resource being described should influence how much metadata is created.

There is room for many approaches in these implications, but not for "the perfect record."

The Imperfect Record: is this what the users want?

> Which helps our patrons more, one perfect catalog record or ten slightly imperfect records that could be created in the same amount of time?[50]

If the perfect record is an object of scorn and derision, an ideal which should be and must be refused and abandoned, will we make our users happy by providing "the imperfect record"? Is this not exactly what has been advocated by proponents of the below minimal level records, Intner with her "faulty records" and Anderson in the quotation above? Not exactly, for to refer to the creation of below minimal level records as "the quest for the imperfect record" would be to engage in the same kind of dishonest rhetorical strategies that the despisers of "the perfect record" do when they write of that. The truth is that below minimal level records work for certain purposes and certain kinds of search strategies. Below minimal level records (and all manner of erroneous, imperfect, incomplete and faulty records) will work perfectly for many library needs (e.g. shelving, circulation), but only a record correctly coded for date, language and country of publication will serve the users who search by any of those elements. While a "perfect record" is meaningless in a bibliographic universe of different needs, goals and purposes, an

---

[50] Rick Anderson, "The Library is Dead, Long Live the Library: Why Everything is Different Now and What We Can Do About It." http://www2.library.unr.edu/anderson/molospeech.htm

imperfect record by whatever standards would seem to be by definition a problem.

One of the constant themes in the articles discussed in the previous section was that what was adequate at one time in one place for the purposes of a particular institution may not and probably will not be adequate for that same institution at a different time, much less other institutions in different places at different times. I regularly use records from the Czech and Polish national libraries because these are "perfect" in my opinion, yet I have to change almost all of the fields because the language of description, subjects and classification are all created according to systems and standards which differ from those in use where I work. It is not simply a matter of the presence or absence of information or of errors, but of fitness for a purpose.

The institution and adaptation of standards for description, subject headings and classification systems, exactly like the creation and elaboration of encoding systems like MARC, Dublin Core and ONYX have been undertaken so that libraries (and other institutions) can share data. Intelligibility, interpretation and interoperability are all facilitated by the various languages (LCSH, AACR, MARC, English, Polish, etc.) which catalogers use in communicating to the world what it is that their particular institution has made available for use. Without those standards and structures, intelligibility and interpretation by human beings would be severely reduced, and interoperability among various brands and generations of technical systems would be impossible.

Conclusion

The cataloger's commitment to useful (accurate, consistent and sufficient to a purpose) bibliographic information is the basis of communication with the users in libraries. Burger insisted that "in spite of the differences among the attitudes catalogers hold toward cataloging, all of them will eventually claim that they are involved in an act of communication."[51] Information technologies require doing this according to shared standards and metadata structures. The increasing emphasis on the system and format of the data led Burger to suggest that "We are spending a great deal of time and resources on the system of data definition and spending less time and resources than is necessary on the substance of the data."[52] We quarrel endlessly over RDA, markup languages, and encoding level standards, but any look at what these technical structures are supposed to support, their only reason for existing, is met with scornful references to "the perfect record."

Disparaging the very part of the bibliographic record which matters most by rhetorically reducing it to the impossible fiction of "the perfect record" is not a step in the direction of understanding what is being done, nor of what can be done, much less of what ought to be done in the service of library users. "The perfect record" is most often employed in an effort to disregard or dispense with one or even all demands for or questions about the adequacy, fitness to purpose, truth and usefulness of all bibliographic information and the standards established to aid librarians in their efforts to interpret the library's materials for machine manipulation as well as communication with the library's users.

Future discussion of database quality needs to refuse the rhetoric of "the perfect record" as it is just as true to suggest that "perhaps there is no perfect record" (Hamaker, 2001) as it is to suggest that "whatever pleases the user" or "whatever pleases the administration" is the perfect record. What we need to discuss instead is the following:
1) What data elements are useful for the kind of library research performed here in this particular institution?

---

[51] Robert H. Burger, "Data Definition & the Decline of Cataloging Quality," *Library Journal* 108 (October 15, 1983): 1924.
[52] Ibid.: 1926.

2) How much, and which elements of that necessary information can this institution afford to support? (This means either creating it initially, correcting or adding it to bibliographic records imported from external sources, and future maintenance in cases of changing standards, new headings, data definitions, etc.)

An honest response to the first question will provide the basis for discussing the second. An honest answer to the second question will put everyone—library administrators, bibliographers, catalogers, reference personnel, library boards, college presidents, bursars, faculty, students and all users—in the same position: knowing what they are paying for and what they can expect. That may not be a perfect outcome, but it would be an honest one, and therefore one on which we could agree.

References

Anderson, Rick. "The Library is Dead, Long Live the Library: Why Everything is Different Now and What We Can Do About It." http://www2.library.unr.edu/anderson/molospeech.htm (accessed May 30, 2007)

Bade, David. (2002). *The Creation and Persistence of Misinformation in Shared Library Catalogs: Language and Subject Knowledge in a Technological Era.* Urbana: Graduate School of Library and Information Science, University of Illinois at Urbana-Champaign. (*Occasional Papers*, no. 211)

Bade, David. (2007). "Structures, Standards and the People Who Make Them Meaningful." Paper presented at the 2nd meeting of the Library of Congress Working Group on the Future of Bibliographic Control, Chicago, May 9, 2007. http://www.loc.gov/bibliographic-future/meetings/docs/bade-may9-2007.pdf (accessed June 18, 2007)

Boissonnas, Christian. (1979). "The Quality of OCLC Bibliographic Records: The Cornell Law Library Experience," *Law Library Journal* 72 nr.1: 80-85.

Burger, Robert H. (1983). "Data Definition & the Decline of Cataloging Quality." *Library Journal* 108 (October 15): 1924-1926.

Campbell, Tony. (1992). "Retroconversion of the British Library's Map Catalogue - The Art of the Possible." *Liber Quarterly* 3:1 (1992): 1-6, http://liber-maps.kb.nl/articles/campbell.htm

"Costs of upgrading cataloging." *Library Journal* 103: 11 (June 1, 1978): 1124.

Deeken, JoAnne Deeken. (2006). "Quicker, Cheaper, Better: Pick Two. A Report on the ALCTS Heads of Technical Services at Medium Sized Libraries discussion group meeting. American Library Association Midwinter Meetings, Boston, January 2005." *Technical Services Quarterly*, 23 nr.3: 81-89.

De Gennaro, Richard. (1981). "Libraries & Networks in Transition: Problems and Prospects for the 1980's." *Library Journal* 106 (May 15): 1045-1049.

Hafter, Ruth. (1986). *Academic Librarians and Cataloging Networks :Visibility, Quality Control, and Professional Status.* New York: Greenwood Press.

Hamaker, Chuck. (2001). "Creating Record Sets For E-content in OPACs." *Charleston Advisor* 2:3 (January), http://www.charlestonco.com/features.cfm?id=52&type+fr (accessed May 31, 2007)

Harris, Roma M. and Victoria Marshall. (1998). "Reorganizing Canadian Libraries: a Giant Step Back from the Front?" *Library Trends* 46:3 (Winter): 564-580.

Intner, Sheila S. (1990). "Copy Cataloging and the Perfect Record Mentality," *Technicalities*, 10: 7 (July): 12-15.
Mason, Moya K. "Copy Cataloguing: Where is it Taking Us On Our Quest for the Perfect Copy?"

http://www.moyak.com/researcher/resume/papers/clog4mkm.html (accessed May 30, 2007)

Mowat, Ian R.M. (1998). "Edinburgh University Library: A Vision For the Immediate Future. Paper presented to Library Committee, 21st October 1998." http://www.lib.ed.ac.uk/about/vision.shtml (accessed May 31, 2007)

National Library of Australia. Libraries Australia. "Cataloguing Workflows Options for Australian Libraries." http://www.nla.gov.au/librariesaustralia/workflowoptions.html (accessed May 31, 2007)

O'Neill, Ed. (1996). "Matching and Validating Personal Names Authority Records." *Cataloging & Classification Quarterly* 22 nr.1: 99-100.

Osborn, Andrew. (1936). "Cataloging Costs and a Changing Conception of Cataloging." *Catalogers' and Classifiers' Yearbook* 5: 45-54.

Robertson, R. John. (2005). "Metadata Quality: Implications for Library and Information Science Professionals." *Library Review* 54 nr5: 295-300.

Smith, Stephen J. (1994). "Cataloging With Copy: Methods for Increasing Productivity." *Technical Services Quarterly* v.11 nr.4: 1-11.

Steinhagen, Elizabeth N. and Sharon A. Moynahan. (1998). "Catalogers Must Change! Surviving Between the Rock and the Hard Place." *Cataloging & Classification Quarterly,* v.26 nr.3: 3-20.

Thomas, Sarah E. (1996). "Quality in Bibliographic Control." *Library Trends* 44 nr3(Winter): 491-505.

Tillett, Barbara B. (1993). "Catalog It Once for All: A History of Cooperative Cataloging in the United States Prior to 1967 (Before MARC)," *Cataloging & Classification Quarterly* 17 nr.3/4:3-38.

Wurangian, Nelia C. (2003). "Dressing the Part..." *OLA*

Quarterly 9:1 (Spring 2003) http://www.olaweb.org/quarterly/quar9-1/wurangian.shtml (accessed May 31, 2007)

Yee, Martha. "Beyond the OPAC : Future Directions For Web-Based Catalogues." http://www.nla.gov.au/lis/stndrds/grps/acoc/documents/Yee_Keynote.doc (accessed May 31, 2007)

VI

The Social Life of Metadata: Arguments from Utility for Shared Database Management (A Response to Banush and LeBlanc)

Abstract

In Banush and LeBlanc (2007) the utilitarianism of Bentham was resurrected and offered as a "philosophical backdrop for dealing with competing library choices." This paper discusses two serious failures in that paper: the failure to situate utility in the current context (shared bibliographic databases, cooperative cataloging programs, automated data manipulation and exchange) and the simplistic assumptions about library users and their diverse needs which allow the authors to reduce all metadata related issues to a simple managerial task of triage.

Part One: Utility, library priorities, and cataloging policies.

1. *Introduction*

The publication of a philosophical examination of library services, priorities and policies arouses expectations of a philosophical discussion: rigorous and systematic, clarifying ambiguities and sorting out confusions, revealing unexpected problems and providing insights into practices and the theories which have been offered to explain and/or justify them. Unfortunately, none of this may be found in Banush and LeBlanc's "Utility, library priorities, and cataloging policies." Instead, the reader is greeted (in the first sentence) with an aphorism attributed to Yogi Berra, and informed that "The question debated ... is how, or even if, academic and research institutions should respond to the rise of technologies" (p. 96). The authors then inform us that "the deliberate approach to change and the existing institutional cultures of academic and research libraries have sound arguments in their defense", but "do not prepare such institutions to change direction swiftly or move into new areas with the rapidity of private sector parties" (p. 97). "Current thinking among many academic library leaders" the authors announce, "dictates that change must occur." They quote the former Bodleian librarian Reg Carr, remarking "User desires, he suggests, should drive library services. Libraries must meet user demands even if the users want contradictory things" (p. 97).

It might be argued that these first three paragraphs should be dismissed as just that: introductory paragraphs and therefore not the place for critical examination. Yet the reader who does not pause in astonishment over these statements would be a poor reader indeed. We are told that the debate is about how or even if we should respond to technological innovation and change, a formulation that immediately casts us all as followers (or worse) rather than critical users critiquing, judging, selecting and cooperating with designers in the development of technologies. This is followed by the criticism that the pace of change in academic life is slower than in "private sector parties" as though institutions of learning and teaching should be evaluated on the same criteria as Toys R Us or criminal organizations, these latter usually being the first to exploit technological developments. "Current thinking"—surely the hallmark and synonym of profound thinking—has it that "change must occur", as though anyone ever thought change could not or would not or ought not occur. *Se vogliamo che tutto rimanga come è, bisogna che tutto cambi.* (If you want everything to stay the same, everything must change.—Lampedusa from *Il gattopardo*) The issue is never simply "change," but what kind of change, when, where, by whom and how. And finally we are told that user desires and demands, contradictory though they may be, should determine library policies, but those users remain so abstract as to provide us no guidance whatsoever, and those users become no more concrete in the remainder of the paper. In fact, this is the root of the authors' failure not only in the introduction but throughout the paper: by stating all of the issues, problems and contradictions as simple abstractions, the authors can pick any sort of change, user, need or utility that they want, understand these in any manner that suits them, and fit everything nicely into these categories of "change, "users" and "utility." Who after all, could object to change, users and utility? The objections and conflicts, and therefore the difficulties arise only when we inquire into the specifics of the changes advocated, the particular users invoked, and the nature and scope of the utilities claimed.

This becomes abundantly clear in the paragraphs which follow. Technical services departments have been targets of both staff and budget reductions, the authors rightly remark, and many library leaders argue that because cataloging is expensive, libraries should rely on Google and use their precious resources elsewhere. The authors then discuss the consequences of this decreasing support of cataloging activities, noting that catalogers who continue advocating support of the traditional goals of cataloging in order to avoid certain negative consequences sometimes do so "even in defiance of the broader policy goals of the library." A little slight of hand there, since those "broader policy goals" being resisted are precisely those which have been formulated in disregard of the negative consequences. Yet Banush and LeBlanc assert that slower turnaround time and growing backlogs are not the results of these policy decisions but are instead the results of cataloger defiance. The authors assure us in the words of Fischer et al. that backlogs and slow processing "exist because cataloging departments still seek to provide a level of service that is not supported by the institution." That statement reveals much about its authors and those who quote it in approval: the level of service no longer supported was formerly supported precisely in order to meet recognized user needs. A more honest formulation by Fischer et al. would have been: backlogs and slow processing exist because cataloging departments still seek to provide a level of service *to users* that is no longer supported by the upper administration. Yet instead of seeing this issue clearly, Banush and LeBlanc assert that as a consequence of these problems, administrators and catalogers are pitted against each other, "each claiming to have only the best interests of users in mind" but lacking "a common vocabulary or mutually understood context ... Acrimony and resentment only grow, and no one wins" (p. 98).

The confusion in this description and analysis of the problems is astounding. It is precisely these kinds of conditions that a careful and rigorous analysis ought to clarify. No philosophy will solve these problems, not even utilitarianism, but at least we should arrive at a clearer understanding than that provided by Banush and LeBlanc. A problem which clearly has its origins in the broad policy goals of the library, is, in the space of a single paragraph, reduced to a simple labor-management dispute in which neither side understands the other and neither side "wins." With the situation, the relationships among agents, the issues and the problems so poorly and confusedly set out in the introduction, there is little chance that the "theoretical or philosophical framework for choices" (p. 98) which the authors seek to provide in this paper will be able to clear up the mess. What will decide the issue for Banush and LeBlanc we know already. The authors complain that neither side understands the other, but Banush (2006) has made it clear that management understands all of the problems and knows what the answers are. The problem from his perspective is nothing other than a conservative and obstinate labor force threatened by change, refusing to understand what management understands already and resisting the progressive ideas and direction offered them:

> The more conservative forces, which seem to include many front-line staff, are vigorously (sometimes stridently) defending the status quo, or even the status quo ante; others, primarily managers and administrators, are trying to move away from the old models toward something very different. ... Like many political and business leaders in Europe, most library leaders have identified the problems and know what needs to be done, at least generally. But they also realize that for the most part, the staff do not want change. (Banush, 2006)

2. *Utility and library priorities*

The principle of utility, which Bentham associated with the greatest happiness for all, is the principle Banush and LeBlanc put forward as a guide for library service. While admitting that utilitarianism failed as a framework for thinking about rights, justice and equality, they follow modern attempts to reestablish the principle of utility on "the axiom of greatest need" rather than happiness. In this understanding of utility, "it is the 'need-satisfaction' of the community at large that is at stake" (p. 99), but their understanding of the community at large to which utilitarian considerations should apply is limited to the library's parent institution, a major blunder in a discussion of shared databases, cooperative cataloging and the Internet.

They offer the practice of triage as a clear example of the application of the utilitarian principle, a manner of working that will be discussed in greater detail in the third section. They then assert "that libraries must first separate users' wants from users' needs," that they must distinguish the basic from the not-so-basic needs, and that with these basic principles they can establish priorities, "since they cannot provide everything for every user" (p. 100). Unfortunately for our two philosophers, rather than using those principles to investigate a variety of user needs and wants, their relation to institutional purposes and their implications for cataloging policy, they simply list what they consider are currently basic user needs: "access to electronic resources and instructional material, as well as online help, which permit users to work independently and outside the library; library space that allows for both private and group study and learning; and extensive multimedia holdings in physical formats" (p. 100). Why these should be identified as needs rather than wants is not indicated, much less why they should be identified as basic needs. (In Banush and LeBlanc's own words, the results of the survey revealed only Cornell library's users' "desired level of access," not their needs.) In addition to these basic needs, they note, "many users still identify books" as something specifically appropriate to libraries. The adverb "still" speaks volumes, as does the relegation of books to a side note about our somewhat conservative (backward? defending the status quo ante? resistant to change?) users, many of whom apparently are still thinking in terms of past realities rather than the 21st century academic library.

Again, as in the discussion of cataloging practices in the service of user needs but in defiance of library goals which deny the validity of those needs, it is precisely at the point where a careful description, discussion, evaluation and ordering according to their utility for the various user groups and their varied needs is specifically called for that the authors offer instead commonplaces and abstractions that are neither discussed, evaluated nor ordered, much less examined in relation to the various user groups (freshmen, graduate students, professors, bibliographers). The practices that academic libraries support are not mentioned, not even earlier in this same paragraph where the institution's mission is mentioned. We get access, work, space, group learning, multimedia formats, and even books, but no discussion of the breadth and depth of research strategies required in a large academic institution like Cornell. How does one provide the greatest good for researchers wishing to discover the nature and number of textbooks in indigenous languages printed in the Belgian Congo under colonialism, reports of cholera epidemics in the Ottoman Empire or references to Jewish Catholics in personal narratives of the inmates or other persons with contemporary knowledge of the Warsaw Ghetto—to mention a few of the research projects that I have been asked to assist with? And indeed, when one evaluates a policy by merely looking at statistics (as in the fifth section of the paper), the real users are always ignored.

3. *Utility, triage, and cataloging policies.*
The triage system is exemplified by emergency room triage in hospitals, a place where the authors have apparently never spent any time. To those who have been there in need of care, backlogs of patients, an eternity of waiting for treatment and an exhorbitant bill are their most obvious traits, but this is not mentioned. The authors tacitly acknowledge that the metaphorical transfer of emergency room triage to libraries cannot be pressed too far, for in the library "this triage entails more than just deciding what must be done now versus what can wait until later. It involves a decision concerning how much treatment a given item needs, either now, later, or perhaps never, within the context of providing adequate access to the greatest number of items." (p. 101). Certainly in a hospital emergency room there may be cases in which no treatment is needed now or ever. The difference is that a doctor examines each patient who enters and makes that judgement because the patient is there with him. Contrary to the authors' assertion, in a library there is never "a decision concerning how much treatment a given item needs" because "items" have no needs: only users do. The misunderstanding is carried further a few lines later: "doing the most

good for the greatest number of items does not necessarily mean doing the most good for an individual title. In fact, it may mean just the opposite..." (Careless language is a problem throughout the paper.) The library users have vanished: the "item" has replaced them.

Triage in a hospital works the way it does (with constant backlogs and long delays accompanied by complaining patients) because need and user are united in a single bodily presence here and now. In the library there is always a temporal as well as spatial disjunction; user needs become evident only when the user arrives. That is, the user may arrive with the need before the item is acquired (perhaps initiating the purchase request), while it is in processing, or 5, 10 or even 100 years after the item has been set out to gather dust on the shelf. In the latter case in which user and need arrive after acquisition, strictly utilitarian considerations would insist on discarding the item since there is no known need for the item. The question then is why the item was acquired in the first place, seeing that there are no known users. And again the answer is simple: some librarian made the decision to acquire the item based on a knowledge of the kinds of research material that future users of that particular library might find useful and the cost of the item; that is, a utilitarian decision made which took into consideration future potential utility rather than immediate needs. It is an understanding of the institutional practices and purposes, not existing user needs that leads to the acquisition of the item, and it is just those practices and purposes that must be kept in mind when cataloging each item the library acquires.

Triage must work differently in hospitals than in libraries because of the difference between a service that treats present users with immediate demands and a service that is being constantly built for unknown future users and their unpredictable needs. Again, the authors' failure to identify this difference let alone investigate the implications of this difference is clear not only by the absence of any remarks on the difference, but even more so by the subsequent discussion of the well-known views of Marcum and Calhoun as these contrast with Thomas Mann's published responses to them.

The authors note that Mann (2006) demonstrates the utility of library catalogs for research, but accuse him of sidestepping "the pragmatic issue of the time and cost required to provide 'full level' metadata access to everything that present and future scholars could possibly need or want" (p. 102). This is of course a falsification of Mann's argument by surreptitiously assuming that the library in Mann's argument is the information universe that Google claims to be organizing: all the world's information. If indeed the library were to feel obligated to collect and catalog "everything that present and future scholars could possibly need or want" the task and associated costs would be not merely staggering but unrealizable, unrealizable because what any future user will consider to be relevant information (e.g. grass stains on a football player's shoulder pads, the chicken hawk population on the Bade farm in 1969) as well as how she will go about searching for it is unknown and unpredictable. But this is not the library Mann has in mind. His library is a collection that is built up one item (or one collection) at a time to support a particular institution's purposes; in such a library an item is acquired because it is deemed worth adding to the collection and therefore deserving of a description enabling its discovery. And as Banush and LeBlanc note for their own library (Cornell), how each library decides to make these items available and accessible to present and future users, the level of description and organization given to individual items or collections within the library will depend upon the purposes and practices which the institution serves, not "everything that present and future scholars could possibly need or want."

Mann is also criticized for his "focus on individual cases, rather than supporting a comprehensive look at discovery issues for the scholarly infosphere as a whole" (p. 102). This is of course perfectly in keeping with the authors' preference for the vague and the abstract since such vague and general goals can conveniently hide a multitude of contradictory goals, needs and desires. On this point, the authors would benefit greatly from even a cursory glance at the literature on reliability, accidents and ergonomics. Dörner (1997) for example found that vague and general goals prevented managers from realizing the contradictions and conflicts that would lead, in the vast majority of the cases he studied, to catastrophic failures. Yet instead of examining the implications of that difference of focus, between their "comprehensive" look and Mann's individual cases, they dismiss both sides of the Marcum-Calhoun versus Mann debate as insufficiently "open-minded" and offer as a model instead... Cornell's cataloging policies between 1997 and 2007 devised and implemented under the direction of Karen Calhoun, a magnificent case of double-speak exactly like the description and analysis of the labor-management misunderstandings discussed in the introductory section.

4. *Utility, library priorities, and cataloging: the case of Cornell University Library.*
In the fourth section of their paper the authors describe cataloging as it has been done at Cornell during the past decade. During this time vacant cataloger positions were transferred to other departments concurrently with the explosive growth of electronic resources requiring cataloging. The discussion of the changes (found on page 104), deserve careful scrutiny.

There is much about "reducing the costs of technical services operations so that funds could be redeployed," of generating "the necessary savings for staff redirection," of accepting available metadata without evaluation, of items "moved to the shelves as quickly as possible," rapid processing by low-level staff, and abbreviated level cataloging. There is only one reference to users: "results showed that users at all levels ... noted significant gaps between their desired level of access to electronic resources and ability to obtain information readily and independently." (p. 104). So the library administration "further reduced staff support for cataloging in order to reallocate these lines to other areas."

Banush (2007) disputed my characterization of the goals of Cornell's COR policy as "rapid processing is the only goal" and "quick decisions are better than intelligent decisions because they are quicker" (Bade, 2007), but in the article written with LeBlanc this is exactly how the authors' describe that policy: Catalogers now "follow one simple, but important directive: no backlog.... In other words, catalogers use professional judgment to make utilitarian need-satisfaction decisions regarding the nature and extent of basic intellectual access required for individual titles, based on time and resources available—that is, bibliographic triage." (p. 104-105). How they can go from catalogers following only one directive—the managerial demand No backlog—to "catalogers use professional judgment to make utilitarian need-satisfaction decisions" by means of an "In other words" might perhaps be explained by one better versed in logic than I, but it seems that the famous non-existent sequitor is missing here as well. In the management's utilitarian logic "No backlogs" is simply equated with "the greatest good for the greatest number," and so it seems that on the part of labor there is only following that directive and no professional judgment at all. Utilitarianism works at the managerial level; only obedience is apparent at the labor end.

The library's objectives, the "seemingly impossible imperative—increase productivity, eliminate a large backlog, and simultaneously reduce staffing levels," were met: staff levels decreased, cataloger productivity increased, the backlog was eliminated, costs declined.[1] The authors are obviously satisfied with these results, but acknowledge that "Only future students, researchers, and librarians will be able to determine whether the policies ultimately prove to be wise or myopic. What we can say now, and with certainty, is that the process used to develop and implement the current cataloging policies reflects quite clearly

---

[1] Increased productivity is something to boast about only if the product is worth increasing. The increased production of errors and useless misinformation is not an accomplishment to brag about, but this was in fact the chief product of Cornell's cataloging policies as I evaluated them in Bade (2003).

the tenets of utilitarian thought." (p. 105). The authors' certainty is ill-founded. It would be more accurate to say that the process reveals the reasons why utilitarianism failed so miserably.

5. *Consequences of cataloging pragmatism*

In the preceding section the authors graciously acknowledged that only future users will be able to evaluate the results of Cornell cataloging policies. In section 5 we suddenly encounter "pragmatism'—a philosophical justification of a markedly different character—but it appears only in the section title, with no discussion of how a pragmatic approach or justification might differ from a utilitarian account. The authors claim that Cornell managers were aware of the potential disadvantages as well as the advantages of a utility-driven approach, and admit that "there is some evidence to justify the fears of those who opposed the strategy." (p. 106). They even mention some severe criticisms of their policy coming "from some catalogers even outside of Cornell," a reference to my own paper (Bade 2007). Yet they dismiss all of these "contemporary conclusions" (because only future users are allowed to judge the policy) as "merely speculative." (p. 106). Instead they offer a variety of statistical data to refute all arguments and allay all fears about any negative consequences of those policies. Only one argument in Bade (2007) was addressed: statistics indicate that COR records prior to upgrading are borrowed through interlibrary loan at seven Ivy League schools even more than PCC records whether full or core. For that to constitute an argument against a negative impact for institutions beyond Cornell one would have to argue that there were no other significant factors (e.g. relative number of COR and PCC records, the presence of fuller descriptions in other databases). If Cornell users are like users in other institutions, those materials may have been located using the upgraded record found in OCLC prior to Cornell's "harvesting" of the same. Those statistics ought also to be compared with interlibrary loan figures for non-Ivy League institutions.

We can trace most of the reasons for the failure of the authors' espousal of utilitarianism (or pragmatism) as a justification for policies in place to this refusal to look at their policy from a perspective not limited by the narrow institutional objectives to "increase productivity, eliminate a large backlog, and simultaneously reduce staffing." The authors (and presumably other administrators at Cornell) refuse to view the policies themselves with a view to utility in the long run and in the wider environment; the only question they ask, the only issue they explore, is whether it will be useful to do X in order to achieve Y, where Y is a policy directive given and accepted uncritically. "Utility" in their policy is simply a blunt instrument for decision making in the face of a given set of priorities; their "philosophy" has no critical but only a justificatory function. It was in this fashion and according to such a philosophy that Eichmann determined how to ship his cargo throughout the Reich. He also had a "seemingly impossible imperative"; he also fulfilled the organization's objectives.

An unfair comparison? No. Certainly what Eichmann did was horrible in ways that cannot be compared to what is being done at Cornell. But from a utilitarian perspective the two are indistinguishable. To understand why is to understand why utilitarianism failed. It is precisely by framing issues and forcing decisions in terms of "the greatest good for the greatest number" that utilitarianism denies the validity of competing claims and contradictory goals. It is not only in matters of rights, justice and equality that utilitarianism fails; utilitarianism fails in the presence of all difference: differences in users, tasks, desires, needs, goals and perspectives. While Banush and LeBlanc depend upon the international context of shared metadata, cooperative cataloging and automated data exchange and manipulation when they have their local objectives in mind, they completely close their eyes and minds to that environment and the claims it makes upon them when it comes to considering the consequences of their policies and actions for all others with whom they are claiming to cooperate. If we view cataloging policies from that wider perspective—global users, a global information system, cooperation, sharing, and automation—the principle of utility bites back.

Part Two: Utility and users in shared and cooperative systems.

We know from experience how capable a utilitarian means-ends-rationality is of giving politics over to inhuman behavior.
(Hannah Arendt, 2007 [1959], p. 193)

1. Who needs a philosophy?
Libraries and cataloging departments do not need philosophical justifications; their justification lies in fulfilling the purposes for which they were established. Nor do they need philosophies as a "backdrop" for policy making. What policy making requires is a clear understanding of the practices and purposes the library is to serve, and that understanding will mean examining library services, organization, policy and practices in light of their usefulness for the particular institutional needs. In the case of libraries participating in cooperative programs, however, usefulness cannot be understood in local terms alone, and it is not philosophy that reveals that to us but our understanding of what cooperation means.

In choosing utilitarianism as the basis for their rationalization and justification of Cornell policies, Banush and LeBlanc join together two long traditions of thinkers and actors: ideologues and management. There is a clear correspondence between enlightenment rationalism, Bentham's utilitarianism and a manner of thinking which avoids the "particular, and thus accidental" (Arendt, 2007 [1932], p.3), facts and evidence, relationships and unintended consequences, denying their importance in favour of abstractions such as "user", "item", "need", "desire", "greatest good" and the "greatest number." Banush and LeBlanc's Figure 1 ("Generic overview of institutional priorities") provides a marvelous example of saying nothing with a diagram, and the text explicating it states everything in general and therefore nothing at all.

The authors do mention briefly a number of general problems facing libraries today, including the difficulty of choosing among and deciding whether and how to support technological innovations, social fads and traditional services, but in the body of the paper none of these difficult and often contradictory possibilities are further discussed. We are simply told that library administrators must make choices and the principle of utility can guide them in those choices. When the goals of the library are themselves in conflict, an appeal to utility cannot help decide how to satisfy those goals; it can only be used to justify abandoning some goals in favour of others. The failure to recognize when goals are contradictory was one of the characteristic features of policies leading to catastrophic failure in the experiments carried out by Dörner, as was the failure to formulate goals in concrete terms. The goal of a "user-friendly library" he insisted, lacked any "criteria by which we can decide with certainty whether the goal has been achieved." (Dörner 1997, p. 51). The vague and the general do not lend themselves to criticism and evaluation: who would oppose utility? Service to the users and their needs? The greatest good? The widest applicability? Yet it is abundantly clear that any policy at all can be justified as being "service to the users" or "for the greatest good."

The policies at Cornell, as in most libraries, were not developed in light of a philosophical examination of the library's goals; on the contrary, they were developed according to a set of unexamined and uncritically accepted presuppositions, the principle one being that "no backlogs" is the greatest good for the greatest number. "No backlogs" is certainly a concrete goal, its meaning clear. It is a goal toward the satisfaction of which definite steps can be taken. Yet if that demand is accepted as the only goal of library policy, only one step is needed to erect it into the "simple directive" which will guide all policy and practice, all other goals having been eliminated.

The "philosophy" at Cornell was all *ex post facto*; what guided policy were accepted and unquestioned presuppositions. Apparently there were those who both examined and questioned those presuppositions, but those persons were, in Banush's words, "disgruntled staff... who feel too threatened by change to consider reforms" (Banush, 2006). As was evident in Banush and LeBlanc's paper, the adoption of a philosophy in an organization is almost always an attempt to control employees, eliminate argument and justify policies. Dissent and argument are unwelcome in any situation where one wants an entire organization to change as rapidly as versions of a software program, and then always by managerial decision. Dissent and argument are, however, necessary to the enterprise of science, and along with paying attention to the facts they constitute the basic prerequisites for scientific understanding in any domain, including the area of librarianship.

The utilitarian approach advocated by Banush and LeBlanc leads to no deeper understanding of cataloging policies at Cornell than could be found in their brief historical description: there were backlogs, upper management decreed "No backlogs" and middle management figured out how to move the items in the backlog onto the shelf to please upper management. User needs only entered the picture in the form of staff resistance and fears of negative consequences. The "needs" identified in the surveys were needs of the most general kind, none of them arising from the particulars of research projects but exactly the kinds of needs one expects as answers to a vague question in a survey instrument: the answers always reflect the formulation of the questions. The only consideration of utility involved in making the policy was the need-satisfaction of the upper management. Perhaps management needs utilitarianism or some other philosophy to justify the changes made, but neither those on the working end nor the users themselves would need a philosophy to figure that out.

If we think of philosophy differently than Banush and LeBlanc, not as a tool for making or justifying decisions but as a manner or mode of investigation leading to the discovery of contradictions and conflicts, the achievement of clarity and increased understanding, then we may indeed be well served not by "a philosophy" but by adopting that mode of experience and investigation historically considered philosophical. It is in that manner of looking at cataloging that I have studied cataloging policies ever since reading Thomas Mann on the "Cataloging must change!" controversy in 1997.

The first direction in which this mode of investigation led me was to try to understand the implications of cooperative cataloging, both how local decisions affect the cooperating institutions and vice versa. This line of inquiry immediately revealed the conflicting needs and goals of institutions devoted to different user communities. On those two aspects of cataloging policy the library literature has much to offer in the way of advice and feel-good stories but very little to offer in the way of critical examination, empirical research or qualitative evaluation. By investigating these two issues vital to the formulation of cataloging policy we can see more clearly the reasons for the failures of cataloging policies at Cornell as well as the utilitarian justifications given for them. The primary consideration in any library policy must be the needs of those for whom the library exists, and to those library users we now turn.

2. User needs: comprehensive views must be based on real use studies rather than managerial assumptions about utility

> *A thing can reveal itself under many aspects only in the presence of peers who regard it from their various perspectives. Wherever the equality of others and of their particular opinions is abrogated, as, for instance, under tyranny, in which everything and everyone is sacrificed to the standpoint of the tyrant, no one is free and no one is capable of insight, not even the tyrant.* (Hannah Arendt, 2005 [1959], p. 169)

The line of arguments that I have pursued in earlier writings, like those put forth by Thomas Mann, have focused on particulars, arguments that depend upon attention to real users and real research needs in all their depth and variety, and not simply statistical data for the latter inevitably reflects and appears to validate the abstractions that counting requires. The implicit philosophy guiding the focus of investigation and the choice of arguments in both my work and Mann's is rooted in attention to the particulars, always demanding an empirical investigation, and is in every aspect opposed to the superficial rationalism and narrow utilitarianism underpinning Cornell policy as explicitly formulated in the paper by Banush and LeBlanc. Nowhere is this difference more noticeable than in the treatment of "the users."

I have argued elsewhere (Bade 2008) that our understanding of library users' needs must be rooted in institutional purposes and research practices—concretely specifiable because normative practices—rather than in the impossible task of knowing and serving all present expressed needs and predicting every possible future need. Libraries are institutions, always answerable to some larger social institution and often established by a constitution that specifically identifies how it is to serve specific communities and their specific practices. What those practices are, and what they require may be known with certainty only by those familiar with those practices from the inside, i.e. as a practitioner. The diversity of those practices one can only encounter in their realization in specific library users engaged in a particular research task.

In the not too distant past many public libraries that had been specifically founded to serve the *reading* public rightly debated whether or not to extend their services to include music listening, video-viewing, game-playing and other computer uses having nothing to do with the library's collections and stated purposes. Similar decisions as to how best to support the library's primary objectives are required in other types of libraries as well. One example from just a just a few years ago: so many computer terminals in the Joseph Regenstein Library were being used for extended time-consuming (and computer-consuming) pursuits like writing, email reading, and Internet surfing for pleasure that those users who came to the library specifically to look for something that the library had (or which they hoped the library would have) were unable to find a single available terminal from which to search the online catalog (there being no other way to search it). The result was angry faculty members and a discussion among librarians which ultimately led to the reservation of a certain number of terminals for library catalog searching only. Let us be clear about this example: this was a restriction of access on public terminals in order to serve a certain practice held to be crucial and central to the university and the library's mission. It can easily be argued that this was for "the greatest good of the greatest number"—so long as one assumes that the primary purpose of computers in the library is to enable searchers to utilize the library's collections, an assumption that both the library administration and the faculty apparently agreed upon. That decision could just as easily have been denounced as not being in the interest of "the greatest good of the greatest number" if the assumption were otherwise. Had the assumption been that the use of the library as physical collection were secondary to its function as study hall or Internet provider, the decision would have been quite different. In matters such as these utilitarianism cannot help us at all: the assumptions concerning the library's purpose will determine the decision, and that assumption must have been determined before any appeal to utility could have any meaning.

If one begins with the assumption that library based research is the primary practice that the library exists to support, then the evaluation of library service will be guided by the support which it provides that research. Library based research, Abbott (2006) argued, is research with records, and this means that the primary goals of the library are to provide the library's users access to those records. The primary means of enabling that access are two: 1) purchase of materials (in any format, whether physically or through electronic subscription, or in the case of freely available Internet resources, simply identification plus linkage); and 2) some form of description enabling discovery, identification and evaluation of suitability for the desired purpose. The former of these tasks is a matter of collection development, and is not the matter under consideration in Banush and LeBlanc, and thus of no concern here either. The second of these and the policies for the creation and management of those descriptions is the topic of interest. Those descriptions for discovery, identification and evaluation in an electronic environment are usually called bibliographic records and the information contained in them metadata. Because the metadata may be embedded in the item itself or specified in more than one location (e.g. name, series and subject authority records) in what follows I shall simply refer to metadata.

The primary issue for library policy regarding the creation, acquisition and management of metadata is the kind and amount of information that should be created, since that information must be created by someone and therefore it is costly. If we ask what information ought to be created, there is a clear source for an answer: the MARC formats. Every valid element that has been established for the various MARC formats has been proposed, its function and uses described, its necessity or desirability argued and its continuing value defended successfully not by some cataloger with nothing better to do but through discussions of committees of librarians in all areas of service and the input of non-committee members from around the world who felt they or their users had a stake in the decision that was important enough to merit their participation in the discussion. The elements defined in the MARC format represent the "many aspects," the "many-sidedness" and the "presence of peers" that Hannah Arendt ascribed to the Greek ideal for the πολιτικός: the greatest possible overview of all the possible standpoints and viewpoints from which an issue can be seen and judged." (Arendt, 2005 [1959], p. 168). What the Greeks called φρόνησις Kant discussed in his *Critique of Judgement* as an "enlarged mentality…, the ability to think from the position of every other person." (quoted in Arendt, 2005 [1959], p. 168). Some elements are necessary in all records because of system requirements; others are required when applicable; many more are optional and to be added by those who want their particular users to be able to use that particular bit of information in their institution. There is room for a great deal of variation in the quantity and kinds of information entered into any MARC record, and every institution determines by policy what its users (including its library staff) require in order to accomplish their purposes and practices. The utility of any element may vary greatly across institutions but will not vary much if at all for a given purpose or practice. In what follows I will limit my remarks to those appropriate to the primary users of a large research library and the practices academic research involves, not because no others are of concern to me, but because both Cornell and the University of Chicago are such institutions, and therefore I can assume that the user purposes and practices at these two institutions are similar in their essentials. Librarians at the University of Chicago, as well as librarians, faculty and students in most academic libraries can indeed judge the Cornell policy now (and not just in the future), since they use on a daily basis metadata originally created at Cornell (an aspect of utility ignored by Banush and LeBlanc.)

I mentioned above three research projects in which I was involved not as the researcher but as a librarian. A brief description and discussion of one those projects, followed by an account of a research project of my own and a quantitative study of circulation at the University of Chicago libraries by Andrew Abbott will provide a basis in both real users and statistical user data for developing a comprehensive view of user needs, i.e. a view not limited to the single aspect of time in the queue. Looking at individual research projects is not intended as an argument for following every possible need of every possible user; on the contrary these two research projects illustrate very common types of research problems and the kind of information required for satisfying such users.

During the research for his book *Jewish Christians in the Warsaw Ghetto* I met almost daily with Prof. Dembowski. What he needed were first hand accounts of the three Catholic parishes within the ghetto and biographical information on the priests and their parishioners, the Jewish Christians who were the sole members of those parishes. While much of this material was gleaned from bibliographies, acquaintances and from his prior knowledge of Warsaw and its population both before and during the Shoah, the crucial information required for the discovery of additional material was subject information relating to the ghetto and the date and language of original composition and publication. It did not matter in what language first person accounts were written as he wanted them all; what he could not read himself he had translated. He needed not only the originals but translations as well in order to see how certain passages were translated (or deleted), and one of the results of our working over the citations and translation histories was the mistaken conflation of two separate primary sources—perhaps the most important of all the available documents—under one heading in the library catalog, not just in the Regenstein Library catalog but apparently in every US library that held those books. Both books, in all their printings, had the same entry in the catalog and notes in the record stating that they were translations of the same work. Only because he insisted on looking at every edition and translation did he identify and make possible the correction of a 50 year old confusion arising from the information originally provided by the publisher/translator in the item cataloged. Language, dates, translation history (e.g. uniform titles), notes, subjects: not too much to ask, and all important for one research project.

My own project began while writing a paper several years ago. I noticed that the discussion of cataloging errors followed either a positivistic approach—errors are things that one can identify and correct straightforwardly and unproblematically—and what I would call a "cataloger's judgement" or subjective approach, i.e. errors aren't really a problem, they are merely differences of opinion. I felt the need to gain a deeper understanding about what we are talking about when we talk (write, sing, cry) about errors. I also wanted to gain a historical understanding so as not to be caught uncritically following current fashion. I wanted a perspective not limited to the Anglo-American 21st century. And I wanted a multidisciplinary basis, not merely a theory developed in the small world of LIS.

The first strategy was to search our local catalog for materials that I could obtain here and now. Subject headings for Error and Errors, as well as for a number of other related terms started me off with great range of materials from many perspectives published over a long period, and most of these including bibliographical references to the earlier literature. Next step was to search OCLC, both the books file and the periodical indexes, but unlike the library catalog one can (only) use keywords, thankfully in particular fields as well as generally. That is both a limitation and a problem. Knowing that many items do not have subject headings and that many relevant items might actually have different headings I searched other terms and variants as both title and subject terms. I found that I had to search the following terms: error, errors, mistake, mistakes, misinformation, quality, fault, failure, mismatch, accidents, misconduct, malpractice, variation, normalization, standardization, wrong, stupidity, risk, slips, integrity, wayward, menace, garbage...and this list gets me through just the title keywords NECESSARY to find *some* of the items in the first 6 of the 50 pages of the final bibliography. Many relevant items are not to be found under any keyword that I could think of using, e.g. the article "When novices surpass experts: the difficulty of a task may increase with expertise" and for locating these I was entirely dependent upon either citation or subject data supplied by the persons creating the bibliographic record. The same process I then repeated language by language to locate the non-English language materials that might lack the subject terms already searched.

At that point, the work of the library catalog became a matter of finding an actual copy to read, whether by checking out the item locally, getting it online or ordering it through interlibrary loan. Once I got these items I followed the trail of references, sometimes to surprising places. Evans' *Getting It Wrong* (found by a subject search) led me to Augustine, and because of the breadth of Augustine's works, I searched an Augustine concordance (found via a subject search) in which the various terms he used are given in context from which I could select just those instances that interested me and then go back to the catalog and find the particular works (found via uniform titles) where those passages were found. I plowed through literatures I had known only from cataloging and had not previously read. Besides the literatures of librarianship and information science, linguistics and philosophy, I struggled through the legal, medical, sociological, psychological, literary, mathematical and theological works as well as studies on "scientific error." In most cases, my entry into the literature was a subject search in the library catalog since I had no prior knowledge of those literatures.

I had originally decided not to look at the ergonomics items which came up in my search results, thinking that I would find nothing relevant to library catalogs in writings about chair design and carpel tunnel syndrome (the limits of my then greatly impoverished understanding of ergonomics). However, while reading James Reason's *Human Error* I realized how wrong my assumption had been. The ergonomics literature turned out to be where most of the really challenging and stimulating work was being done. So I ended up looking for material on industrial safety, high reliability organizations, nuclear power plant management, air traffic controllers, fire-fighting, and all kinds of things that ergonomists discuss.

That is the kind of research and those are the kinds of searches that I expect academic libraries, at least the large ones, ought to be supporting. An important part of the literature I could find readily because of and only because of the subject headings and index terms provided in the library catalog and the various databases made available through the library website. I stress subject headings because in my work with those bibliographical records acquired from Cornell which were created according to the Cataloging on Receipt procedure, those headings and their associated classification numbers were among the most frequently deficient elements.

It is perhaps easy to dismiss the experiences of David Bade and Prof. Dembowski as exceptional cases. We are *not* undergraduates writing term papers for an introductory class. We *are* the long tail. However, we do represent exactly the kind of user that the University of Chicago Task Force on the University Library determined that the libraries at the University of Chicago should be dedicated to serving, in fact its primary user base. Although it is possible that the library administrators at Cornell have determined their user base to be of a different character, the materials collected by Cornell (as evidenced in the bibliographic records in OCLC that have been produced by Cornell) suggest that they are in fact collecting for a group of academic users much like myself and Prof. Dembowski. What is different, apparently, is that at the University of Chicago we have accepted a mandate from the university administration to serve the most demanding of the library's users, and we try to satisfy that administrative directive. At the Joseph Regenstein Library it is not so easy as simply "No backlogs."

The mandate accepted by the librarians at the University of Chicago is not to determine the greatest good for the greatest number; it is to consider as paramount the support of the research needs of from 500 to 1000 of the libraries' more than 90,000 registered card holders: its heaviest users. I have attempted to give some idea of the nature of that research in my brief accounts above; an account of a different kind, a statistical account, was recently provided by Prof. Andrew Abbott in a December 13, 2007 memorandum to the library director. In that memo he noted that, for the period beginning 14 October 1998 and ending 18 October 2006, 21% of the items in the collection in the Joseph Regenstein Library were charged out by patrons (not by the bindery or other housekeeping accounts) while the figures for the other libraries on campus were 15%, 9%, 34%,

46% and 47%. This is a different story than that we are used to hearing about the long tail. And there is more: 16% of all charges were for items circulating only one time during that period. This is the kind of figure that opponents of the long tail love to wag, but Abbott's interpretation differs:

> The 431,395 "once-only" charges from JRL are an especially important figure. Typically, these are the books being used by scholars for cutting-edge library work, work with materials only rarely touched. These are the kinds of materials that, were they missing (as they are in lesser libraries), would force scholars to make interlibrary loan requests (or travel to libraries that have better holdings). There are 2922 days in eight years ... This means that there were 148 of these "once-only" charges PER DAY over the eight years of data.

Were utility defined as the greatest good for the greatest number, these 431,395 items would get less than full level cataloging, or more likely, never acquired in the first place; what a savings in time, staff and money that would be! But when utility is defined as serving the institution's objectives—in this case the heaviest users, cutting-edge research—these same items will be both purchased and provided with metadata to the same extent as more heavily used materials.

That is what we strive for at the University of Chicago, but our efforts are made more difficult than they would be if other academic libraries shared our objectives. That, in a nutshell, is the problem of the shared and cooperative database. The less than full treatment provided by institutions where the objectives are other than service to the heaviest users counts for a large percentage of the bibliographical records available from our shared databases and presents the library with difficult organizational problems, particularly in the matter of triage. How can utilitarianism help us decide here? It cannot. In a shared database there is no shared understanding of utility; rather an experience of futility (if not a philosophy of futilitarianism) seems to be common to many librarians involved in cataloging and database maintenance. Far from being disgruntled staff, those librarians are, in some libraries at least, the persons who most clearly understand the diversity of user needs that the library catalog must strive to meet.

3. *The social life of metadata: cooperation and information exchange in technical networks*

> *If someone wants to see and experience the world as it "really" is, he can do so only by understanding it as something that is shared by many people, lies between them, separates and links them, showing itself differently to each and comprehensible only to the extent that many people can talk about it and exchange their opinions and perspectives with one another, over against one another.*
> (Hannah Arendt, 2005 [1959], p. 128)

"All acting," Hannah Arendt wrote, "is situated in a web of relations in which anything intended by individuals is immediately transformed, and is thus prevented from being brought about as a set goal" (Arendt, 2007 [1959], p. 194). She was returning to a theme she had discussed earlier in a 1953 lecture in which she remarked that "we never quite know what we are doing when we begin to act into the web of interrelationships and mutual dependencies that constitute the field of action" and quoted Bossuet's comment that there is "no human power which does not, against its own will, further other plans than its own" (Arendt, 2005 [1953], p. 56-57). This knowledge of the "tragic element in all action" persists throughout most of Western intellectual history, being lost "only with the sudden and disconcerting onrush of the gigantic technical developments after the industrial revolution" (ibid., p. 58). The loss of that understanding has been characteristic of the assumptions and logic of technological development and many of the social and ecological problems following technological innovation and diffusion have been linked to actions undertaken on the assumption that the results of the insertion of technologies could be predicted by a knowledge of the technical potential alone. Arendt links the loss of awareness of this uncertainty directly to production oriented thinking, claiming that "the experience of fabrication achieved such an overwhelming predominance that the uncertainties of action could be forgotten altogether" (ibid.).

In his study of large-scale technical systems the sociologist Alain Gras pointed out that "*a priori* and *a posteriori* control proceed from two different logics: only regulation '*ab initio*' really appears in large systems, but everyday usage of the technologies they support involves a larger social environment that changes the rules of the game" (Gras, 1993, p. 219). "Technique imposes itself as a manner of thinking the world, it is a system of the production of ideas and representations of nature far more than a system of actions on that nature" Gras (1993, p. 13) wrote, and that manner of thinking is all too often not only simplistic but considers technology "isolated out of the context in which it is found, rendering it autonomous in relation to its human context. Technique is situated beyond culture; it goes on of its own accord." (ibid. p. 247).

That manner of thinking is clearly evident in the essay by Banush and LeBlanc. When considering their description of Cornell's cataloging policies the strangest aspect of all is the incoherence of their stress on external resources, external users, remote access, automated processes and an unquestioning reliance on cataloging from elsewhere with the refusal to address any and all matters that would indicate how their policy affects all those external users, processes and systems. The wider information environment in both its social and technical aspects is welcomed as providing resources to be exploited, but the effects of their participation in that wider environment and the responsibilities participation entails are ignored in the formulation of the policy and denied in Banush and LeBlanc's article. Even though the authors admit the potential for risk and negative effects, the insistence upon accepting copy without review, the use of automated upgrading programs and the statistical data of usage offered as evidence in favour of the policy are indisputable proof that for the Cornell administrators there are no potential risks not worth taking.

In an earlier paper (Bade 2007) I discussed a number of reasons why the Cornell COR policy is an irresponsible policy doing damage not only to Cornell but to the entire network of library metadata sharing throughout the world today. Those arguments need not all be repeated here, but I would like to reiterate one argument. The COR policy is completely dependent upon at least one other institution both having the same items catalogued according to this policy at Cornell, and providing full cataloging for them within two years. It is very clear that such a policy could not possibly be adopted by all institutions for if it were no complete metadata would ever be created anywhere. No database can effectively support both data mining or harvesting à la COR *and* copy-cataloging without review for these two activities are mutually exclusive: the latter is only possible if metadata created to support the former practice is not in the database. Copy-cataloging without review requires a reliable database; COR explicitly requires that someone else pay attention to the record and insofar as other cooperating institutions use metadata without review COR MUST FAIL. The radical incoherence and incompatibility of those two policies could not be clearer, but to see that incoherence one must understand that *every contribution to a shared database effects policies in every other participating institution.* The policies at Cornell mean that no other institution can adopt a policy of copy-cataloging without review. Since other institutions do accept metadata without review, we know that COR fails at Cornell. A society of exploiters is an ecological disaster.

It could be argued that the characteristic trait of the "information society" of the early 21st century is exploitation and its overt desire theft. Mechanical *re*production rather than production predominates, as this is the *modus operandi* of information technologies; recent assaults on copyright law (e.g. the Google Books project) are indicative of that orientation, as is COR. Whereas copy-cataloging and shared databases were some of the main topics of the late 20th century library world, today's hot topics are data mining, harvesting, and reusability, this latter called the Holy Grail of content engineering (Breure, 2005). For many librarians, metadata always already exists; it is something found, purchased, copied, downloaded and manipulated, never something created, evaluated or interpreted. That metadata has a social role and must be created for or adapted to that role is denied in every policy that ignores evaluation and interpretation. Like searching systems, metadata must ultimately serve the library user's purposes. Yet in spite of the ubiquitous appeals to and arguments from cooperation, data sharing and "users", both the social context and user purposes are ignored or even denied whenever policy is subordinated to a simple managerial objective such as No backlogs.

The industrial revolution as a mode of thinking has overtaken libraries, and as a consequence the uncertainties of action of which Arendt wrote are no longer acknowledged in the library literature. Just as tailor made clothes to fit unique needs were replaced by mass produced items for a market, the librarian's dialogue with the library's users has been replaced by automatic data transfer and relevance ranking; the acknowledged uncertainties of the former dialogue have been discarded for the unacknowledged, hidden and much greater uncertainties of the latter.

Part III: Conclusion

Ideologies embodied are invariably totalitarian; that is their nature: the refusal of the other, of difference, dissent, the new, the particular. Technologies are also the embodiment of ideas. As ideas, they must be totalitarian since they have no human capacities for judgement, change or forgiveness; as implemented, they are characterized by accidents and unforeseen outcomes, for what they produce when employed by human beings depends not only upon the designer's specifications but also upon all those factors that human action brings into play: psychological, economic, social, intellectual, legal, political and religious as well as the physical environment itself. The intelligent use of technologies in any social setting requires attention to all of the environmental factors that may influence or be influenced by the technologies. Banush and LeBlanc's "philosophical backdrop"—whether utilitarianism or pragmatism—refuses to look at anything other than management demands for moving stock; all uses and users, those at Cornell and everywhere else, were rendered out of sight and out of mind by that reduction of all of the goals of academic libraries to a single demand: no backlogs.

Library administrators do indeed have difficult choices to make, and those choices will undoubtedly become more complex and difficult. Making those choices within an ever more tightly integrated socio-technical world will require much clearer thinking than is evident in Banush and LeBlanc (2007), and above all will require a larger perspective. If we are to speak of a "bibliographical ethics" it will have to be founded on something other than utilitarianism. No principle of utility can be invoked by the library to arrive at its goals since the goals of the library are determined by the practices of the library's users. Utility (whatever that is) may indeed be invoked when choosing between competing and contradictory goals, but only as a justification for discarding certain of those goals; it can be of no value in determining how to satisfy any given goal. Not even for the elimination of backlogs.

REFERENCES

Abbott, Andrew (2006). *The University Library*. http://www.lib.uchicago.edu/staffweb/groups/space/abbott-report.html#VIA

Abbott, Andrew (2007). Memorandum, December 13, 2007.

Arendt, Hannah (2005 [1953]). "The tradition of political thought." In her: *The promise of politics*. New York: Schocken Books, pp. 40-62.

Arendt, Hannah (2005 [1959]). "Introduction *into* politics." In her: *The promise of politics*. New York: Schocken Books, pp. 93-200.

Arendt, Hannah (2007 [1932]). "The Enlightenment and the Jewish question" in her: *The Jewish writings*, p. 3-18.

Arendt, Hannah (2007 [1959]). "Culture and politics." In her: *Reflections on literature and culture.* Evanston: Northwestern University Press, pp. 179-202. (Originally published as "Kultur und Politik" in *Merkur* 12, pp. 1122-1145.)

Bade, David (2003). *Misinformation and Meaning in Library Catalogs.* Chicago: The Author.

Bade, David (2007). "Rapid cataloging: three models for addressing timeliness as an issue of quality in library catalogs." *Cataloging & classification quarterly*, v. 45, nr. 1, pp. 87-123. (Reprinted in this volume)

Bade, David (2008). *Responsible librarianship: library policies for unreliable systems*. Duluth, Minn.: Library Juice Press.

Banush, David (2006). Posting to PCCPOL, 24 May 2006.

Banush, David (2007). "Rabid cataloging: response to David Bade" *Cataloging & classification quarterly*, v.45 nr.1 pp. 126-127.

Banush, David; LeBlanc, Jim (2007). "Utility, library priorities, and cataloging policies" *Library collections, acquisitions, & technical services*, v. 31, p.96-109.

Breure, Leen (2005). "Reuse of content and digital genres" in:

Herre van Oostendorp, Leen Breure and Andrew Dillon, *Creation, use, and deployment of digital information.* Mahwah, NJ: Lawrence Erlbaum Associates, p. 27-53.

Dörner, Dietrich (1997). *The logic of failure: recognizing and avoiding error in complex situations.* Reading, Mass: Addison-Wesley. Translation of: *Die Logik des Mißlingens.*

Gras, Alain, avec la participation de Sophie L. Poirot-Delpech (1993). *Grandeur et dependence: sociologie des macro-systèmes techniques.* Paris: PUF.

Mann, Thomas (2006a). *What is going on at the Library of Congress?* Available at: http://www.guild2910.org/AFSCMEWhatIsGoingOn.pdf

VII

Irresponsible Librarianship: A Critique of the Report of the Library of Congress Working Group on the Future of Bibliographic Control and Thoughts on How to Proceed

Part 1. Critique
The Guiding Principles

The report of the Working Group offers three "guiding principles," these being new rules for the discourse and practice of librarianship. Briefly paraphrased, they are:

1) Bibliographic control means managing global information systems from Amazon to Google to Wikipedia. It no longer has anything to do with bibliographical description, i.e. analytical bibliography or cataloging, nor with scholarly communication.
2) The Bibliographic Universe consists of all the world's information. It recognizes no local difference of purpose or action, it no longer has any boundaries whether of place or purpose; all activities of bibliographic control are global activities.

3) The Library of Congress must cease to consider its own goals and purposes as its primary mission and follow what everyone decides is best for everyone. The role of the Library of Congress is now to conform. By implication and in accordance with the rest of the report this applies to all libraries everywhere.

These redefinitions guide the report in its recommendations, but there are other, equally important assumptions, including: 1) the inevitability and desirability of a global socio-technical system in what I think are its most undesirable aspects —control without borders, disregard of the local and of differences— 2) the primacy of efficiency as a value, and 3) exploitation is an efficient means of cooperation.

The report adopts a rhetoric that confidently asserts what the future will be, what we must do, and must do without delay. The future is predicted to be a global system based on two decades old technology. The Working Group is repeating the perennial folly of identifying tomorrow's technology with today's.

The demand for efficiency begs the question of what we are trying to do in our activities of bibliographic control, i.e. efficient at doing what? If the goal of bibliographic control is understood to be an activity in support of the scientific and scholarly practices of citation, literature search and exploration then the evaluation of efficiency cannot be separated from user success in those activities.

The Working Group Calls for a Unified Philosophy of Bibliographic Control

We read that "Users would be better served if access to these materials were provided in the context of a unified philosophy of bibliographic control" but there is no philosophy here, just the management of a network of technical systems. What might a unified philosophy of bibliographic control be? Would it not have to deal with language (which the report simply regards as a problem to be solved by URIs) and with communication as human activities, rather than simply with the technical aspects of communication systems? Human communication plays no role whatsoever in the Working Group's understanding of the library.

R.G. Collingwood argued that the meaning of any statement must be related to the question it is intended to answer. This understanding of meaning was further developed by philosopher Michel Meyer and the linguist Roy Harris, the latter stating the matter succinctly: meaning is radically indeterminate. In Meyer's understanding of human communication, questions are always prior and they always arise from the problems of living in a universe in which we do not know the answers but wish to understand each other and act in the world together. The answers we give are not only always provisional but they are also always debatable because the questions themselves arise from our problems, our not knowing something.

If librarianship involves an engagement with users and their questions, then it cannot be understood as simply the management of technical systems and the information given. What is relevant to any particular question will be determined by the question, and that question cannot be present to any information system. All that is present to the technical system is a string of text and a universe of information that contains only answers given to previous questions arising in different situations.

Go to the University of Chicago library website and open up LENS. Type in "Roy Harris" and see what comes up. I did this with the question in mind "What do we have on or by Roy Harris the linguist?" That my question was not present to the system is evident not only in the results given—arranged by a system definition of "relevance"—but in the absurd word cloud associated on the side and the suggestion of 1273 different authors who "matched" my query. Typing "Michel Meyer" will produce very similar results, yet in his case I have already done a lot of authority work and error correction on most of the records for his works.

If communication presupposes cooperation understood as doing something together for a reason, then we can understand why the information system has such difficulty in making any sense: the information system cannot cooperate with anyone for it is not doing anything for a reason. Roy Harris' word cloud in LENS presents a perfect example of the operation of the technical system. It suggested *par, qui, que, les, pour* along with other French words, and as spelling variants, *rye, ryoi, charris* and *farris*. Now that is truly what I call ARTIFICIAL INTELLIGENCE: automatic generation of responses totally unrelated to MY question. For systems engineers this is perhaps no problem, just an indication of the need to refine some algorithm, etc. But what is the effect of such responses on the human user of the system? Cultural theorist Paul Virilio suggested a defeat of facts, a tragedy of knowledge, a global accident of meaninglessness.

Roy Harris' word cloud does not mean that LENS is useless. Far from it. LENS is a very valuable tool that any intelligent user can use. Ignoring the items by and about Roy Harris the composer, the catalogues of California earthquakes and many other irrelevant items, the user can find enough books by and about Roy Harris the linguist to get what he or she needs. And that is precisely my point: an informed user who intelligently interprets and responds to the information given can accomplish what he or she set out to do. But let us not confuse the successful results of that intelligent *user* behaviour with the *system's* behaviour and describe the "bibliographic control system" as intelligent.

The technical system does not cooperate with the user, rather the user uses the system for his or her purposes. Those with whom the library user is really cooperating are the persons who create the information entered into the system and the designers who attempt to develop a system in response to known practices. These forms of cooperation are what make the system work, but this cooperation depends on real relationships among users, librarians and designers or else the problems and questions of the users will remain poorly understood or simply unknown to those creating and managing the information system.

Communities of Practice
Of particular interest to music librarians is that the Working Group's single vision of our future as a technical production/problem gives no attention to the place of non-technical knowledge in the library. In this future, librarianship has nothing to do with any disciplinary knowledge except LIS. The redefinition of bibliographic control considers that activity to be a matter of managing rather than establishing relationships, a shift definitely reflecting the reorientation away from institutional purposes and user practices and towards management of abstractions as though those abstract entities posited by FRBR have no special relationships to communities of practice.

On page 10 of the report we read that "separation of the communities of practice that manage [different resource types] is no longer desirable, sustainable, or functional," and "Consistency of description ... is becoming less significant than the ability to make connections between environments." The implications of this are difficult to grasp. The "different communities of bibliographic practice" mentioned refer to those who manage different formats in the library; there is no reference here to user communities, nor to disciplinary differences. Do music librarians manage stuff or do all of their activities relate to user communities of interest and their needs? Your answer ought to be that you do both: the former to serve the latter. The Working Group simply failed to consider the latter.

The Old versus The New
Further on we read that "bibliographical control cannot continue to be seen as being limited to library catalogs" but of course it never was. The authors of the report wish to make this claim in order to present all that other bibliographic information as now, thanks to the World Wide Web, finally available for library reuse.

Legacy data—data "not designed for the current and emerging machine environment"—is data created for other uses, for past practices involving past technical systems and their users. The problems we are now experiencing with legacy data are the same problems that we now encounter and will always encounter with any data created elsewhere, by others and at times other than our present needs. It is the problem of reuse. This includes not only technical problems of interoperability but problems of differences in purposes, practices and user communities. Metadata reuse is not the solution as the Working Group insists, but the source of many of our problems, itself a problem to be dealt with.

By calling for the harvesting and reuse of information produced in other areas of the library and outside it, bibliographic control must now extend over and include all information including citation, quotation, criticism and computational analysis. That seems to be a big move: it is nothing less than claiming that the research process is now to be performed by the bibliographic control system, not the user. But how much will future practices of users and librarians differ from current and previous practices even given such a system? Whereas formerly the librarian and the user went from one card or volume or shelf to the next depending on the sources consulted, now the move is from link to link. Yet the practice of research remains the same as always: determining what you want to look for, deciding how to go about looking for it, evaluating what turns up and so on. Looking only at the technical process, then yes, the report rightly describes this as a "dramatic transformation"; if we look at research in libraries as an intellectual activity, then it has hardly changed at all. Perspective in this matter is everything.

Cooperation or Reliance?
The assumption that "bibliographic control" is the management of a technical system global in scope requires the Working Group to stipulate its organizational prerequisites. Thus the report overflows with calls for coordination, cooperation, decen-

tralization, taking responsibility, eliminating barriers to sharing and reuse of metadata, all of which sounds so nice to our ears. I, at least, am all for it! Yet this language serves to hide the problems rather than reveal them. The Working Group offers cooperation and reuse as solutions that must be adopted, but any of you who have tried to cooperate, decentralize, take responsibility, or reuse metadata will know that our main *problems* proceed from these activities—not our solutions.

The Working Group's understanding of cooperation is that we can create basic records that serve our institution well enough and they will also be available for other institutions to enhance or otherwise alter to suit their purposes. This is all splendid except that we notice that this is not an option, it is obligatory. Sharing and cooperation is an obligation now because LC (and all of us) have to *rely* on the work of others. That little word **RELY** slipped in there because it had to. We have been told that the information is already there and all we have to do is decide how to utilize it. But as soon as LC and other libraries can create basic records that others will find it *necessary* to enhance, in order for it to serve their purposes, cooperation and sharing become obligatory because what the report does not say and even denies is that those basic records indicate the absence —not the presence—of information just waiting to be tapped. A more carefully considered understanding of cooperation would see that cooperation requires not only commonly agreed upon goals and standards, but that everyone involved must fullfil those goals according to those standards in every action they undertake.

We should also especially note that last admonition for LC to consider when to discontinue its efforts. It is one thing to discontinue efforts when changing circumstances mean that the goals of the library are no longer served by those efforts; it is quite another matter when those efforts are discontinued on the assumption that someone else will take over the burden of making just those efforts for us, for that is not cooperating with others, it is exploiting them.

The relationships created by relying on others within a system designed for exploitation of given resources are praised as cooperation and collaboration in one paragraph but decried as dependencies in another. Compare the following statements:

LC may need to be able to rely on the work of others (p. 11)
Long-term dependence on Library of Congress bibliographic services leaves the users of those services increasingly vulnerable to any changes in them. (p. 17)

How are we to comprehend a report that demands that LC must depend on bibliographic data produced by others for their purposes when at the same time we are warned that our dependence on LC leaves us increasingly vulnerable to any changes? This warning applies to all dependencies on external data sources and is a major problem for understanding and implementing the proposed recommendations of the Working Group.

Difference in the Bibliographic Universe
Cataloging and collection development according to the demands of local purposes, users and budgets is replaced by the demand that everything be controlled. We may recall Deanna Marcum's earlier statement "the intellectual integrity of collections built and nurtured by knowledgeable individuals is a lasting tribute to the scholarly community. This is the function that may not be readily accommodated in a digital library."[1] The report assumes that the "explosion of materials" must be under our "bibliographic control" and since we cannot afford to control all of it item by item "the model of item-by-item manual transcription can no longer be sustained." What the report fails to note is that the past model of item by item description was coupled with policies regarding collection development. Collection development, we know, has long been regarded as impossi-

---

[1] Deanna Marcum, "Digital libraries: For whom? For what?" *Journal of academic librarianship* v.23, March 1997, p.81-84.

ble in a web environment, and undesirable at that, since we now want everything.

The universe of information is assumed to be a given commodity which libraries will exploit, NOT a developing resource which we are creating together for a particular purpose. By treating the differences among the various creators and users of information as irrelevant to bibliographic control, all information in the bibliographic universe can be treated as simply given to us ready made and available for exploitation. But libraries have some difficulties exploiting publishers and when they want cooperation they find that it presupposes common goals and purposes, neither of which exist in the bibliographic universe.

Significant differences among the actors in the bibliographic universe are denied or declared insignificant in some recommendations, but emphasized and remedies proposed in others. Compare the following recommendations.

1.1.1.1. Be more flexible in accepting bibliographic data from others ... that do not conform precisely to U.S. library standards
1.1.1.6. Demonstrate to publishers the business advantages of supplying complete and accurate metadata
1.2.1.1. Share responsibility for creating original cataloging according to interest, use and ability
1.1.3. Develop content and format guidelines for submission of ONIX data to the CIP program and require publishers participating in the program to comply with these guidelines.
2.1.2.1. All: Adopt as a guiding principle that some level of access must be provided to all materials as a first step to comprehensive access, as appropriate. Allow for different cataloging levels depending on the types of documents, their nature, and richness.

The first and fifth recommendations allow for differences in cataloging levels but the second and fourth refuse to admit them. We are asked to share data that does not conform to our local standards (1.1.1.1) but at the same time to share responsibility for creating data according to the local context, i.e. interest, use and ability (1.2.1.1). And so on, and so forth. Given that we are urged to share all "changes that might benefit the broader community" (p. 13) and to take advantage of the "many other sources of data" including user-contributed and computationally derived information that might be useful, what can "complete and accurate metadata" possibly mean for anyone in the "supply chain"? The notions of complete and accurate are inseparable from purposes and the practices which support them, and thus this appeal across "communities of bibliographic practice" constitutes the denial of the fundamental problem which is then proffered as the solution to a different problem, the interoperability of technical systems. In this global fantasy all differences among "players" are ignored or their importance denied.

The allowance for different cataloging levels according to "the types of documents, their nature, and richness" in 2.1.2.1 is made in reference to rare, unique and non-print materials and must be read in connection with the demand that item-by-item description is no longer a sustainable model. We are called to redirect resources towards these materials instead of those materials that have received priority in the past, but unique and non-print materials require not only item-by-item description but far more description as well, due to their nature, and even more if they are digitized. The issue here is straightforward: libraries have "hidden collections" because they at one time decided that certain materials had a lower priority at their institution than some other kinds of materials. The Working Group is simply telling us that we have all got our priorities backwards. I do not deny the importance of the diverse materials held in "hidden collections," but the relative importance of materials is a decision that individual institutions ought to make, not the Working Group.

In regard to recommendation 1.1.3.2. concerning the automatic acceptance of publisher data, the Library of Congress response shows a much clearer grasp of the realities of the technical situation than does the Working Group. There we read *Do not support, because incompatibilities between ONIX and ECIP programming and publishers' workflows make this unworkable at this time. ... not all resources will lend themselves easily to this treatment.* It is good to see that LC understands not only lack of use of ONIX but technical incompatibilities make accepting "these data in a fully automated fashion" unworkable, but it is disappointing to see that issues related to user purposes and their communities of practice are not considered in either the recomendation or the response.

The Working Group has a clear understanding of the necessities of standards for data transmission but has no corresponding understanding of any standards related to social practices and communities of interest. Differences among the various "players" were ignored by the Working Group apparently on the assumption that those differences can be accomodated within the right technical system. With all differences and therefore all problems for cooperation abolished, acceptance of the system as imagined by the Working Group appears as the sole rational option available for all involved. Everyone in the world will willingly adopt the system with all of the demands and constraints imposed on them by US libraries and when everyone has complied with our wishes we will "accept these data in a fully automated fashion." Once this system is in operation the possible discrepancies between publishers' definitions of *full* and *accurate* and any particular library's understanding of the same qualitative matters is an issue that cannot arise, nor will the issue of the value of any user contributed metadata be considered.

The Missing Link, or Qualitative aspects of Bibliographic Control

All qualitative aspects of bibliographic control are related to users, institutional purposes and normative practices and therefore invisible and irrelevant to the functioning of the technical system as such. The system is imagined to work in a manner analogous to email: the message is delivered no matter what the content. Is it possible to consider a scholarly information system in this manner alone? To put the issue in different terms, information and misinformation are equivalent in any technical information system, but can they be understood as equivalent in a system used for scholarly communication?

Scholarly communication is not the only form of communication that occurs in libraries, but it is a very important form that relies on normative practices such as citation. In a report that the Working Group ignored, Malcolm Wright & J. Scott Armstrong begin with the statement "The prevalence of faulty citations impedes the growth of scientific knowledge."[2] This paper brings together three aspects of the problem: the problem of data reuse (drawing citations from sources other than the item in hand), violating the norms of a practice (bad research practices), and the social consequences of these errors (obstacles to the growth of knowledge). The Working Group ignores all these aspects of the practice of bibliography that have previously informed and guided our work as librarians. By rejecting item-by-item description the Working Group has repudiated the cardinal rule of bibliography in scholarly reseach: *de visu* inspection.

The report contains no evidence of seriously considering either bibliography as a practice or quality of data intended for human rather than machine interpretation. The system will ensure data quality through cooperation, Uniform Resource Identifiers and standards. The authors of the report demonstrate an extraordinary confidence in the cooperative tendencies of people who do not agree, a global willingness to adhere to a standard of our choosing, and the capabilities (present or future) of information technologies for dealing intelligently with problems of meaning. I do not share their confidence on any of these issues.

---

[2] Malcolm Wright and J. Scott Armstrong, "Verification of Citations: Fawlty Towers of Knowledge?" MPRA Paper No. 4149, posted 07. November 2007.

What if the available information is incorrect, inadequate or missing? Obviously if "the particular needs of the communities concerned" are to be satisfied by "allowing display and indexing of data elements to vary" as the Working Group suggests, then there must be someone locally devoted to the creation of that additional or variant information and the modification of existing information to fit those local needs. Yet those persons have been eliminated as inefficient in other recommendations and replaced with automatically generated or externally obtained information.

Academic Library Users
In responding to recommendation 1.1.4.2. that the Library of Congress "promote widespread discussion of barriers to sharing data" it is noted that users expect more information than the library ever attempted to provide in the past. Hundreds of tags are not unusual in web resources "so some users have expectations for hundreds of subject headings." Yet while insisting that we meet this expressed desire for more information, the Working Group dismisses as an "unproven assumption" (is that not an oxymoron?) the argument that all users will benefit from information created to support the most demanding users. "Users" everywhere want much more—and we must provide it! the Working Group insists—but the value for the broader community of providing much more is an "unproven assumption" which we must reject. Another glaring contradiction.

On page twenty-seven the Working Group identified the library community's basic problem but it ought to be redirected to the Working Group itself. The Working Group, we must conclude, *needs to focus on identifying and addressing real needs with workable solutions and to guard against having unvalidated assertions or professional ideology be the main drivers of development.* It appears that when real needs are expressed by real users, they are attended to selectively and ignored or rejected when they contradict the professional ideologies so clearly set forth in the Working Group's report. And the solutions the report sets forth have already revealed themselves to be unworkable as I have been documenting in detail for the past five years.

One particularly revealing paragraph of the report may be found in the Background section on page eight. A number of recent library reports on our topic are mentioned and some of their findings and recommendations noted. Conspicuously absent from this discussion are any references to the report commissioned by the University of Chicago.[3] Unlike the reports mentioned by the Working Group, the University of Chicago report was neither undertaken nor written by librarians but rather by a group of faculty members appointed by the Provost. Unlike those other reports the University of Chicago report is a document in which the faculty make it clear what they want from the library. It is the perfect document to help us inform ourselves about user desires in the context of academic research, yet again unlike the other reports, the University of Chicago report was not promoted nor even publicly announced. The report was buried in silence as though it were regarded as simply user resistance to the library of the future. Is this how we librarians in our infinitely superior wisdom regard the expressed desires of our users? For the Working Group at least, the answer must be: Yes.

The University of Chicago Provost's report reads nothing like the report of the Working Group. For instance, the second general principle guiding the Provost's report is *Any plans for the future of Regenstein [i.e., the Joseph Regenstein library at the U. of Chicago] should be flexible. We are unable to predict the future demands with clarity.*

The fifth particular principle is the following:

The rapidly changing technical environment means that we need to develop serious instruction in library research. ... Yet most of our entering students of all levels have relatively minimal expe-

---

[3] http://www.lib.uchicago.edu/e/about/finalreport.html

rience with library work. The Task Force is persuaded that there remain crucial skills of knowledge assembly that students do not learn on their own, and that a serious effort must be made to teach them.

Rather than recognizing the rapidly changing technical environment, the Working Group foolishly declares what the future will be, and although they go on at length about the importance of education for librarianship, user education is never mentioned. Instead, on page 31 of the Working Group's report we read that libraries must orient themselves towards the lowest common denominator and not seek to satisfy the sophisticated users.

The Working Group rejects user education as it does service to its heaviest users. The Working Group assumes that the "crucial skills of knowledge assembly" noted by the University of Chicago report are no longer important in the research process, for **the system will perform all of the work for our users, exactly as the Working Group assumes that the system will perform all of the librarians' work for the library**. Had the Working Group a little more self-knowledge, there would have been a single guiding principle:

We must let someone else do the work and be satisfied with whatever we get, for our users do not care and neither do we.

The Problems We Face
You will have noticed that my talk has been neither resistance to nor advocacy of past, present or hoped for future practices, standards or technologies. The primary issues that the report raises are not those of MARC, Dublin Core, LCSH, RDA, FRBR, Web2.0 or any other structure, standard, operating platform, technique or economic model. The primary issues are related to *what* we are doing, for *whom* and *why*, i.e. matters redefined by the working group in the Guiding Principles. These three questions will be answered differently by every community of bibliographic practice but the Working Group has presumed to

answer for all of us. The real problems we face are precisely what the Working Group offers us as the solutions.

The Working Group's philosophy of bibliographic control is based on its understanding of what happens in libraries: What happens in libraries is the manipulation and exchange of data.

In opposition to this fundamental assumption, I insist that what happens in libraries is communication among members of communities of practice occupying various roles in a system of communication: academic publishers, students, faculty and librarians in the system of scholarly communication; cartographers, commanders and programmers in military communication systems; and musicologists, copyright lawyers, musicians and music publishers in the music industry and music libraries. The problem of bibliographic control is not solely a matter of transport and warehousing but facilitating and improving that human communication.

Although the Working Group declared that the future of bibliographic control will be dynamic not static, the Working Group has understood the system of bibliographic control in terms of its architecture alone, ignoring its dynamics. It is in their misunderstanding of the social dynamics of the purposeful use of technical systems that the members of the Working Group demonstrate their inattention to the use of the system, their lack of research on socio-technical systems, the inadequacy of their model of the system and the debilitating effects of their assumptions about socio-technical systems in general and shared information systems in particular. Because the Working Group understood the problem to be a simple technical problem, like Vannevar Bush they offer the current technical system as the solution to all tomorrow's problems: problems of human communication are solved by data transfer, problems of meaning are solved by URIs and computational analysis, and the social problems of organization and conflicting purposes are solved by simply demanding that everyone do what the Working Group thinks everyone ought to do: Cooperate!

Part 2. How Now Brown Cow? or The Future of MOUG

A matter that has been a concern of mine for a long time is the relationships between communities of practice and cataloging, bibliography and reference work. When it comes to resources for specific communities of interest I believe, to quote the Working Group, the "separation of the communities of practice that manage them is no longer desirable, sustainable, or functional.

Whether or not the future develops according to the vision of the Working Group, it seems to me that for music cataloging, as for all cataloging, bibliography and reference work, the division of work among librarians ought to be determined by the user communities of practice rather than along the lines of library practices. You will already know my reason why: in order to meaningfully communicate with library users about their needs and desires we must be involved in the same community of interests and practices. While this is the rationale for departmental libraries, we need to realize that the segregation of music collections from other types of materials as well as the functions related to them has been standard practice in many libraries mainly because of their physical characteristics and the necessity of having these managed by persons who can read music. In a digital library where all access is through metadata, the differences among these various types of materials is, at least in the thinking of the Working Group, no longer significant enough to merit special communities of bibliographic practice for their management.

What then? The selection, cataloging and reference work once performed by a librarian who was an integral part of the departmental life will become the responsibility of the main library and its generalists. The various aspects of library work will then be divided according to the library oriented tasks rather than united in the coherent management of a specific collection. From then on the collection will simply be a fragmented subset of the main library and the system considered as a whole will be expected to serve the user. In that system the management of what was once a carefully, deliberately and intelligently developed and managed collection will be the responsibility of an ever changing roster of persons with no knowledge of the collection as a collection and probably no involvement in the practices of those for whom the collection was being developed. The same cataloger and the same reference librarian will deal with both Roy Harris the linguist and Roy Harris the composer. But fortunately for most of you here, that is not the situation in music libraries, and that precisely because of the special position of music.

If we assume the vision of the future outlined in the Working Group report and an administration that still considers it important for someone in the library to have a knowledge of music, what might change? I think probably that the collapse of cataloging, bibliography and reference will be an attractive option for administration, and assuming enough such librarians for any given collection, a real step forward. A persistent critique of catalogers, classification systems and subject heading terminology is that they are oriented toward the librarian and incomprehensible for the users. There is a lot of truth to that. If the music librarian is involved in all aspects of music librarianship, then his or her participation in reference work will be a constant source of knowledge and ideas for improvement of cataloging and cataloging tools from the users' perspectives, as well as guiding the selection of materials to support the interests and needs of a constantly varying student body and faculty. In turn, the practice of cataloging will be an extraordinary aid in understanding the potential and limitations of the information available to the searching technologies in reference work. It will also, I hope, lead the librarian as bibliographer to carefully consider the costs and expertise required for cataloging in every purchasing decision since she will be doing the cataloging. And of course responsibility for developing a collection will provide an excellent perspective from which to provide consistent cataloging as well as advance knowledge for reference work.

What about the worst case scenario? If the big heads in the library world follow the mixed chorus of voices declaring that both collection development and cataloging are impossible and unnecessary in a digital library whose boundaries are imagined or intended to coincide with the limits of all the world's information, then I cannot see where there would be any room for music librarians. The question for music librarians is therefore whether there is any justification for a digital departmental library or at least a music specialist. If you would agree with me in thinking that the universe of all the world's information is too large a universe for anyone to navigate via the single box provided by a search engine, if you would agree that collection development conceived as limiting the universe of all the world's information to materials selected to support a particular community of interest and practice is not only justifiable but highly desirable, then your future library and the future of your problems of bibliographic control are yours to decide, develop and perhaps most of all to fight for.

Thank you. La lucha continua.

VIII

Carlo Revelli on the (Non)Autonomy of Cataloging

For many years I have been amazed at the number of people, including some catalogers, who sincerely believe that with a couple keywords—in English—typed into a search box, everything that needs to be considered will be handed to us. In an environment saturated with claims about access to all the world's knowledge and demands for international standards and cooperation, the universe of discourse is more often than not reduced to whatever is online and in English: nothing else counts. An international approach to libraries ought at least to seek out ideas expressed beyond the confines of the English language. Unfortunately, getting to that literature—in spite of our wonderful search engines and specialized databases—is not always easy.

A few years ago in his review of "*Le catalogue*," a special issue of the *Revue de la Bibliothèque nationale de France*, Michael Carpenter wrote "For reasons that are not entirely clear, finding information on the cataloging practices of other countries, even Western European countries such as France, is always a difficult task for those working in American libraries."[1] He concluded his review with the remark "It is perhaps a sign of linguistic provincialism that only eleven American libraries are currently recorded as holding issues of the *Revue*. Given the utility of the material in journals such as the one under review, such collection development failures cannot help American librarianship learn from other traditions."[2] While book review editor of *Cataloging & Classification Quarterly* Carpenter brought to the attention of the readers of this journal a number of important works on cataloging that were written in European languages and this new column is an attempt to take a step further in that direction.

The International Observer will be an occasional column in *Cataloging & Classification Quarterly* modeled on and named after Carlo Revelli's column *Osservatorio Internazionale*. Revelli's column has appeared regularly in *Biblioteche Oggi* since 1994, and in it he reviews the non-Italian periodical literature on a particular topic, weaving a diversity of perspectives and problems together in a running commentary and questioning of that topic. It is a column that represents the thinking of a distinguished scholar of cataloging theory and history as well as the perspectives and problems of a public library director. Revelli does not suffer from provincialism but pays attention to the special needs of "provincial" and special libraries of all kinds, as well as special classes of library users. More than just a survey of a topic and the literature about it, each article combines Revelli's careful selection from the literature with his intelligent discussion, the result being something very different from (and an excellent supplement to) any set of items captured by keyword. It is a column that I have enjoyed so much that I have often wondered why no such column appears in any Amer-

---

[1] Michael Carpenter, Review of: *Revue de la Bibliothèque nationale de France* no. 9. "Le catalogue." *Cataloging & Classification Quarterly* 36, no. 2 (2003): 102.
[2] Ibid., 106.

ican or other English language publication. Hence my proposal to CCQ and the initiation of the column you are now reading.

The nature of this column will differ slightly from that of *Osservatorio Internazionale*. Whereas Revelli's column appears in a journal devoted to librarianship in general, the primary goal here will be to discuss recent literature on particular topics relevant to cataloging and classification, whether managerial issues, standards, tools, practices, cooperation, or any topic at all that may appear in the literature related to librarianship, information science, or any other field that an open mind can relate to cataloging.

Furthermore Revelli generally devotes a great deal of space to publications from the Anglo-American provinces whereas here the object will be to focus on publications not in English and published outside the Anglo-American world. In a world in which globalization is often assumed to be Americanization, a knowledge and appreciation of the differences that actually exist among us appears to me to be an urgent necessity. Michael Carpenter wrote in his review of the first edition (1996) of Revelli and Visintin's *Il Catalogo*, "For those whose outlook on librarianship is parochially American, I definitely recommend the book as a sovereign antidote to the unjustified preconception that all the world holds to the same views on cataloging that the English-speaking world has."[3] It is my hope that this column will function in a similar manner by introducing readers to the great range of perspectives, problems, research, and experiences that exist today.

The most appropriate topic for the first column is the writings of Carlo Revelli himself. Although Revelli has been writing about cataloging since 1960 I will focus on three books published during the past decade: *Il Catalogo* (with Giulia Visintin, 3rd ed., 2008), *Citazione bibliografica* (2002), and *La biblioteca come teoria e come pratica: antologia degli scritti*

---

[3] Michael Carpenter, Review of: Carlo Revelli, *Il Catalogo*, *The Library Quarterly* 70, no. 3 (2000): 403.

(2006). Rather than review these books independently, I will follow Revelli's method of looking at them together with a particular topic in mind. The topic I have chosen arose directly out of my reading these books in close succession, and I will formulate it as a question: Is it possible (or desirable) to understand cataloging as an autonomous activity?

The question took a while to form in my mind; initially I reflected on the experience of *déjà vu* while reading his *Citazione bibliografica*. Nearly all of the issues discussed in that book were familiar as topics in cataloging, but the treatments discussed by Revelli varied. He begins by distinguishing quotation from citation (*citazione* is used for both in Italian), limiting himself in this book to the latter. He then proceeds to discuss footnotes, again noting that his topic is limited to bibliographical footnotes. Having established the limits of his study, he differentiates between bibliographical description and citation in the section "The description of the document."

> We know that the description of a document, whether this be physically independent or contained within the publication, in itself does not present problems of availability but only of identification and comprehensibility.[4]

This "double necessity of describing and identifying" a document in the practice of citation differs from the practice of descriptive bibliography in being more modest "in so far as the minimum of information that allows identification and finding the document is sufficient."[5]

From here he moves on to the elements of citation, discussing these in the context of International Standard Bibliographic Description (ISBD), the Italian cataloging norms (RICA, or *Regole italiane di catalogazione per autori*), and the Anglo-American cataloging standard *Anglo-American Cataloguing*

---

[4] Carlo Revelli, *Citazione bibliografica* (Roma: Associazione italiana biblioteche, 2002), 8.
[5] Ibid., 10.

Rules, Second Edition (AACR2). The many descriptive elements that one may include in a citation vary in their importance, and "Therefore the opportunity of offering greater detail depends upon the importance given to the text, to its characteristics."[6] He proceeds to discuss the various elements that may and variously are included in bibliographical citations, concluding his remarks with a discussion of punctuation, capitalization, the use of italics, and so on. Punctuation in ISBD, he notes, is not really punctuation but a system of signs to qualify the meaning of what follows. ISBD punctuation conceived in this manner calls into question not only many discussions of punctuation but the very different status of punctuation in Resource Description and Access (RDA). I will not pursue the implications of this interpretation here, but his final observation in this section "We ought to seek not an absolute coherence, but coherence within the document, and this coherence should be compatible with comprehension and legibility"[7] hints at the role of punctuation as a system of signs that work in an international setting.

We move on to problems regarding the order of elements within a citation and access to the citation within a document such as a bibliography or catalog. Description by itself, he notes

> does not offer points of access, or in other words, it does not function to find information relative to the document, except in the case of the online catalog within which one can find it by means of any word the description contains. If we consider a bibliographical compilation or even more simply the bibliographical citations at the end of a text, these conditions require the descriptions to be organized according to fixed criteria. Every description can be ordered according to a determinate access point, compatible with the other entries assigned to the other descriptions in the same bibliography. The criteria can be

---

[6] Ibid., 13.
[7] Ibid., 26.

> alphabetic by author, alphabetic by subject, systematic, chronological, by type of material and so on.[8]

Here Revelli is reprising an argument from one of his most brilliant papers, "L'intestazione principale: un reperto archeologico?" [Main entry: an archeological relic?], published originally in 1996 and reprinted in *La biblioteca come teoria e come pratica*. In that article Revelli examines citation practices in the contexts of printed bibliographies, card catalogs, and online databases. He discusses a number of writers from Domanovszky to Gorman and beyond on the obsolete and "arbitrary distinction between main and added entries"[9] (quoting Nora Tamberg from a 1974 paper), and among the quotations he provides we read R. Conrad Winke's remark "Catalogers no longer have the luxury of continuing out-dated practices solely for the sake of tradition."[10] To this unanimous chorus Revelli responds:

> In fact, we are not dealing with a luxury that is perhaps even superfluous and devoid of utility: the issue here is to evaluate whether this norm [the concept of main entry] retains any meaning when transported into an environment different from the one for which it was established. Olivia M.A. Madison notes the frequent doubts concerning the utility of the principal of main entry in the online catalog, but in spite of the costs associated with it, considers it useful for controlled access . . . as the principal element of the citation that identifies a publication since author-title form of citation is preferred. The alternative would be to present incoherent solutions: "deleting auth-

---

[8] Ibid., 26–27.

[9] Carlo Revelli, "L'intestazione principale: un reperto archeologico?" in his *La biblioteca come teoria e come pratica* (Milano: Editrice Bibliografica, 2006), 204.
[10] Ibid., 205.

orship as a prominent part of the citation process would only create greater confusion with catalog organization."[11]

With this argument, the question that forms the topic of this first installment of *The International Observer* hit me with full force. Is cataloging an autonomous, purely technical operation carried out in libraries, to be changed at will to accommodate whatever technical possibilities arise without regard to practices or contexts outside the library? Are the historical theories, practices and norms of bibliography, citation, and cataloging irrelevant in all contexts simply because in one technical context they are no longer important for certain kinds of activities?

With these questions in mind I looked at a number of textbooks, handbooks, and general treatises on cataloging and metadata to see how the activity of cataloging was related to practices of citation and bibliography in the world outside the library. The result was a revealing look at what may be the chief source of disconnect between cataloging practice and the world of library users; it is not the conservatism of catalogers that holds back progress in cataloging theory and cataloging practices, but the common conception of cataloging as an autonomous activity unrelated to other practices, the view of cataloging as a technical operation that follows technical developments while ignoring existing (and longstanding) social practices arising from literacy.

Bakewell, in his *Manual of Cataloguing Practice*, began his book with a chapter on "The nature and purpose of catalogues" in which we read "The principles of cataloguing apply equally to the entry of items in catalogues, bibliographies, indexes and abstracts."[12] In the paragraph that follows this commendable statement Bakewell mentions Andrew Osborn's call

---
[11] Ibid.
[12] K. G. B. Bakewell, *A Manual of Cataloging Practice* (Oxford: Pergamon Press, 1972), 1.

for considering "bibliographies and book-trade lists, as well as library catalogues, when formulating codes of cataloguing rules"[13] and with that we are done with the relationships between cataloging and any other activity.

In his 1983 monograph *Katalogkunde: Formalkataloge und formale Ordnungsmethoden*, Klaus Haller offered the reader a few paragraphs on bibliographies and their relation to catalogs on page 21–22;[14] in even fewer words Bolognini and Pedrini[15] begin with formal definitions of cataloging as distinct from bibliography, and Isabelle Dussert-Carbone and Marie-Renée Cazabon offer no remarks on bibliography or citation at all.[16]

Arlene Taylor (*Wynar's Introduction to Cataloging and Classification*, revised 9th edition) begins right away with chapter one "Cataloging in context," the purpose of which is "to set the context in which cataloging takes place."[17] Neither bibliography nor citation nor any user practices are mentioned; instead we are introduced immediately to "bibliographic control": "Cataloging is a subset of the larger field that is sometimes called bibliographic control, or organization of information." She defines bibliographic control in the words of Elaine Svenonius first ("the skill or art . . . of organizing knowledge (information) for retrieval") and then Smiraglia ("the creation, storage, manipulation, and retrieval of bibliographic data").[18] The only practices and context considered is that of the librarian working with a technical system, not with a user or user practices.

The literature on metadata is too vast and my knowledge of it too limited for me to make any kind of generalizations.

---

[13] Ibid.
[14] Klaus Haller, *Katalogkunde: Formalkataloge und formale Ordnungsmethoden* (München: K.G. Saur, 1983).
[15] Pierantonio Bolognini and Ismaela Pedrini, *Manuale del catalogatore* (Milano: Editrice Bibliografica, 1986).
[16] Isabelle Dussert-Carbonee and Marie-Renée Cazabon, *Le catalogage: method et pratiques* (Paris: Èditions du cercle de la librairie, 1988).
[17] Arlene Taylor, *Wynar's Introduction to Cataloging and Classification*, revised 9th edition (Westport, Conn.: Libraries Unlimited, 1994), 3.
[18] Ibid.

What I have read, browsed, and checked the indexes to reveals a literature situated entirely within the context of computer architecture and programming; citation and bibliography are words nowhere to be found, and cataloging is treated as an irritating and limiting term fit for past situations, not the present much less the future. Even where "the users" are trotted out on nearly every page (e.g., in Weinberger's *Everything is Miscellaneous*), this literature is theoretically grounded in a technical process and "the users" are considered only as users of some particular technical system.

Perhaps the most revealing remarks appear in Lois Mai Chan's *Cataloging and Classification: An Introduction* (2nd edition). Chan describes both cataloging and classification as "operations," not as practices, and neither are related to any practices outside the library. At the very beginning she notes that she will discuss "cataloging and classification in terms of three basic functions: descriptive cataloging, subject access and classification"[19] and a couple pages later we read that "one cannot prepare a bibliographic description of a document without resorting to AACR, nor can one classify an item without using a classification scheme."[20] This is an astonishing claim, and Revelli offers us abundant evidence of alternatives, both historical and theoretical, to such a truly insular view of cataloging and classification.

Revelli's discussion of cataloging is remarkable for the extent to which it is founded upon an understanding of cataloging as one of many practices, past and present, that must be integrated in order to be able to use a catalog (of whatever form) or bibliography, as well as when reading and writing. Cataloging is a practice that presupposes a literate culture and all of the practices associated with and arising from the activities of writing and reading.

---

[19] Lois Mai Chan, *Cataloging and Classification: An Introduction*, 2nd edition (New York: McGraw-Hill, 1994), xix.
[20] Ibid., xxi.

For Revelli, citation is both the historic justification for such principles as main entry and a continuing practice itself arising from our concepts of authorship, which is in turn rooted in the practice of writing. In an essay written before the online catalog appeared in his library ("Divagazioni sul concetto di autore" [Remarks on the concept of the author], originally published in 1976) Revelli made this point clear: "The principal card is compiled entirely on the basis of the concept of the author . . . while the secondary cards are composed on the basis of the probable reasons for searching."[21] In the aforementioned essay "L'intestazione principale: un reperto archeologico?" Revelli returns to this theme, remarking "The conflict between bibliographical entity and literary entity persists and assumes a new vitality appropriate to the alternatives facilitated by the online catalog."[22] Revelli concludes by noting that he is averse to predicting the future and joining the chorus agreeing that the principal of main entry "no longer has any reason to exist in a catalog, whether a card catalog or online."[23] In certain forms of organizing information, in the case of musical compositions with generic titles, depending on the design of and policies regulating the implementation of the technical system and the data that we put into it, we may find that the concept of main entry still has a role to play in a wide variety of situations. The future, after all, is not something any of us know with any certainty.

Revelli was a much better prognosticator than that chorus he would not join. Technical systems and their requirements seem to be more clearly understood now than when Revelli was a rather lonely voice arguing for the significance of the concept

---

[21] Carlo Revelli, "Divagazioni sul concetto di autore," in his *La biblioteca come teoria e come pratica: antologia degli scritti* (Milano: Editrice Bibliografica, 2006), 99.

[22] Carlo Revelli, "L'intestazione principale: un reperto archeologico?" in his *La biblioteca come teoria e come pratica: antologia degli scritti* (Milano: Editrice Bibliografica, 2006), 208.

[23] Ibid.

of the author and the principle of main entry. The desirability of indicating the nature of a person's relationship to a work is now acknowledged, as is the technical necessity of making that relationship explicit. Just having a name in a bibliographical record is not enough; if we want to know why that person is associated with a particular item, that information has to be provided for it to be available to the searching system: automated means for discovering and identifying those relationships are wholly inadequate. With RDA we have not only a relator code for author— "A person, family, or corporate body responsible for creating a work that is primarily textual in content" (RDA, Appendix I)[24] —which is the old principle of main entry, but for hundreds of other kinds of relationships that may hold between a person and a particular item.

Cataloging rules (e.g., for the determination of main entry) are not arbitrary rules invented by catalogers and retained only because we are conservative, but practical responses to those readers who still insist on referring to and searching for publications by their authors and their titles. The long list of writers who have insisted on the uselessness of any concept of main entry have simply thought about catalogs in only one form—as electronic databases—and in no relation to any of the social practices surrounding the creation and use of bibliographical information. This is a mistake Revelli never makes. For him, citations "should be comprehensible and permit one to search for the corresponding document in a bibliography or in a library catalog."[25] That is, the citation practices of authors, the cataloging practices of librarians and the searching practices of library users cannot be considered in isolation.

In *Il catalogo* Revelli comments on the connection between automation and the fate of the principle of main entry, and brings us back to the user and the world in which the library user lives:

---

[24] ttp://www.rdatoolkit.org/constituencyreviewfiles/Phase1AppI 10 27 08.pdf
[25] Revelli, *Citazione bibliografica*, 54.

> We will not consider the changes as a path towards an actual or future perfection, but as corresponding to the changing exigencies of a changing culture. The one who consults the catalog has already his own information for verifying the existence or not of a publication, a work or simply the name of a person: the reader has therefore the necessity of finding a publication or of retrieving a series of documents and has his own knowledge on the basis of which he searches the catalog.[26]

Citation, bibliography, cataloging, reading, and searching a library catalog using that citation form a single complex of a wide variety of persons, practices, and tools that must be integrated in our understanding as well as in those practices. That brings us to a second characteristic feature of Revelli's approach to cataloging.

In regard to the question of autonomy, Revelli and many writers of the past decades are in agreement rather than disagreement on one matter, and that is that the library and its catalog must not be considered autonomous with respect to the library's users. While few writers on cataloging and metadata pay attention to bibliography and none discuss citation, it seems that everyone these days is referring to library users, their desires and practices, often scolding anyone who disagrees with them—real or imagined—and holding up "the users" as proof that they are right. Here again, however, reading Revelli one comes up with a very different attitude and approach to "the users." Instead of claiming that "the users" want this or that and hauling them out to justify his approach, Revelli always brings us back to the users to remind the reader that his (Revelli's—or anyone else's) way is not universally binding nor eternal but may be adapted or abandoned according to the needs of those users in

---

[26] Carlo Revelli, in collaborazione con Giulia Visintin, *Il Catalogo*, Nuova edizione con aggiornamenti (Milano: Editrice Bibliografica, 2008), 185.

the reader's library whom Revelli does not know and about whom he makes only one claim: their practices and needs should inform the way you do things in your library. The development of norms, international or otherwise, and their adoption and application are very different matters.

This approach to the users of the library was in fact the most overwhelming feature of *Il catalogo*, and is no less evident in the essays in *La biblioteca come teoria e come pratica.* It is perhaps most spectacularly revealed in the appendices to *Citazione bibliografica*, where Revelli reproduces about fifty pages of various forms of bibliographic citations. At one point in the text Revelli makes the casual remark that his examples M and N in the appendices "confirm the great variety of solutions" to the problem under discussion.[27] At another point he asks "And if it were necessary to indicate a title in the absence of an author? Well, whether outside or inside the parentheses, in whatever manner it has to be present. . . . Let's try to have some faith in the intelligence of the reader."[28] Perhaps the most direct statement to reflect this approach is his remarks on his own practice of citation in the book itself:

> In homage to the liberty so often recommended, the method of citation applied in this publication is not intended to be prescriptive. Apart from being coherent with this publication itself, it is only intended to offer ease of using the citations in the text and the bibliography at the end, to render the documents recognizable for the purpose of finding them. In order to give an idea of the variety of criteria for citations, I have thought it convenient to present a certain number of examples furnished with notes.[29]

---

[27] Revelli, *Citazione bibliografica*, 37.
[28] Ibid., 43.
[29] Ibid., 50.

Revelli's awareness and acceptance of "the great variety of solutions" is in stark contrast with an attitude prevalent these days and recommended by the Library of Congress Working Group on the Future of Bibliographic Control.[30] According to this opposite view, all the "players" in the bibliographic universe should be encouraged to adopt our standards (in some matters at least), and in other matters librarians are called on to accept—all of us—the standards in use by some other group of "players." In this view of things what is important is that the technical system function as it is designed to function; standards are created or changed to promote technical interoperability, and cooperation means everyone must adapt to that system now, and change with it as it changes. Revelli—no stronger nor more intelligent advocate of standards and international cooperation can be found—does not think about standards and cooperation in the manner of the aforementioned Working Group.

> New instruments create new exigencies and the modalities with which information about documents are formed and modified, but the necessity of collecting and distributing information about documents persists, and the recognition of that necessity is common to the compilers of bibliographies and of catalogs of all times. Cataloging norms themselves are the result of the recognition of an exigency and it has always been the result of a professional deformity to consider them as ends in themselves. Without them, we could not bring together information

---

[30] Revelli's "great variety of solutions" refers to the practice of citation, not to cataloging, which was the object of the Working Group's report. Revelli does not suggest that the same kind of variety of solutions available in citation is possible in cataloging. My intention here is to contrast the general openness in Revelli's work for the necessity of local institutions to develop policies appropriate to their mission, where the great variety of institutions means that there are indeed a "great variety of solutions," with the approach of the Working Group, which seems to argue that theirs is a single solution and it is not a local solution.

in a coherent manner. From the necessity of fitting a norm to new situations and exigencies follow the ruptures in the coherence of the catalog, the convenience of constructing new catalogs when they reveal themselves incompatible with the old ones, and the opportunity for establishing new norms more convenient in the new situation. These are contradictions that it would be dishonest to ignore, but which will be more easily surmounted if considered in light of the purposes of the catalog.[31]

For Revelli, cataloging does not exist to enable technical systems to operate; on the contrary our technical systems—and they are many and varied, not single—as well as our cataloging practices have always been, are now and must remain rooted in practices such as citation, a practice that, as he demonstates so clearly in *Citazione bibliografica*, reveals an enormous variety at present and historically. In the practice of citation an author describes a resource in a manner which permits the reader to evaluate the source, locate it, and read (or listen to) it; a technical system does not describe anything for anyone. A technical system follows its user's actions according to a program, and offers its users whatever that programmed response produces. Citing a resource using a Universal Resource Locator (URL), for example, may sometimes give the reader some clues as to what and where to find the resource to which it "points" but often does not. A Digital Object Identifier (DOI) tells the reader nothing, and a broken link only reminds the reader of the limitations of a technical system poorly integrated with the practices it is supposed to support.

---

[31] Carlo Revelli, in collaborazione con Giulia Visintin, *Il Catalogo*, Nuova edizione con aggiornamenti (Milano: Editrice Bibliografica, 2008), 18. In an email to me Revelli noted that he does not feel that his approach to standards and cooperation contrast so sharply with the recommendations of the Working Group. Since I agree with what Revelli has written, I assume this means that Revelli and I disagree on how to understand the report of the Working Group.

No other writer on cataloging or metadata has integrated the library user so completely into the theoretical foundations of cataloging; Revelli does not bring library users into his discussion to justify his arguments but as the ones whose practices should provide us with the objects of our endeavors as well as determine which among the many possible alternatives, orientations, methods, and policies available to the library will be chosen. Revelli's users are not abstractions, any more than his norms or his technologies. They figure prominently not only in the arguments he makes, but in his bibliography, and we learn in his preface that his relationship to the library's users is the experience that has formed his theorizing. He acknowledges

> the librarians, in large part not known to me personally, but who have conversed with me through their writings on cataloging questions and on the relations between the catalog and the public, that public being the end and reason for being of library catalogs. . . . And I offer my thanks to those who frequent the Torino Public Library, whose uncertainties, observations and requests have convinced me to consider the value of the catalog as one of the essential components of the library. . .[32]

The library's users are not creatures of no particular time, of no particular place, and engaged in no particular practices. Nor are library users a homogenous group: "for the library public no single necessity exists, but the necessities vary" according to the kind of library.[33] The public for any particular library, Revelli insists, "does not correspond to a single person cloned thousands of times, but is composed of individuals with different personalities, needs and knowledge."[34] Nor is any library

---

[32] Ibid.
[33] Carlo Revelli, "Il catalogo per soggetti e le aspettative dei bibliotecari nei confronti dell'automazione" in his *La biblioteca come teoria e come pratica* (Milano, Editrice Bibliografica, 2006), 125.
[34] Carlo Revelli, in collaborazione con Giulia Visintin, *Il Catalogo*, 334.

such a no place in no time for no particular purpose: "In other words the public uses the catalog not only according to the needs they have, but according to what information is there."[35] People come to a library because of what they think the library offers them, and that may or may not be what we think we have to offer them or even want to offer them. We may find we are dealing with

> contrasting, when not directly contradictory, needs: what information about what materials for what users? Even if the problems relative to the catalog are presented on the basis of general interests common to all, the actual realization of the catalog is strictly conditioned by the specific characteristics of the library. . . . Each library has its own reason for being, on which depend its complex organization, the acquisition of materials, their availability to the public to which it is devoted, and the information related to that material.[36]

Thinking about the library's mission requires "the recognition of a strict relationship between the materials it possesses, its growth and its public."[37] In cataloging, "not all documents are of equal value for everyone and once again we find ourselves faced with the question of why this library exists, what its public desires" and this means that "each library must formulate cataloging policies appropriate to its own nature and its own public."[38] In cataloging, access points "permit communication between the user and the catalog: the cataloger provides the information and the user finds it."[39]

For Revelli it is clear that cataloging cannot be autonomous with respect to library users, nor with respect to the wide

---

[35] Ibid.
[36] Ibid., 22.
[37] Ibid., 23.
[38] Ibid., 39.
[39] Ibid., 51.

range of social practices associated with a literate culture. And there is yet another sense in which cataloging must not be understood in isolation, as an autonomous activity. In the paragraph "Indexing and cataloging" we read:

> Let us recall that the cataloger cannot call himself such if he limits himself to describing isolated documents and establishing relative access points, without evaluating the accumulation of information within a catalog in which the products of such individual operations must result in compatibilities among them. The catalog in fact is a joining of information and not simply the sum of isolated information, and therefore it must be homogenous and not present contradictions: "we are not faced with the isolated cataloging of a single document: the real problem is how it is to be integrated into the particular information system of which it is to become a part."[40]

Again, Revelli's approach to the problem of catalogers working with a technical system differs radically from that which we have come to expect. Here the cataloger takes responsibility for seeing that the whole system—cataloger, cataloging data, cataloging system—is to be coherently and effectively integrated for the users of that system. That integration, bringing coherence and meaningfulness for the library user is not something the information system does but something the cataloger and the users themselves do, and experience with the library users ought "to lead the cataloger to modify his own behavior."[41] In a discussion of the differences between alphabetic and systematic organization Revelli remarks that this is a matter

> of various ways of organizing information, that in a certain sense we can consider complimentary: the choice of one or the other strategy of searching depends on the

---

[40] Ibid., 55, quoting Teresa Grimaldi.
[41] Ibid.

> knowledge and the necessities of the users. . . . In reality it is a matter of alternative methods and the library that refuses to combine means of access to information significantly limits the possibilities of research on the part of the public.[42]

"Cataloging descriptions do not function autonomously, but are ancillary instruments for identifying documents in order to find them."[43] The catalog, he wants us to understand, "is one of the means for bringing together the materials of a library or library system, but not the only means. . . . there are other means for informing readers."[44] Catalog maintenance "cannot be considered in isolation and is open to and connected with problems related to other aspects of library service."[45]

The papers in *La biblioteca come teoria e come pratica* provide us with many further perspectives on the non-autonomy of cataloging. There we find cataloging related to library management, cooperation, censorship, conservation, minorities, the disabled, special libraries, and public libraries. With so many diverse activities, constituents and problems, Revelli is not easily convinced by the slogans coming from other quarters. "We say that each publication should be cataloged only once? Well, let's try to keep our feet on the ground."[46] Such an attitude, he suggests, is based on the belief that everyone needs the same thing, that needs do not differ from one community or from one kind of user or from one time to another. The irony here is that this "once and forever"—the ultimate dream of the ultimate conservative—approach to cataloging is being preached by folks who think of themselves as the progressive members of the libr-

---

[42] Ibid., 295.
[43] Ibid., 125.
[44] Ibid., 27.
[45] Ibid., 427.
[46] Carlo Revelli, *La biblioteca come teoria e come pratica* (Milano: Editrice Bibliografica, 2006), 224.

ary world. To be sure many of these prophets assume that the catalog record will change automatically, or that nothing need be cataloged at all: everything will be done on the fly by software operating over a multitude of autonomous but always available and flawlessy interoperable databases. This scenario assumes that all problems of interpretation and human interaction with the system will be adequately dealt with in a reasonable amount of time by improvements in software, as for example by a subject access system the structure of which would be "independent of language, having instead a multilingual vocabulary that would not be based on any vocabulary but on conceptual differences."[47] Revelli on the other hand argues that "the diversity of languages and above all cultural variety" impede the rigid adoption of international norms and "make the possibility of putting together terms and lists of authorized headings for different linguistic communities" unlikely unless local situations (geographical and temporal) as well as minority populations are disregarded.

Revelli argues for standards that should be adapted to local circumstances and must change as often as the world changes, for catalogs and cataloging practices that must take account of local circumstances and must change as often as the world around us changes, and for catalogers who adapt accordingly. Revelli's discussions about how these changes should be considered, planned, implemented, and evaluated are based not on fantasies, futurology, and prognostications of technologies to come, nor are they tied to existing technologies. They are based on a deep and intimate knowledge of the great range of past and present practices associated with recording and studying the human experience using all the means we have had at our disposal, a knowledge which brings with it an expectation of change and the necessity of integrating that past world of practices and

---

[47] Revelli, in collaborazione con Giulia Visintin, *Il Catalogo*, 481.

expectations into a new situation that we are making one move at a time.

> Everywhere people are raising questions about the future of paper, the book, of libraries, of librarians . . . but we cannot, today, abandon paper, the book, the library or even the librarian because these exist and function today. . . . . That is not to say that things are destined to remain the same into some distant future, but in view of any future we cannot abandon current reality: I do not see why in this crisis of values and of certainties we must regard the library as something eternal.[48]

Manos a la obra!

* * **

This brief romp through three books by Revelli has not touched upon his 1970 monograph on subject cataloging (a reprint of which will appear soon), nor on most of the nearly 250 items mentioned in the bibliography in *La biblioteca come teoria e come pratica.* By writing so much of liberty I risk misrepresenting him by barely mentioning his stress on cataloging norms as necessary "for making possible the compatibility and integration of cataloging information without limiting their area of application" (e-mail to the author, July 12, 2010). My only defense is that my focus was on the necessity of seeing these practices—citation and cataloging, as well as bibliography and catalog searching—as related activities, and that the role of norms in cataloging as well as library cooperation is another topic, too much to deal with here. I hope I have written enough to turn the attention of many more librarians—not just catalogers—toward

---

[48] Carlo Revelli, *La biblioteca come teoria e come pratica* (Milano: Editrice Bibliografica, 2006), 233.

the work of one of the most extraordinary librarians and theorists of cataloging of the past century.

References
Bakewell, K.G.B. (1972). *A Manual of Cataloging Practice.* Oxford: Pergamon Press.
Bolognini, Pierantonio and Ismaela Pedrini. (1986). *Manuale del catalogatore.* Milano: Editrice Bibliografica.
Carpenter, Michael. (2000). Review of: Carlo Revelli and Julia Visintin, *Il Catalogo*, The Library Quarterly 70, no. 3:401-404.
Carpenter, Michael Carpenter. (2003). Review of: *Revue de la Bibliothèque nationale de France* no. 9. "Le catalogue." *Cataloging & Classification Quarterly* 36, no. 2:102-106.
Chan, Lois Mai. (1994). *Cataloging and Classification: An Introduction*, 2nd edition. New York: McGraw-Hill.
Dussert-Carbonee, Isabelle and Marie-Renée Cazabon. (1988). *Le catalogage: method et pratiques.* Paris: Èditions du cercle de la librairie.
Haller, Klaus. (1983). *Katalogkunde: Formalkataloge und formale Ordnungsmethoden.* München: K.G. Saur.
Revelli, Carlo. (1976/2006). "Divagazioni sul concetto di autore," In: *Studi di biblioteconomia e storia del libro in onore di Francesco Barberi.* A cura di Giorgio De Gregori e Maria Valenti. Roma: AIB, p. 463-475. Reprinted in his *La biblioteca come teoria e come pratica: antologia degli scritti.* Milano: Editrice Bibliografica, 2006.
Revelli, Carlo. (1986/2006). "Il catalogo per soggetti e le aspettative dei bibliotecari nei confronti dell'automazione." In: *Il recupero dell'informazione: atti del Convegno-esposizione bibliografica "Indicizzazione per soggetto e automazione", Trieste, 21-22 ottobre 1985.* A cura di Adriano Dugulin, Antonia Ida Fontana, Annamaria Zecchia. Milano: Editrice Bibliografica. (Atti e documenti; 8), p. 27-53. Reprinted in his *La biblioteca*

come teoria e come pratica. Milano: Editrice Bibliografica, 2006.

Revelli, Carlo (1995/2006). "L'intestazione principale: un reperto archeologico?" In: *Il linguaggio della biblioteca: scritti in onore di Diego Maltese*. Raccolti da Mauro Guerrini. Firenze: Regione Toscana. Giunta regionale. (Toscana-Beni librari; 4). vol. II, p. 589-610. Reprinted in his *La biblioteca come teoria e come pratica.* Milano: Editrice Bibliografica, 2006.

Revelli, Carlo. (2002). *Citazione bibliografica.* Roma: Associazione italiana biblioteche.

Revelli, Carlo. (2006). *La biblioteca come teoria e come pratica.* Milano: Editrice Bibliografica.

Revelli, Carlo. (2008), in collaborazione con Giulia Visintin. *Il Catalogo*, Nuova edizione con aggiornamenti. Milano: Editrice Bibliografica.

Taylor, Arlene. (1994). *Wynar's Introduction to Cataloging and Classification*, revised 9th edition. Westport, Conn.: Libraries Unlimited.

IX

Jakobsonian Library Science?
A Response to Jonathan Tuttle's article "The aphasia of modern subject access"

Abstract

This article responds to Jonathan Tuttle's article "The Aphasia of Modern Subject Access" in which Roman Jakobson's semiology of "shared codes" consisting of preexisting signs is offered as the explanation for two redundant linguistic tools associated with cataloging: LCSH and LCC. The article criticizes Tuttle's terminology, his semiology, and his argument that selection and combination are both necessary for the operation of language but each are associated with only one of these tools.

1. Linguistics for catalogers

Unlike Saussure, Jakobson was no theorist.[1]

Far too often and for far too long cataloging has been theorized and discussed as though it were a technical operation that could be satisfactorily understood without reference to the material and social conditions of libraries, their users, and the corresponding issues in linguistics, semiology, epistemology, ergonomics and the many other areas of inquiry that would seem to be relevant to anyone considering the practices involved. In a recent paper published in *Cataloging & Classification Quarterly* Jonathan Tuttle seeks to go beyond a technical and practical discussion of cataloging with his proposal for a theoretical explanation for why catalogers do what they do. While I laud his attempt to bring some theoretical understanding to discussions of cataloging, that is unfortunately the only positive comment I can make about his essay.

2. Tuttle's terminological muddle

Tuttle's theoretical problems arise partly from his choice of theoretical point of departure: Roman Jakobson's linguistics. Or, as I suspect, a single distinction drawn in one paper by Jakobson, since Tuttle betrays no evidence of ever having read any other paper by any linguist at all, unless one also counts Hutchins as a linguist.[2] Yet even before we get to his discussion of Jakobson, Tuttle treats us to considerable evidence of his own theoretical confusions. He begins, for instance, by posing the question that his theoretical investigation will supposedly answer: "Why do

---

[1] Roy Harris, *Saussure and his interpreters*. 2nd ed. (Edinburgh: Edinburgh University Press, 2003): 94.

[2] Tuttle does mention a statement by W.J. Hutchins from his *Languages of Indexing and Classification: A Linguistic Study of Structures and Functions* (Stevenage, England: P. Peregrinus, 1975), but Hutchins was far from offering a theory of language. His linguistics was a linguistics of classification systems and indexing only.

catalogers use two systems, one notational like *Library of Congress Classification* (LCC) and the other terminological like *Library of Congress Subject Headings* (LCSH), to reach the same goal: subject description and access?"[3]

That opening sentence of his abstract conflates two very different activities—subject description on the one hand, and indication of location information for access to some object on the other—and identifies that conflation as the single goal of two different tools used in those activities. Yet even here, "the same goal" is described as *two* goals: *subject description* and *access*. The failure to distinguish these two quite distinct goals and considering them as a single goal allows him to simplify and restate this "same goal" as a single goal which he takes as his point of departure. The one goal of both LCC and LCSH is, he claims, "to distill the aboutness of an item."[4] What happened to access? With this simplification Tuttle simply denies that access to the items described is a goal of LCC, LCSH and their associated practices. Why he needs to simplify in this fashion becomes clear as his argument develops, for it is only by eliminating all reference to the material and social conditions of libraries, catalogers and library users as these have changed over time that his chosen theory of language can in any way 'explain' these two tools involved in modern cataloging practice.

The conflation of systems, activities and goals in his second paragraph is bad enough, but the means by which he arrives at this position—that classification using LCC and subject description using LCSH share the same goal—is even more breathtaking. The opening two sentences of his introduction inform us that "In every library, language is used to represent language. Between the user and the resource, a record stands as surrogate for that resource, combining the language of an item's content

---

[3] Jonathan Tuttle, "The aphasia of modern subject access" *Cataloging & Classification Quarterly*, v.50, no. 4 (2012): 263.
[4] Ibid., 264.

with the language a patron might use in searching for that item."[5]

The first sentence made me stop to try to understand what he meant. Without the benefit of his subsequent explanation I could not fathom what he meant by "represent"; with the explanation in the following sentence it became clear that he did not mean "language is used to represent language" but rather "language is used to represent (i.e. create a description of) some resource." Unfortunately it seems that Tuttle does not realize that he is confused about what he means, and it is that confusion that permits him to write "represent language" when he is discussing the representation of objects (items or resources in his terminology), and not language. Apparently he has made a series of intellectual moves from library item through subject of item to subject is a concept, eventually ending up with a group of signs and symbols standing for concepts, which is his definition of "system of language." This sliding through equivalencies is an inexcusable confusion on his part, but it is not the only mess he makes in the second sentence: we have yet to investigate "record" and "surrogate."

At a first reading Tuttle's reference to a "record" seems straightforward enough, at least for a reader acquainted with libraries and the language of librarianship. "Surrogate" will probably not raise any eyebrows either (other than my own), but the following clause calls both terms back for reconsideration. The record combines "the language of an item's content with the language a patron might use in searching for that item."[6] Two remarks are necessary here. The first is that the language one finds in a catalog record is a description of an item in which the language of the author or creator of the item in question is interpreted and a new statement is created according to standard practices of description. Thus the language of the title page—"the language of an item's content"—may be transcribed in the

---

[5] Ibid., 263.
[6] Ibid.

catalog record but it is not simply transcribed: it is represented to the reader as specific information about the author, title, producer, publisher, and so on of the item. That indication of the contextual meaning of the various written symbols on the title page (opening frame, container, etc.) is not always present on the item itself but rather the product of the cataloger's interpretation. Furthermore, the subject headings assigned, the names of those involved in the production of the item, and other descriptive information may be and usually is rendered in the language of the cataloger rather than merely transcribed from the item. The latter cataloger-supplied information is not merely the hypothetical language that "a patron might use in searching for that item" but is in some cases a standardized form of name, subject term or note. Current developments in cataloging technologies and theory suggest that transcription of the item's content will be increasingly replaced by cataloger interpretation accompanied by links to information not taken from the item at all.

The second matter to note about the language of Tuttle's catalog record is even more important, namely that the "record" does nothing like combining languages, for records do not do anything; catalogers and library users do things including making and using records, but the records themselves do nothing. This is neither a trivial point, nor is it a red herring, for the question that Tuttle wishes to address is "Why do catalogers use two systems... to reach the same goal" (from the abstract), or put differently in the second paragraph of his introduction "why do catalogers, in effect, perform the same work twice?"[7] The whole point of Tuttle's paper is to argue that "catalogers, in effect, perform the same work twice"—which he eventually argues is not really the same work twice—because language requires them to do that. We are not discussing something that "records" do but something that catalogers do. If we put the makers of the catalog record back into the description of what is happening in

---

[7] Ibid., 264.

this first paragraph of Tuttle's, we get something not at all like "language is used to represent language." What we get instead ought to be something like "catalogers create language to communicate to someone concerning the nature and location of a certain physical or digital object."

And "surrogate"? A common enough way of referring to records that catalogers create, but what does it imply? Something that stands for (or substitutes for) something else. Instead of forcing the library's users to walk along the miles of shelves in the library, they can make their way through yards or meters or pages of "surrogates," catalog records that describe those items arranged on miles of shelves or hidden in some computer. The key issue here is what that "surrogate" actually is. In one sense only it is a replacement for the item, namely the catalog record can inform the library user about an item instead of the user being required to read that information in the book itself, and that presumes that the information recorded in the catalog record is also recorded in the book in that fashion. If that information is not also present in the same form in or on the item itself, then whatever the catalog record is, it is something different from the item. In any case a catalog record is NOT a surrogate understood as a replacement for the book, score, recording or electronic document; in so far as one may write of it as "standing for" an item it does so only as a semiological creation in its own right. Rather than understanding the catalog record as a surrogate, it is better to understand it as a message or sign emanating from the library and created by some person according to local policy for the purpose of communicating to future users of the library the nature of the material available (on the shelves or online). It exists for those who for one reason or another do not wish to look through all the objects in the library in order to find something, whether a known item or anything that fits a certain set of criteria. That is, a library record is not a surrogate standing in for concepts, nor is it a surrogate standing in for a book (electronic document, etc.), but is itself a message made to accomplish the goals of the library which are to serve the goals of the library's users.

I have no trouble with writing about bibliographic records as surrogates in everyday practice, but when the word appears in theoretical discussions it brings much trouble and confusion in its wake, and Tuttle wastes no time in bringing both of the latter into his discussion. In his third sentence we are informed that "the language in a surrogate record appears in the form of a list" (LCSH) and in alphanumerical notation (LCC), noting further that both LCSH and LCC are systems of language. Tuttle defines "a system of language" as "a group of signs and symbols standing in for concepts."[8] For practical considerations one may indeed wish to consider LCC and LCSH each to be "a group of signs and symbols standing for concepts," but this seems to be a particularly poor definition of *a language,* and wholly inadequate for understanding language as a social practice. What Tuttle seems to be defining is not "language" as we know it but "a system of language," i.e. a restricted code of some sort that someone has developed for specific purposes. And indeed I would argue that both LCC and LCSH are restricted codes developed on the basis of standard written English, but a theory of restricted codes is not the same as a theory of language.[9]

The whole of the discussion so far—and we are still on the second page of Tuttle's essay—has been an exercise in terminological confusion, the result of carelessly making words mean too little, too much, and nothing in particular as the author slides around with language, systems of signs and symbols, representation, standing for, surrogate, record, item, concept and aboutness, while none of these terms are rooted in any theoretical framework. All of these terms have meanings which are either rooted in everyday library practice or float freely in the no man's land where refugees torn from their theoretical homeland

---

[8] Ibid.
[9] For a critical examination of theories of language, see Roy Harris, *Integrating Reality* (Gamlingay: Authors Online, 2012).

wander about in confusion. The only terms that have any theoretical foundation in Tuttle's article are two selected from Roman Jakobson: *selection* and *combination*. What Harris wrote of Jakobson's mistake describes the nature of Tuttle's mistake as well: Jakobson's mistake, Harris wrote, concerned "the role of theory and the status of technical terms in a theory."[10] None of the terms in Tuttle's theory have any theoretical relation to the others, least of all his borrowings from Jakobson.

3. Redundancies in Cataloging
Tuttle argues that Jakobson's theory of language offers us a way to understand the apparent redundancy of LCC and LCSH. For Jakobson, language is a code and nothing else, while communication is simply the result of using the code. Tuttle switches between language as code and language as communication throughout his article, always drawing upon the theory of language appropriate to a restricted code when what he wants to explain is language of a much broader scope, namely communication between catalogers and library users. Jakobson's theory followed that of the electrical engineers of his day in thinking of language as being a mental process with all the characteristics of an early database understood as something like a filing cabinet used in an office:

> The communication engineer most properly approaches the essence of the speech event when he assumes that in the optimal exchange of information the speaker and the listener have at their disposal more or less the same "filing cabinet of *prefabricated* representations": the addresser of a verbal message selects one of these "preconceived possibilities" and the addressee is supposed to make an identical choice from the same assembly of "possibilities already foreseen and provided for". Thus

---

[10] Harris, *Saussure and his interpreters*: 98.

> the efficiency of a speech event demands the use of a common code by its participants.[11]

We have a common code—in this case two of them, LCC and LCSH—each of which is for Tuttle "a group of signs and symbols standing in for concepts" from which catalogers and library users select, combine and exchange elements in order "to distill the aboutness of an item." Or rather those signs and symbols were standing in for concepts in paragraph one while they "stand in for subjects, the myriad topics each item is 'about'" in paragraph two.[12] The novelty of Tuttle's argument is that he argues that there are two such systems not because of the needs of libraries and library users but because of the nature of language: "The unique functions of language itself,... illuminate the purpose and use of classification numbers and subject headings."[13] His conclusion: "language must have two co-existing functions to operate, one selecting symbols and the other combining them."[14] LCC and LCSH, being languages, are each deficient (aphasic) since they each carry out only one of the two necessary functions of language, and therefore we require both in order to effectively find our book or ebook in the library. Thus for Tuttle, linguistic behaviour and communication in libraries are both explained by the nature of language rather than by human social life and the nature of libraries, their materials and the activities carried out within them. This seems to me to get everything backward.

Why does Tuttle feel the need to consider both LCC and LCSH as redundant to begin with, only in order to argue that

---

[11] Roman Jakobson, "Two aspects of language and two types of aphasic disturbances" in his *Selected Writings* (The Hague: Mouton, 1962-), v. 2 (published 1971): 241. In this passage Jakobson is quoting from the paper "In search of basic symbols" by D.M. MacKay published in *Cybernetics, Transactions of the Eighth Conference* (New York, 1952).
[12] Tuttle, "The aphasia of modern subject access," 264.
[13] Ibid.
[14] Ibid., 274.

they were never redundant? Did anyone really need twelve pages of linguistics to see that classification systems order things systematically (that is why we call them systems) and that whatever criteria one chooses for ordering, the cataloger orders (collocates, combines—choose your synonym) the items classified according to that criteria, thereby effectively precluding any other ordering? And that with a given system of subject headings the cataloger can both discriminate and bring together items with as fine a discrimination or as broad a category as you allow your system to reveal but can never order anything? Tuttle's perception of two systems of description and classification as redundant was the result of his analytical method: "But analyzed one by one, each of these differences between numbers and headings only betrays more redundancies: both systems refer to disciplines; both can be loosed from physical objects.[15]

Tuttle offers a brief history of the parallel developments of these two systems, but his brief history—like all histories—is both selective and an interpretation of the selected facts. His 21st century myopia is glaringly evident in his dismissal of "The Location Device View," the explanation of the difference between subject headings and classification schemes: "Online habits of organization then suggest physical location was never the main reason for a single subject identifier. It was always more important for an idea to be placed between two ideas than for a spine to be placed between two spines."[16]

Neither youth nor theory are any excuse for such an anachronistic misreading of the past. Tuttle dismisses all of the material and social conditions of research in libraries in the 19th century because those conditions are no longer constraints (he believes) in the world of information online. In fact it remains the case that without an indication of physical location in a catalog record there is not now nor ever was any means of accessing the item that the catalog record describes. In his reduction of the

---

[15] Ibid., 264.
[16] Ibid., 268.

Library of Congress Classification system to a system for indicating "aboutness" Tuttle denies the centrality of all issues of access and location. As for suggesting that placing an idea "between two ideas" being more important than placing a book in a specific place, I suggest that placing an idea "between two ideas" is a mental activity that relies very heavily on the material existence of both bodies and the material products of human intellectual life. In any case, the intellectual activity of placing an idea in a context is an activity quite different than finding a book on a shelf no matter how it is ordered, or finding an online resource using a searching system based on relevance ranking rather than any human description and classification.

What Tuttle fails to appreciate is the great variety of "location devices" used in the past as well as the present, and even more how these were combined with various other systems, tools and physical means of marking and organizing library materials in order to enable library staff and other library users to find specific items in libraries small and large. Library systems for locating and therefore finding items have been based on many criteria, not simply on "aboutness." There are systems utilizing accession numbers, systems based in part on language or script, imprint date and date of acquisition, systems based on religious and political understandings of the world and systems for technical retrieval such as Uniform Resource Locators (URLs), as well as various means of classification by subject. The classification of all publications in the Czech national bibliographies of the socialist era followed political alignments depending on whether the item concerned a socialist or a non-socialist nation, the classification differing sometimes from one issue to the next. The University of Chicago Library utilizes not only the LCC system but at one time or another has also used (and in some cases continues to use) Dewey; Harvard-Yenching; government document numbers; music publishers names and numbers; locally developed systems for law, literature and biblical studies; and probably other systems that I am not even aware of.

Why have libraries developed "location devices" based upon an analysis of subjects? The answer, Tuttle suggests, lies in the nature of language. May it not be that it had much to do with the adoption of open stacks policies, the spread of public libraries, and the increase in library patrons asking where they might find books on baseball, romance novels, tuberculosis, gardening, and so on? Items in a library have to be ordered in order to be found; providing an order based upon an analysis of their subject is only one means of providing that order, but it is an extremely useful means.[17]

Prior to the rise of electronic documents available online, the question "where?" was crucial in every library request. One practice that reveals this crucial question by its absence is that in a classified library some library patrons never ask "where"; they simply wander about, find the areas of interest to them and return there regularly, completely bypassing the catalog record while making use of the classification to the exclusion of all other systems of description and organization that the library may offer. Similarly in the online environment many users of libraries rely on links to electronic documents, neither using nor even being aware of the classification and subject description systems in use. Yet exactly as in the case of the 19th century library user, if the URL fails to work, the modern online library user is as helpless as the patron searching for a misshelved book. Location in cyberspace is as important as it is in any other space.

4. Jakobson and his filing cabinets
One of the primary difficulties in offering language as the determining factor in processes of "selection" and "combination" is that neither process is tied to language, both are behaviours of humans and other creatures without language; one might even

---

[17] For nineteenth century arguments for that wonderful new idea of "le catalogue systématique" see F. Nizet, *Notice sur les catalogues de bibliothèques publiques*. 3e éd. (Bruxelles: Impr. Vanbuggenhoudt, 1888).

describe certain actions of machines with such words. Should we not turn the equation around? Classification and subject systems are designed in order for librarians to be able to order and describe library holdings because library users wish to select from the library's stock of possible (available) items or gather together (combine) a collection of items on a particular topic (or by a particular author, or editions of a particular item, which are also functions of classification systems that Tuttle ignores). The library user comes to the library to do something; language left to itself will never select or combine, not even restricted codes like LCC or LCSH.

Returning to Jakobson to understand language including the language characteristic of library cataloging and library searching is to return to a theory of language from the early 1950s. It is also to return to a theory of language that was heavily influenced by technologies and theories of information of the late 1940s. Furthermore, Jakobson's linguistic theorizing was as carelessly fashioned as it was widely read and highly praised; in the essay Tuttle discusses, Jakobson mistook Hjelmslev's terminology for Saussure's.[18] The paper in question draws on an understanding of computers published in 1952 and research on aphasia from 1939 to 1952. There would be nothing wrong in going backward were there something worth going back to, but is there? Have there been no breakthroughs in understanding the use of information systems since 1952? Are neurologists still

---

[18] See Arby Ted Siraki, "Problems of a linguistic problem: on Roman Jakobson's coloured vowels" *Neophilologus*, 2009, 93:7. Siraki refers to the first edition of Harris's *Saussure and his interpreters* on this matter but a direct accusation does not appear in the second edition that I consulted. Siraki also notes that Jakobson has often been accused of cherry-picking and omissions, an accusation Harris does make and elaborate upon in the second edition. [When this article was published in *Cataloging & Classification Quarterly* someone at Routledge substituted "article" for "essay" and inserted "how" into the footnoted sentence ("in the article Tuttle discusses how Jakobson mistook...") making it appear that Tuttle in his article identified Jakobson's mistake, but he did not. Siraki claimed that the mistake was identified by Roy Harris; as I indicated in my footnote, I was unable to verify that.]

thinking about aphasia in terms of problems of selection and combination of items in a mental filing cabinet? (I do not know.) As for linguistics and semiology, much has happened since 1952 and Jakobson has had nothing to do with it.

Any understanding of signs and language—such as Jakobson's and Tuttle's—which holds these to be prefabricated and pre-existing items that are then selected and combined, and the meanings of which have been determined in advance of any person's desire to say or write something is an understanding of signs and language that cannot allow for any person to speak or write appropriately to the situation at hand. In spite of Jakobson's claim that combination creates new meaning, there can be no possibility of making new meanings if the meanings of the signs are "prefabricated representations" of "preconceived possibilities." What Jakobson offers us is a semiology that is valid only for computer-computer communication, a semiology that is never adequate to human communication which "depends upon the freedom of man and his capacity to change the world and its natural course."[19]

Combining subjects and selecting concepts were, Tuttle claims, "the paths that led users to resources at the end of the nineteenth century and they will be the paths that lead users to resources in this century."[20] What Tuttle has left out of this picture of library users are the two activities that truly are linguistic in nature: writing the bibliographic description and reading it. Writing and reading, we should not forget, are also social activities that we engage in only because we desire to communicate, and it is our attempts to communicate that creates both the the signs written and the signs read. Combining subjects and selecting concepts never have and never will lead anyone to any resource; the only things that will lead you to a resource are your legs or someone who knew where to find just what you are

---

[19] Hannah Arendt, "Franz Kafka, appreciated anew" in her *Reflections on literature and culture* (Stanford: Stanford University Press, 2007): 101.
[20] Tuttle, "The aphasia of modern subject access,": 274.

looking for and wrote down the directions. A semiology that understands that signs are products of communicative activity will be adequate for an understanding of the creation and use of indexes in books, card catalogs, online catalogs, search engine algorithms, URLs, railroad signs, body language, spam, glossolalia and abstract art as well as human behaviour in the face of misshelved and missing books; Jakobson's filing cabinet on the other hand is 60 years behind the curve...and counting.

5. Beyond filing cabinets

Librarians whose understanding of communication in libraries is modelled on computer architecture are unlikely to go beyond the filing cabinet/warehouse model of libraries as storage and retrieval systems. Creative thinking is something wholly other than selecting and combining the information given, but it is only in creative activity that we will find a model of human communication adequate to the activities of librarians and library users. However accurate the filing cabinet model may be for describing the physical dimensions of libraries real and virtual, and perhaps even the activities of some librarians, it fails as a description and even moreso as an explanation of the creative actions of librarians and library users.

Cataloging is not a simple activity of selecting and combining subject headings. Certainly there are approved lists of terms to use, but those lists are not closed—many of us add to the lists regularly—nor are the relationships between the terms in those lists and the materials to be described predetermined: the cataloger *makes* that association, and makes it for reasons that have nothing to do with the functional limits of language understood as a technical system. It is only if one ignores completely the reasons for catalogers doing anything at all that one can explain the activities of catalogers as due to the nature of language or of a technical system or tool. The same consideration applies to the activities of library users. People come to the library to do many things, but I know of no one who has ever come to the library to select and combine words, concepts or anything else. Whatever value Jakobson's theory of language may have for understanding certain pathological conditions, it has no value for understanding communication in libraries. A semiology adequate for understanding what happens in libraries must be founded not on a theory of language but on a theory of human action and communication. Jakobson will be of no use in developing such a semiology.

References

Arendt, Hannah. (2007). "Franz Kafka, appreciated anew," in her *Reflections on Literature and Culture*. (Stanford: Stanford University Press, 94-109.

Harris, Roy. (2003). *Saussure and His Interpreters*. 2nd ed. Edinburgh: Edinburgh University Press.

Harris, Roy. (2012). *Integrating Reality*. Gamlingay: Authors Online.

Hutchins, W.J. (1975). *Languages of Indexing and Classification: A Linguistic Study of Structures and Functions*. Stevenage: P. Peregrinus.

Jakobson, Roman. (1956/1971). "Two aspects of language and two types of aphasic disturbances" in R. Jakobson and M. Halle, *Fundamentals of Language*. Mouton & Co., The Hague. Quoted here from the 1971 reprint in his *Selected Writings*, v. 2. The Hague: Mouton.

MacKay, D.M. (1952). "In Search of Basic Symbols" in Heinz von Foerster, M. Mead, & H.L. Teuber (Eds.). *Cybernetics: Circular Causal and Feedback Mechanisms in Biological and Social Systems. Transactions of the Eighth Conference*. New York: Josiah Macy, Jr. Foundation, 181-221.

Nizet, F. (1888). *Notice sur les catalogues de bibliothèques publiques*. 3rd ed. Bruxelles: Impr. Vanbuggenhoudt.

Siraki, Arby Ted. (2009). "Problems of a Linguistic Problem: On Roman Jakobson's Coloured Vowels" *Neophilologus* 93, nr.1:1-9.

Tuttle, Jonathan. (2012). "The Aphasia of Modern Subject Access," *Cataloging & Classification Quarterly* 50, no. 4:263-275.

www.ingramcontent.com/pod-product-compliance
Lightning Source LLC
Chambersburg PA
CBHW071347290426
44108CB00014B/1464